The Bible Speaks Today

Series Editors: J. A. Motyer (OT)
John R. W. Stott (NT)

The Message of Amos
The Day of the Lion

Titles in this series

The Message of Amos

The Day of the Lion

'There is no need to cry: the Lion . . . has triumphed'
(Rev. 5:5, JB)

J. A. Motyer

formerly Principal of Trinity College, Bristol

Inter-Varsity Press
Leicester, England
Downers Grove, Illinois, USA

Inter-Varsity Press
38 De Montfort Street, Leicester LE1 7GP, England
P.O. Box 1400, Downers Grove, Illinois 60515, USA.

Inter-Varsity Press, England, is the book-publishing division of the Universities and Colleges Christian Fellowship (formerly the Inter-Varsity Fellowship), a student movement linking Christian Unions in universities and colleges throughout the United Kingdom and the Republic of Ireland, and a member movement of the International Fellowship of Evangelical Students. For information about local and national activities write to UCCF, 38 De Montfort Street, Leicester LE1 7GP.

InterVarsity Press, USA, is the book-publishing division of Inter Varsity Christian Fellowship, a student movement active on campus at hundreds of universities, colleges and schools of nursing in the United States of America, and a member movement of the International Fellowship of Evangelical Students. For information about local and regional activities, write Public Relations Dept., InterVarsity Christian Fellowship, 6400 Schroeder Rd., P.O. Box 7895, Madison, WI 53707-7895.

Text set in Great Britain

Printed in England by Clays Ltd, St Ives plc

UK   ISBN 0-85110-731-1 (*paperback*)
USA ISBN 0-87784-283-3 (*paperback*)
USA ISBN 0-87784-925-0 (*set of* The Bible Speaks Today, *paperback*)

25	24	23	22	21	20	19	18	17	16	15	14	13	12	11
13	12	11	10	09	08	07	06	05	04	03	02	01	00	99

TO
Mark
9 August 1973
Stephen and Valerie
11 August 1973
Beryl
30 August 1973

General preface

The Bible Speaks Today describes a series of both Old Testament and New Testament expositions, which are characterized by a threefold ideal: to expound the biblical text with accuracy, to relate it to contemporary life, and to be readable.

These books are, therefore, not 'commentaries', for the commentary seeks rather to elucidate the text than to apply it, and tends to be a work rather of reference than of literature. Nor, on the other hand, do they contain the kind of 'sermons' which attempt to be contemporary and readable, without taking Scripture seriously enough.

The contributors to this series are all united in their convictions that God still speaks through what he has spoken, and that nothing is more necessary for the life, health and growth of Christians than that they should hear what the Spirit is saying to them through his ancient—yet ever modern—Word.

J. A. MOTYER
J. R. W. STOTT
Series Editors

Contents

CONTENTS

Author's Preface

AMOS must have put in hours of study before he went preaching in Bethel. He took the trouble to become well-informed about world history and current affairs, so that he was able to capture and hold his audience's attention by deft allusions to surrounding nations. How his hearers must have loved it, until it came too close to home for comfort! But that too was part of the slog of preparation: his sermons were so well and so cleverly constructed, with closely-argued points made in such ways and in such sequence that the whole had a compelling cogency. Amaziah, that worldly ecclesiastic, saw the mind of the nation coming under Amos' spell, and even if his judgment was suspect about other things, at least here he could be trusted to take the national temperature.

What a pity, then, that Amos left us only the distilled essence of what he said and not his sermons in their full development and application! Look at it this way: suppose we think of 1:3—3:2 as one discourse. It can be read in five minutes without undue haste, but it could not be preached as it stands. It covers too much ground too quickly; no mind could follow or grasp what was being said. To affect his hearers, Amos must have developed his themes, made his connections clear, opened and applied his message, and rubbed it home. But all he left us was his notes.

There are therefore two tasks to be performed on any passage from the prophets. The first is exegesis: to elucidate what is there, to establish the meaning of each word, to balance shades of meaning against each other, to explore grammar and syntax, until, as clearly and confidently as may be, we can believe that we know what it was Amos said. The second—and consequent—

task is exposition. Starting from the meaning which nas been established, exposition seeks to draw it out into a total message so that we today begin to feel its truth coming home to us with force and application.

But the point to be insisted on is this, that both exegesis and exposition are serious exercises in Bible study. They are not sworn enemies, as the jargonistic distinction between 'academic' and 'devotional' would have us believe; neither is the poor relation of the other. Exegesis without exposition is like a deep-freeze, full of good things but, as it stands, out of touch with reality and devoid of nourishment; exposition without exegesis is like a space-rocket, enjoying itself in its own orbit but oblivious now of the launching-pad from which it started.

My aim in this book is exposition. I trust that I have not skimped the task of exegesis—indeed I have ventured to show some of the workings in the margin, and some more in the commentary on Amos in NBCR (though on some points it will be noted that I have changed my mind)—but I have laboured to clothe the bones of exegesis with the flesh of exposition whereby Amos may again speak to the church.

His message is relevant, humbling and frightening. It rebukes the 'eleven and six-thirty' of our formalism; it offers the salutary reminder that a tradition of the church may have lasted two hundred years only to be as false at the end as it was at the beginning; it insists that the church loses the centrality of the Word of God to its eternal peril; it exposes the sin of religious self-pleasing; it describes a religion which is abhorrent to God and calls for its replacement by a resting upon divine grace in faith and repentance, a commitment to God's law in obedience, and a ceaseless concern for the needy among men. Without these, there is nothing so effective as religion to separate us from God's love and to cement us to His wrath.

Expositions should grow out of pulpit work. St Luke's, Hampstead, gave me a choice proving-ground for what has finally become this book. St Helen's, Bishopsgate, lent a helpful ear to a refashioned form of the material. After I had tried to cover the whole book in five studies at the Keswick Convention in 1970, the rumour flew round that by now even Amos was saying that he was sorry he had written it in the first place! I hope this is not true, even though, having now spent a great deal of time in the company of this gentle giant among the prophets, I can only testify to feeling like a very small mouse who has had the good fortune to nibble at a very large and nourishing cheese.

May He who is Amos' God and mine graciously stoop to use this book for the benefit of His church!

Trinity College,   J. A. MOTYER
Bristol.

August 1973

Chief Abbreviations

BDB	*Hebrew and English Lexicon of the Old Testament* by F. Brown, S. R. Driver and C. A. Briggs (OUP, 1906).
BHS	*Biblia Hebraica Stuttgartensia: Liber XII Prophetarum* praeparavit K. Elliger (Stuttgart, 1970).
Cripps	*A Critical and Exegetical Commentary on the Book of Amos* by R. S. Cripps (2nd ed., SPCK, 1955).
Hammershaimb	*The Book of Amos: A Commentary* by E. Hammershaimb (Blackwell, 1970).
IB	*The Interpreter's Bible, Vol. 6: The Book of Amos, Introduction and Exegesis* by H. E. W. Fosbroke (Nelson, 1957).
JB	The Jerusalem Bible, 1966.
KB	*Lexicon in Veteris Testamenti Libros* by L. Koehler and W. Baumgartner (Leiden, 1958).
LXX	The Septuagint (pre-Christian Greek translation of the Old Testament).
Mays	*Amos, A Commentary* by J. L. Mays (SCM Press, 1969).
NBCR	*The New Bible Commentary Revised* edited by D. Guthrie, J. A. Motyer, A. M. Stibbs and D. J. Wiseman (IVP, 1970).
NBD	*The New Bible Dictionary* edited by J. D. Douglas (IVP, 1962).
NEB	The New English Bible, Old Testament, 1970.
Pusey	*The Minor Prophets, II: Amos* by E. B. Pusey (Funk and Wagnalls, 1906).

RSV   American Revised Standard Version, 1946–52.
RV   English Revised Version, 1881–84.

The General Introductions

This commentary follows the division of Amos into three parts which is to be found in NBCR. Each of the parts is here prefaced with a general introduction to its contents and its place in the message of Amos. The hope is that the reader will be thus encouraged to read through the whole section in the light of the general introduction before becoming immersed in the detailed studies. In this way, each separate study will be more clearly held in its place in the total argument of the book.

The Name and Titles of God as printed in RSV

The words LORD and GOD, when printed entirely in capital letters, represent the divine Name, Yahweh. Yahweh is the personal name of the God of Israel. This name was known throughout patriarchal times but its significance (*i.e.* what it tells about the God who owns it as His name) was not revealed until the time of Moses and the Exodus. In the redemption of Israel and the overthrow of Egypt, Yahweh revealed Himself as Redeemer and Judge. The revelation of His name has the same significance as when, in a developing friendship, we begin to use each other's first names. It stands, therefore, for the intimacy with Himself into which the Lord brought His people by redemption. Sadly our English Bibles (except for the Jerusalem Bible) continue to observe the ancient scruple which supposed the name of God to be too holy to be used. Hence we find the printed forms LORD or GOD.

'Lord', printed with capital 'L' only, signifies another Hebrew word meaning Sovereign or King.

Introduction

Why?

AFFLUENCE, exploitation and the profit motive were the most notable features of the society which Amos observed and in which he worked. The rich were affluent enough to have several houses apiece (3:15), to go in for rather ostentatiously expensive furniture (6:4) and not to deny themselves any bodily satisfaction (3:12; 4:1; 6:6). On the other hand the poor were really poor and were shamelessly exploited: they suffered from property rackets (2:6, 7), legal rackets (5:10, 12) and business rackets (8:5) and the defenceless man with no influence came off worst every time. When the poor could not contribute to the rich they were simply ignored and left to be broken (6:6). Money-making and personal covetousness ruled all: the men lived for their offices (8:5), the women lived for excitement (4:1), the rulers lived for frivolity (6:1–6).

When Amos turned his gaze upon the church he found a religion which was very religious, which adored what was traditional but which had shaken free from divine revelation. The religious centres were apparently thronged (4:4; 5:5, 21–23; 8:3, 10), sacrifices were punctiliously offered, the musical side of worship was keenly studied. But it had no basis outside the mind of man. It continued the counterfeit cult of Jeroboam who had set out nearly two centuries earlier to establish a viable alternative to Jerusalem (1 Ki. 12:25 ff.), and, with this length of tradition behind it, by the time of Amos it all seemed to be a self-justifying enterprise. The shrines of Jeroboam at Bethel and Dan were still in full operation (4:4; 5:5; 8:14) but under the analytical gaze of Amos they were but exercises in self-pleasing (4:5), abhorrent to

God (5:21–23). The priest, Amaziah, offers us a case-history of the best sort of worshipper, but, when all came to all, what was he? Establishment-minded (7:10), careful for the ecclesiastical proprieties (7:13) but supremely disinterested in any word from God (7:12, 16).

Standards had gone to pot. Authority and the rule of law were despised (5:10, 12), and national leadership, while revelling in the publicity and dignity of position (6:1) and quick to score debating-points (6:2), was not facing the real issues (6:3a) but seemed even to be contributing to the complete breakdown of law and order (6:3b) by allowing personal likes and dislikes to take primacy over caring for the nation (6:4–6). Public standards of morality were at a low ebb: Amos could speak of sexual indulgence (2:7), transgressions and sins (5:12) and commercial sharp practice (8:5, 6) as matters on which he could not be proved wrong.

These things provided him with grounds for speaking and then for writing, and they also provide us with grounds for considering that he will have something to say to us today. These are the things which mark our society also: some more, some less. None of them is true about everybody; each of them is true about somebody. Amos might well have been walking through any of our great cities.

When?

Looking at these things, Amos saw a society and a church on its last legs, but nobody else did. It was not only a time of affluence but also of political strength and national stability and expansion. He dates his prophecy broadly in the days of Uzziah of Judah and Jeroboam (II) of Israel, and particularly with reference to a notable earthquake (1:1). Unfortunately we do not know the date of the earthquake, but the two kings mentioned enjoyed long reigns in the first half of the eighth century BC. Including co-regencies with their respective fathers, Uzziah reigned from about 790 till about 740, and Jeroboam from about 793 until 753. Circumstances dictated that they should both be expansionist and consolidating monarchs. In 805 BC Adad-Nirari III of Assyria defeated Syria, thus disposing of the power which more than any other would have set limits to Jeroboam's plans. But having thus unwittingly served the interests of Israel, Assyria entered upon a period of quiescence from which it did not rouse until the accession of Tiglath-Pileser III in 745 BC. Jeroboam, a vigorous and able man, was thus given a virtually free hand. He restored the Solomonic boundaries of his kingdom for the one and only time since the death of Solomon (*cf.* 2 Ki. 14:23–29). With the control this afforded him over trade routes, wealth began to accumulate (as we have seen from the incidental evidence in Amos) but mainly in the hands of the commercial barons. In this setting, the warning shots of divine displeasure (4:6–11) went unnoticed, and Amos was initially alone in seeing that the social, ecclesiastical and moral evidence was all pointing one way: this nation and church were doomed.

To whom?

Obviously, seeing things like this, Amos addressed himself to all who would hear, but if we say it like that we will miss the real thrust of Amos' ministry. The people of the day were accustomed to think of themselves as the people of God. They did not think in distinct terms of Church and State as we do. This people, Israel, had had ancestral dealings with God: He had brought them out of Egypt (3:1), constituted them as His people and given them their religion. It was for this reason and on this ground that Amos spoke to them. We will feel the burden and force of his words if we say that he addressed the church. As a whole as well as individually they professed religion, they thought of themselves as walking with God, they held themselves to have quite a precise arrangement with Him, they looked forward (5:18–20) to the day when He would in a unique way exert Himself to bring the whole world to His heel, for they were confident that on that day they would receive all the honours. The word of Amos is a word to the church, and it touches on three central points.

First, Amos insisted that privilege brings peril (3:2). The claim of the day clearly was that privilege brings security. They had been privileged to have direct dealings with God (2:9–11). At certain dates in the historical past God had shown that He was on their side. The particular stress of Amos is this: the nearer to God the closer the scrutiny and the more certain the judgment. Far from their privilege saving them, more will be required from those to whom more has been given; the greater the light the greater the risk. The church is not exempt from judgment; far from it, the judgment begins and rages most severely there.

Secondly, past history cannot take the place of present spiritual and moral commitment. A stale testimony of what happened years ago is like a lesson in history. God looks for up-to-date commitment to Himself (5:6), to moral values (5:14, 15), to personal and social ethics (5:24).

The third emphasis in Amos' message to the church is that religious profession and religious practice are invalid—to be more precise, repulsive to God and therefore not just useless but also dangerous—unless verified by clear evidences. Throughout his book, by implication, but in a succinct fashion in 7:7—8:10, Amos makes clear what the evidences of true religion are. It is the task of the expository studies at that point to explain them, but here they are in summary. In personal terms, true religion is to respond fully to the grace and law of God, living out the law in a life of obedience, resting on the grace both for ability and forgiveness; towards God, true religion is a reverent hearing and receiving of His Word; and towards other people it appears as honesty, considerateness and unfailing concern for the needy. Take these things away and what remains does nothing more than invite the adverse judgment of God.

In all this Amos speaks directly to the church today, and we must banish any thought that he speaks primarily to some other people or to other situations and that it is only by some exegetical gymnastics that there is a message here for the Christian. Amos addressed 'Israel' and we are 'the Israel of God' (Gal. 6:16). It is to be noted that Paul does not say 'the new Israel', and nowhere in the Bible does such a phrase (or notion) occur. Jesus designated His people as the inheritors of the new Covenant predicted by Jeremiah (31:31–34; cf. 1 Cor. 11:25); Paul spoke of them as the children of Abraham, along with Isaac (Gal. 4:28); he also said that 'we are the circumcision' (Phil. 3:3). It is precisely because this is the true situation that James can take the prophecies of Amos as a handbook for the church's mission (Acts 15:15 ff.). In doing this he sets an example in the realms of both principle and practice: in principle, in that Amos brings a Word of God directly (not mediately) to us for our direction, admonition and instruction, and in practice, in that we are to see all that he says in the light of the kingdom of Jesus Christ, a kingdom not of this world, not promoted by the methods of the world, nor seeking political fulfilments in a geographical location.

How much?

Amos was aware of himself as a man gripped by God for the purposes of being His prophet (7:14, 15). He could not but speak, for God had spoken to him (3:7, 8). He was convinced that not just the substance or 'drift' of his message, but the very words he used—the words which were natural to his highly-developed and well-informed mind—were more truly God's words. It is, therefore, in the highest degree unreasonable to doubt that Amos himself committed his message to writing and himself edited it into its present coherent and cogent form. Happily the world of specialist study appears to be moving away from the older and rather doctrinaire disbelief in Amos, the Writer and Editor, but there is still a great deal of dispute whether he can be credited with the whole book as it stands or whether the evidence does not rather suggest that certain passages were inserted by later editors to meet the needs of later situations.

The notion of later insertions is not at all an easy one to handle. If, for example, a supposedly inserted verse, fragment or passage disagrees with its context in subject-matter (and thus declares itself to be inserted), why should anyone have put it there in the first place? If the reply is made that it was inserted in order to adapt the message of Amos to a later situation, the question must be asked how the introduction of extraneous or irrelevant thoughts can be considered to 'adapt': to say something different is to 'add', and to say it in a passage where it proclaims its irrelevance is editorial madness. Again, if a passage is adjudged insertional on stylistic grounds, but is harmonious enough with the message of the context, why should it not be a quotation used by the first author rather than by a later editor?

Many of the allegations regarding insertions in Amos have been noticed in footnotes to the following studies, though, of course, other commentaries must be consulted as well for a full treatment.

It will be found, however, that in this commentary three grounds commonly appealed to, now or formerly, as identifying this or that passage as an insertion have been put aside as inadequate in themselves. The first is evolution of religion. On this ground it used to be common form to excise 4:13; 5:8 and 9:5, 6 because they asserted a doctrine of God the Creator which could not have been current until the best part of two hundred years after Amos. This nonsense has now been exposed by archaeology. The similarity of style shown by these three passages and their possible dissimilarity from the style of Amos are best explained by assuming that he was quoting here from some hymnic source.

Secondly, allusions to Judah (2:4, 5; 6:1) have come under needless suspicion. Certainly, Amos was a prophet to Israel, the northern kingdom, but why should he, any more than any other prophet, have a restrictive view of his ministry? On this ground, not only the oracle against Judah but the whole series against foreign nations (1:3 ff.) should be excised! The fact of the matter, however, at least in regard to his main oracle against Judah (2:4, 5), is that he dare not omit it. Had he left out Judah he would have lost all credibility with his Israelite audience, as a tendentious and biased person. Verses like 3:1 indicate that Amos had a total view of the people of God, and this becomes evident when he turns to the hopeful future (9:11 ff.).

Thirdly, it is customary to exclude the note of hope from the message of Amos, but here this ground also has been rejected as in itself insufficient. It is inconsistent with any theology centring on the name Yahweh and resting on the idea of the covenant to blacken the whole sky with the clouds of wrath and to forget mercy and hope.

The approach adopted throughout this present commentary is that illustrated by Hammershaimb's comment on 3:7. Faced with the allegation that the vocabulary of 3:7 is in part exemplified only in writings later than Amos and that therefore the verse must be judged a later addition, he replies that 'V.7 can, however, be interpreted as a far from superfluous element in the context' and, proceeding to do so, he rejects the insertionist view. This is simply asserting that exegetical and expository arguments take precedence over all others. If a passage is coherent, if a whole book is coherent, it is needless and pointless to multiply hypotheses whereby that unity is fragmented. Whether this method has been applied with success and good sense to the book of Amos must be decided by the reader.

What ?

In the section above dealing with the audience to whom Amos addressed his sermons and subsequently his book, a great part of the central message of Amos was indicated. We must now add a word about the framework of belief within which Amos preached.

One question concerns us here:[1] in what terms did Amos think about the covenant and, especially, did he think that it was capable of entire dissolution?[2] The majority reply to this can be stated in the words of R. E. Clements:[3] 'The message which Amos brought meant a judgment which embraced the entire kingdom, and which implied the end of the covenant with Yahweh and Israel . . . the doom which Amos preached meant the end of Israel . . . He was not thinking any longer of a purge of sinners within the covenant . . . Yahweh himself was Lord of the covenant and was about to bring it to an end.' Clements takes the concept of the 'curse of the covenant' (cf. Dt. 28; 29; and especially Lv. 26:14 ff.) seriously, adding: 'Just how far the curse of the covenant was ever visualized as actually threatening the break-up of the covenant relationship we do not know, but it was certainly held out as a possibility.' He then calls attention in a footnote to 'Ex. 19:5–6 (E) for the contingent nature of the Sinaitic covenant'.

It seems important, however, to ask at what point the concept of contingency applied within the covenant. The sequence of covenants from Noah through Abraham to Moses gives the impression of a fixity of divine purpose: the Lord is committed to taking and keeping a people for Himself, and to finding that

---

[1] For a fuller introduction to the thought of Amos, see NBCR, pp. 726 f.

[2] Cf. J. A. Motyer, Covenant Theology of the Old Testament, Theological Students Fellowship, 1973.

[3] In his most helpful book, Prophecy and Covenant (SCM Press, 1965), pp. 40 ff.

people in the family of Abraham. Nothing else, for example, explains why He should have bothered with such an unattractive and thankless crowd as the people who were slaves in Egypt and who became the incessant grumblers of the Mosaic age. Deuteronomy 7:7 ff. relates the covenant policy of the Lord to the unexplained love which He has for this people. It is hard (indeed impossible) to believe that contingency exists at this point, and it is to be noted that when the great rebellion arose over the Golden Calf, the Lord purposed a fresh start within the family of Abraham (Ex. 32:9 f.), not a wholesale, sweeping destruction.

The contingency to which Clements calls attention in Exodus 19:5, 6 is typical of all that is said or implied on the topic: it is a contingency of enjoyment of the covenant. In the mind of God the covenant is settled for all eternity and cannot be unsettled. It is He who has committed Himself to save and to keep a people for Himself. He has predetermined its membership and all the elect will without fail come into their inheritance. But when it is presented to the mind of man the covenant is a promise suspended on a condition: obedient faith in the promises of God expressed in the covenant. Thus the question of covenant membership was settled in Amos' day on the same grounds as when Paul wrote to Timothy, and they remain the same today: on the divine side, *'The Lord knows those who are his'*, and on the human side, *'Let every one who names the name of the Lord depart from iniquity'* (2 Tim. 2:19).

The question whether Amos was teaching that the Lord had decided to change His covenant purposes, or whether he was foretelling purgative judgments designed to sweep out of the covenant-people all whose profession was a pretence and whose lives did not show the marks of true membership, must be settled by the study of chapters 7–9. The view that the Lord was committed to the absolute termination of the covenant can be sustained only by a surgical approach to these chapters which removes all that suggests any notion of a remnant according to grace and a hope for the future. It also, incidentally, makes Amos a false prophet who foretold what did not happen, the end of the covenant. On the other hand, the view that Amos sees in operation the curses of the covenant, designed to purge out false members and to purify true members, accords with these chapters taken exactly as they stand. It accords also with subsequent history: the preservation of a covenant people until the day of the raising up of the booth of David in Christ Jesus and the blessed forecast of the final consummation of all the purposes of God in Him.

Part One
THE ROAR OF THE LION
Amos 1:2—3:8

General Introduction

IT is a stylistic trick used by Amos to divide his book into its main parts by returning at the end to some thought to which he gave prominence at the beginning. The first part is bracketed between two references to the roaring lion (1:2; 3:8). Each of the subsections (apart from 3:3–8) may be taken as a separate roar: the divine lion first denounces the sins of the Gentile world (1:3—2:3) and then of the Israelite world, addressing first the southern kingdom of Judah (2:4, 5), Amos' own home, then the northern kingdom of Israel (2:6–16), the people to whom he was sent, and ending by binding them together in a concluding oracle (3:1, 2).

The lion metaphor, of course, speaks of judgment and the series of oracles serves to show at point after point the things which come under divine displeasure. Nevertheless, at this point the judgment is still a future threat, and in the subtlest possible way Amos blends the roar of the lion at the end into the voice of the prophet (3:8), his own voice calling out in God's name to the people to heed before it is too late.

Amos 1:2
In God's Name

THE human spine has an endless capacity for being chilled, provided only that the chilling takes place from an entirely safe vantage-point! If it were not so, would we plan our tour of the local zoo so that we arrive at the lion house at feeding time? Even the guaranteed protection of strong plate glass or stout bars does little to diminish the effect of the roar and pounce, the rippling muscles and the tearing claws.

But now remove the bars, restore the lion to its habitat, replace the dead carcase by living prey, revitalize the caged ferocity until it matches again its unfettered and native intensity—and that is the portrait of God with which Amos chooses to open his book.

Samson would be the best commentator on Amos at this point, for he experienced the reality which Amos turned into a metaphor. He heard just such a roar (Jdg. 14:5) as he walked through the vineyards at Timnah. 'Attacked' would, in some ways, be a better translation than 'roared', for the roar in question is the pouncing roar, the roar of a lion already committed to the attack, the roar intended to paralyse its victim with terror. Never did a lion make a greater error of judgment! Samson's action in tearing the beast apart was not a wanton cruelty. The issue of life and death was thrust upon him by the roaring, springing animal. But Amos says that it is *the Lord* who thus *roars*.

It is a savage, vicious word. Can it have any relationship to the divine nature? Can God be like that? It is a word which points forward to imminent suffering, destruction and death. Can such things be the acts of God? These questions are important, for Amos comes before us as a prophet, a man with a word from God, and if the God in whose name he speaks is not the God we worship, then Amos' book may remain as a tract for his times but cannot be a tract for ours. It ceases to have relevance because it is unrelated at source. Who, then, is the God of Amos, this roaring lion of a God?

The divine name

The first word which Amos wishes us to hear him speaking is the name of God: *The Lord roars*[1] so that our gaze is first engaged with the Agent, and it is only when we have contemplated Him that we are allowed to consider what He is to do. Who is *the Lord*, Yahweh?

Like the rest of the Bible, Amos associates (*cf.* 3:1) the name of God with the revelation of Himself which He gave to His people through Moses and the Exodus.[2] The first move in this revelation was the declaration of God's holiness (Ex. 3:5), a truth clearly implicit in Genesis but never before explicitly stated. The first great narrative sequence in Exodus reaches its climax in a colossal restatement of the same truth (Ex. 19), the flame of holiness burning within the bush becoming the mountain of fire blazing up into the heart of heaven. It is necessary to grasp very clearly the significance of the fact that the revelation of the name of God is thus bracketed about by the declared holiness of God. When God declares His name He is offering a summary statement of His essential character. Two things, therefore, converge in the opening chapters of Exodus: the revelation of that divine attribute, holiness, which both Exodus and the rest of the Bible insist to be the fundamental truth about the divine nature, and the name, Yahweh, in which God chooses to express the eternal truth (Ex. 3:15) about Himself. The developing narrative of Exodus fills out the theme.

---

[1] A sentence in Hebrew follows a fixed order of words. The verb comes first and the subject of the verb follows. In the present instance, therefore, the regular order of words would be 'He roars, (namely) the Lord . . .'. Amos inverts the order. The subject, the divine name, comes first and is therefore emphatic.

[2] Two questions are by-passed here: the 'literal' meaning 'Yahweh' considered simply as a word, and the dispute whether or not the name itself was known before the time of Moses. See J. A. Motyer, *The Revelation of the Divine Name* (Tyndale Press, 1959); U. Cassuto, *Exodus* (OUP, 1968); R. de Vaux, 'The Revelation of the divine Name, Yahweh' in J. I. Durham and J. R. Porter (Eds.), *Proclamation and Presence* (SCM Press, 1970), pp. 48 ff.

First in the words He spoke to Moses, and secondly in the great deeds by which those words were authenticated, Yahweh, the holy God, is declared to be the God who saves His people and overthrows His enemies. Salvation and judgment are equally aspects of His holiness, and both together constitute the abiding definition of His holy character which is expressed in His name.

The altar of God

It is one of the indications that Amos is thinking very precisely in terms of the God who revealed Himself to Moses that he should threaten over and over again the judgment of fire (1:4, 7, 10, 12, 14; 2:2, 5). This is not a very apt description of what happens when a lion pounces! But there is nothing quite so consistent with the revelation of fiery holiness which is the essential setting of the name Yahweh. Amos prepares us for this when he lays such considerable stress on the location from which Yahweh roars: *from Zion . . . from Jerusalem*.[3] There is more to this than an implied rebuke to the northern tribes for their schism (1 Ki. 12:16, 26 ff.). Rather the symbolism of fire continues: just as in the narrative sequence in Exodus the flame in the bush (Ex. 3:2) evolved first into the great fire at Sinai (Ex. 19:18) and then into the undying fire upon the altar of God (Lv. 6:13) which accompanied the people from Sinai, so Amos portrays Yahweh as speaking from the place where He had chosen to set His altar, itself the visible expression of the wrath and mercy which together define His holy nature. It was the place of wrath, for there death, the price of sin, was paid;[4] it was the place of mercy, for there the sinner found the balm of divine forgiveness and atonement (Lv. 17:11).

Patient, moral providence

To us, of course, mercy and wrath appear as irreconcilable op-

[3] Here again an inversion in the order of the Hebrew words throws the place-names into prominence. There is therefore a double emphasis: first the using of two names, and secondly the emphasis upon each in turn.

[4] See, *e.g.*, NBD, art. 'Atonement'; A. M. Stibbs, *The Meaning of the Word Blood' in Scripture* (Tyndale Press, 1948).

posites, the one cancelling out the other. The perfect blending of
both in one divine nature is something beyond our ability to
fathom. As Amos perceived the character of his God, he saw that
the lion-roar of condemnation and judgment came only when the
patience of mercy had long, but vainly, waited for repentance and
amendment of life. This is the significance of the repeated phrase
for three transgressions . . . and for four.[5] On the part of man, the cup
of sinfulness has been filled to the brim; on the part of God, there
has been no hasty action: the first transgression well merited
divine wrath, but mercy waited and patience watched. One way of
expressing this truth about God is to say that He never punishes
the sinner except after prolonged personal observation and ample
opportunity for repentance.[6] Another way of stating the same
truth is to say that the face which God turns to the world is
predominantly one of mercy, that wrath comes, when it comes at
all, late and overdue, and, as the Bible permits us to say, accompanied by the tears of God over recalcitrant and impenitent
sinners (*cf.* Lk. 19:41, 42). The God of Amos is a God of patient,
moral providence.

One world, one God

It is easy and correct to describe Amos' God in the words 'patient,
moral providence', but they are impossible to explain and hard to
justify. The inequalities of life are too enormous, the gulf between
the haves and the have-nots too wide and deep, and the evidence of
apparently undeserved suffering and undeserved freedom from
suffering too pervasive for anyone to make an easy assumption of a
single moral purpose governing the world. It can, of course, be
too readily assumed that problems such as these lend their weight
unequivocally to the cause of atheism: for if there is a good God
how can there be such inequalities and sufferings in His world?
But, on the other hand, if there is no good God, while the sufferings

[5] 1:3, 6, 9, 11, 13; 2:1, 4, 6; *cf.* Jb. 33:14; Ps. 62:11; Pr. 30:15, 18, 21;
Ho. 6:2; Mi. 5:5. Throughout, the idea behind the ascending numeral is
that a complete count has been taken, and the result may be accepted with
confidence.

[6] *Cf.* Gn. 6:5, 6; 11:5; 18:20, 21; Ps. 50:21; Ec. 8:11; Is. 30:18; 57:11;
Lk. 13:6–9; 20:9–13; Acts 17:30, 31; 2 Pet. 3: 8, 9, 15; Rev. 2:2, 9, 13, 19,
etc.

remain they are no longer a problem, for the alternative to the biblical teaching that one good God rules all is that chance rules all, and if chance rules, then inequalities, sufferings (deserved or undeserved), injustices and all else are no more than the spin of the wheel: they are facts, not problems. A convinced and consistent atheist may well be ready to say that chance rules all, but if he does so he must give up using the 'problem of pain' as part of his anti-God argument and he must also tell the rest of the world why suffering is universally held to be a problem and not just one of those things.

It is the crowning evidence that Amos is speaking of the God of the whole Bible, the God of the Bible-loving Christian, that in the name of his God he faces a whole world, in all the reality of its cruelties, its unresolved injustices, its privileged and underprivileged peoples, and submits it totally and without reserve to the sway and judgment of the one and only God.

He first states this in a metaphorical way very typical of the prophets. When *the Lord roars*, then *the pastures of the shepherds mourn, and the top of Carmel withers* (1:2). From the luscious meadows in the river valley to the height of Carmel, from Amos' own shepherd-haunts in the far south to the Carmel range in the north, from the tender blade of grass to the luxuriant vegetation of Carmel (*cf.* Is. 35:2), all comes under the blight and blow of judgment.

That is the metaphor. It is one of totality. The reality is spelt out in terms of nations: the whole world is under divine observation, subservient to divine assessment and subdued without refuge before divine judgment. Feel the weight of the monotheism of Amos! When he reviews the world of the have-nots, the nations who have never received any revelation of Yahweh (1:3—2:3), he takes absolutely no cognizance of the fact that each worshipped a god of its own. Such information was quite irrelevant. It was not to that god that they were answerable, nor could that god save them in the day of Yahweh's wrath. There was only one God over the whole earth, and to Him they must and would render account.

But much more is it the message of Amos that this truth has its foremost and more abundant application to the people of God themselves (2:4—3:2). To whom much is given, of him much shall be required. Judgment will not only come to but will begin at the house of God,[7] and will be manifest there in a seemingly pitiless and all-destroying intensity.

The more we have found ourselves (and with grateful hearts) acknowledging the God of Amos as our God, the more we ought to bow humbly before this truth also. Truly He is our God: the holy One, manifesting His holiness in just wrath and righteous salvation, the Lion of the tribe of Judah who is also the Lamb as though it had been slain: He is the God of the altar of Calvary's cross, that final and eternal meeting of mercy and wrath, the one sacrifice for sins for ever.[8] It is true that we can sing with Toplady that 'the wrath of a sin-hating God with me can have nothing to do', since 'my Saviour's obedience and blood hide all my transgressions from view'.[9] Yet it is also true that the wrath of a sin-hating God ought to be part of the permanent consciousness of the Christian, for God never hates sin more than when He sees it defiling the life of His people. The Fatherhood of God, the supreme privilege of our redeemed position, is also the ground of perpetual fear.[1] More than in any other matter, the message of Amos has abiding relevance at this point—to force us to make our calling and election sure, to remind us that it is one thing to claim God's promises but another to inherit them, and to teach, seven hundred and sixty years before a greater than Amos used the words, that many will call out 'Lord, Lord' only to hear the words in reply 'Depart from me, you evil-doers' (Mt. 7:22 f.).

Two dangers

It would not, however, be true to Amos to conclude this opening study without further comment. There are two dangers into which we may easily fall. The first is that of blurring our awareness of his sharp condemnation of sin in God's professing people; the second is the danger of failing to keep this particular message within the context of the total message of Amos. The majority of writers on Amos treat 1:2 as a heading or 'text' for the whole book. In one sense this is true, and in another it is false. As we have

---

[7] Cf. 9:1; Ezk. 9:5, 6; 1 Pet. 4:17.
[8] Cf. Rom. 3:23–26; 2 Thes. 1:5–10; Heb. 10:12; 12:22–24; Rev. 5:5, 6.
[9] From the hymn by A. M. Toplady, 'A debtor to mercy alone'.
[1] Cf. Phil. 2:12; 1 Pet. 1:17.

seen, 1:2 is primarily the opening verse of the first section of the book: it heralds the lion's roar, and 3:8 concludes the section by looking back on the lion's roar. It is this observation that gives rise to the necessity to emphasize Amos' message of judgment upon the church, for over half the material in this section is engaged in statement and condemnation of the sins of Israel and Judah, and indeed, as we shall see, to a considerable extent the sins of the nations of the world are mentioned in order to win the attention of God's people to listen to the message of God's wrath against their own sins.

Nevertheless it is not wholly untrue to view 1:2 as the heading to the whole book, for it is a remarkably exact summary of the total message, especially when we recall that Amos' first word is the divine name, Yahweh, the name spelling both privilege and requirement. What a privilege to know the holy God as Saviour! What a task to dwell with the holy Adversary of sin! That the emphasis in Amos falls on the latter was occasioned by the circumstances of his day. The people of God had fallen asleep in the comfort of the privileges of salvation and needed to be jolted into the awareness that the only assured certainty of the possession of those privileges was the evidence of a life committed without reserve to being holy as their Saviour God is holy. And it can hardly be held that this message is an irrelevance for the church today.

There are (we speak humanly) two sides to the revelation of God given in the name, Yahweh, and there are two sides to the life of the people of God in their response to that revelation.[2] Yahweh primarily denotes the holy God, and therefore the primary response of God's people to knowing Him is commitment to

---

[2] The view held by so many students of Amos that his message is wholly one of judgment—even to the extreme position of making Amos declare without qualification the end of the covenant relation between the Lord and His people—stems from failure to recognize the two facets of the revelation of Yahweh. In the Exodus-situation God acted in salvation-and-judgment. A prophet who announces his message with the trumpet note of the name, Yahweh, and proceeds to link that name so firmly with its original Exodus-context (cf. 2:10; 3:1; 5:25) cannot isolate within the divine nature the single facet of judgment and say that henceforth this is all the divine name is going to mean to God's people—a name for their rejection. Yahweh cannot forget to be gracious.

resemble His holy nature.[3] On the other hand, the holiness is that of a Redeemer, a Saviour of sinners, and the proper response to this revelation is to live before Him in a spirit of penitence, to frequent the place of forgiveness and cleansing, to use to the full the means of pardon and grace.

It is the blending of these truths that made Amos the particular prophet he was, and it is in terms of these truths that his call leaps the centuries to address us. As ever, the Bible speaks with one voice. Looking back to the great acts of salvation in which God has revealed His name and nature, it says 'My little children, I am writing this to you so that you may not sin'; looking into the fickle, wayward and often-defeated lives of God's people, it adds 'but if any one does sin, we have an advocate with the Father, Jesus Christ the righteous; and he is the expiation for our sins' (1 Jn. 2:1, 2).

[3] *Cf.* Ex. 19:4-6; Lv. 20:26; Dt. 7:6; Mt. 5:44-48; 1 Pet. 1:15; 1 Jn. 3:3.

Amos 1:3—2:3
The Fourth Transgression

CONSCIENCE is a God-given faculty, part of the image of God in man. Like every other aspect of this image, it was tampered with, diluted and depraved as soon as human nature gave house-room to rebellion against God, and the process of sin-hardening, now countless generations old, has not improved the sensitivity of conscience as an instrument of moral judgment. Hence it is true that history could well be told as a catalogue of crimes committed in the name of conscience—a narrative which is still in process of being written in our own day.

But it is much truer to say that greater and more numerous crimes have been committed through silencing the voice of conscience. The image of God in man has not been eradicated. What the Bible teaches about fallen human nature is well expressed in theological shorthand as 'total depravity', and is intended to assert the pervasiveness of sin throughout human nature, so that no part or aspect is untainted by corruption. The whole is indeed corrupt, yet Scripture equally insists that the common grace of the Creator God, extending to the whole of creation, has mercifully seen to it that the requirements of His law are written on men's hearts (Rom. 2:15).

Be a man

Consider this in terms of Jesus' statement that the Father gave the Son authority to execute judgment 'because he is the Son of man' (Jn. 5:27). There would be legitimate ground for us to complain if the final word in this quotation was 'God'. God could not reasonably expect us to rise to divine heights! But it is in His character as Man that Jesus executes judgment; He acts as the One in whom is fully realized the perfection of God's human design, the very Image of God Himself. Jesus stands forth as judge, Himself embodying the law on the basis of which judgment will be pronounced: men will be judged for failing to be men, in the day when the books are opened and the deeds of all declared. This is what Scripture says, and this, precisely, is what Amos says.

Indeed, when we read our New Testaments we find ourselves compelled to conclude that its writers were familiar with their Bible! Paul's structure for the opening chapters of Romans, showing as they do the guiltiness before God of both the Gentile world and the Jewish world, is a straight lift from the first two chapters of Amos. And, when he deals with the Gentile world, the apostle offers us a perfect summary of Amos' assessment of their position: *When Gentiles who have not the law do by nature what the law requires, they are a law to themselves, even though they do not have the law. They show that what the law requires is written on their hearts, while their conscience also bears witness. . . . .*[1] We must take care, however, to understand the phrase 'a law to themselves', for it is sometimes used nowadays of a person who defies convention and makes up his own rules, a sort of ethical maverick. Paul's meaning, however, is quite different. No human being can escape the obligation of being human, and even those who have never received spoken or written precepts as from God still sufficiently bear the marks of their Creator upon them that they are not wholly without moral guidance. There is a voice speaking within.

The passage now lying before us for study is a roll-call of the nations surrounding Israel.[2] They have one negative common

---

[1] Rom. 2:14, 15. On the question of 'natural' awareness of moral and religious truth, *cf*. Gn. 26:10; Ps. 19:1 f.; Acts 14:17; 17:28 f.; Rom. 1:19 f.

[2] Commentators commonly deny to Amos three of the oracles which follow: Tyre (1:9 f.), Edom (1:11 f.) and Judah (2:4 f.). (a) They are shorter than the other four. But if a later editor was deceitful enough to try to palm off his own material as the work of Amos, would he fall into the elementary error of adopting a different form? (b) In the Edom and Judah oracles there is supposedly evidence of later forms of expression. On Edom, see p. 38 below. In the Judah oracle, some expressions characteristic of Deuteronomy occur, and since it is assumed that Deuteronomy is post-Amos, these expressions point to a later date. This argument has no value, of course, if Deuteronomy's own testimony to Mosaic origin is accepted. Even so, however, the actual evidence amounts to little: divine revelation is called 'law' and 'statutes'

denominator: none of them had ever received any special revelation of God or of His law; He had never sent prophets to them; there was no Moses in their historical past; the voice of God had never sounded in the ears of their founding-fathers. Yet Amos presents them as nations under judgment. They were without special revelation but not without moral responsibility; they were without direct knowledge of God but not without accountability to God; they were without the law written upon tables of stone but not without the law written in the conscience.

Enquiry into relationships

As far as this passage in Amos is concerned, the law written in the conscience is spelt out in terms of human relationships. Without a doubt the heathen nations named here held many erroneous—even revolting—religious beliefs and practised hideous religious rites. Such are not even mentioned in passing. The spotlight falls not on what they may or may not have done or held in relation to God, but on what they have done man to man: barbarity (1:3) in the course of Hazael's military campaigns half a century earlier;[3]

---

which are to be 'kept'; apostasy is 'walking after' other gods. Mays (an advocate of this line) admits that Is. 1:10 shows that 'law' was current in Amos' day; Hammershaimb (rejecting the whole procedure) says that 'walking after' originates in participating in pagan processions. But at any rate 'walk' signifying 'manner of life' is commonplace. (c) It is alleged that the later editor was motivated by a desire to complete the encirclement of Israel by a full roll-call of nations. But it would certainly have called forth the adverse opinion of the commentators had any of these obvious candidates for rebuke been omitted! And Amos could not have dared omit Judah if he wished to remain objective and credible to an Israelite audience.

[3] *Cf.* 2 Ki. 8:7-15; 10:32, 33; 13:3, 7, 22. Hazael's dates were 842-806 BC. Elisha thoroughly forewarned him against the course which he adopted, but, as Pusey (*in loc.*) tellingly remarks, 'Hazael seemingly hardened himself in sin by aid of the knowledge which should have been his warning ... Elisha read him to himself ... he very probably justified himself to himself....' The details in verse 3b may be a literal description of the brutality practised or figurative of some outrageous method of terrorism. Verses 4 and 5 describe the spread of divine destruction throughout the kingdom until all is destroyed: the dynasty is gone (Ben-hadad was the son and successor of Hazael, 2 Ki. 13:24); neither barred city nor open valley provides refuge; *Beth-eden* may be Bit-Adini on the Upper Euphrates, the significance being that there will be no escape through flight to another kingdom; and finally the Syrians

pitiless slave-trading involving total populations (verse 6b),[4] promise-breaking (verse 9),[5] unnatural and persistent hatred (verse 11),[6] and finally sickening atrocities against the helpless (verse 13)[7] and the dead (2:1).[8]

return to the unknown obscurity from whence they first came (*cf.* 9:7), figurative here of the blotting out of their name.

[4] Gaza is to be understood as the slave-trader acting in conjunction with Edom as either the market or the retailer. Gaza is selected to typify Philistia either as a well-known centre of trade and therefore the one primarily involved in this traffic in human life, or else because of the meaning of its name ('Strength'), suggesting that no human power can stand against God in judgment. Note that Samson was brought to Gaza (Jdg. 16:21): it must have been recognized as the acme of Philistine strength. Failure to mention Gath among the Philistine towns in verse 8 has led some commentators to date this oracle after 711 BC (when Gath fell to the Assyrians) and therefore after the time of Amos. But equally one might say that Gath was still suffering eclipse after its defeat by Hazael (2 Ki. 12:17). *Cf.* J. L. Mays, *in loc.* See also 2 Ch. 26:6.

[5] Verse 9b opens with the identical accusation as verse 6b but adds the particular charge of covenant-breaking. Literally the words are 'the covenant of brothers'. Calvin understood the brothers in question to be Israel and Edom (*i.e.* Jacob and Esau): Tyre contracted guilt by association in that they took sides in Edom's well-known violation of brotherly obligations. But it is better to follow the clue provided by the references to a covenant relationship between Tyre and David, renewed with Solomon (*cf.* 2 Sa. 5:11, 12; 1 Ki. 5:1–12, where in verse 1 'always loved' is to be understood of preserving loyalty within a covenant relationship). As we shall see below, it is important for our understanding of Amos that he makes no reference to hurt done to Israel or Judah by name but simply specifies the sin of breaking a pledged word.

[6] Mays (*in loc.*) speaks for many commentators when he says that the attitude here ascribed to Edom finds its best reflection in Ob. 10–12 and La. 4:21 f., and that since these belong to the time of the fall of Jerusalem (586 BC) this oracle against Edom must belong to the same period and cannot be ascribed to Amos. But it ought to be noted that while these references specify a particular act of Edomite hostility, Amos is concerned with a persistent and maintained hatred. Hammershaimb (*in loc.*) notes the fact of Edomite wars throughout the century up to the time of Amos and the possibility of widespread Edomite aggression during the rebellion against Joram (2 Ki. 8:20 ff.) within that period.

[7] NEB, without comment, proffers the translation 'because in their greed for land they invaded the ploughlands of Gilead', which neatly exposes the sinfulness in God's eyes of expansionist policies. But there is sadly no ground for toning down or avoiding the atrocity committed against pregnant women, as RSV. It was part of the terrorist enterprises of the contemporary war-machines (*cf.* 2 Ki. 8:12; 15:16; Ho. 13:16). If it had any purpose other than to subjugate by brutality it was to destroy the future hope of the enemy.

[8] Hammershaimb notes that burning the dead was an expedient resorted

When we examine this list of broken relationships we find that it is not a haphazard collection of charges but a carefully-structured statement. Six nations are brought under review. In the cases of the first two (1:3–5, 6–8) nothing is stated except the fact of gross cruelty; the next pair, however, strike a rather different note in linking themselves together by the word 'brother' (1:9, 11); and the final pair, associated as they are by the contrasting ideas of destroying the future (as represented by the unborn children, verse 13) and desecrating the past (2:1), are firmly linked by bringing before us two categories of helplessness, the pregnant woman and the dead body. Thus we may say that Amos first examines violations of the general relationships of life, human being to human being, then the particular responsibilities of life, brother to brother, and finally the special claims of life, the attitude of the strong to the weak. In this way he speaks out on behalf of six basic principles of human conduct.

People and things

It is not difficult to think ourselves into the frame of mind cultivated by the war-effort of Hazael and his Syrians (1:3–5). Had he been subjected to interview the royal commander-in-chief would undoubtedly have said, 'There's only one way to make war: you hit the enemy with everything you've got in every way you can.' And if anyone raised a voice of humane protest against carrying the war to the extreme of the deliberate torture of captives, sooner or later the reply would have come, 'There's a war on. Didn't you know?' Exceptional circumstances justify exceptional measures and remove conventional limitations.

Man may think so, but God does not. War or no war, Hazael had no liberty to treat people as if they were things. It is the first absolute moral principle for which Amos campaigns: people are

---

to only 'in cases of especially serious offences where it was impossible to regard the simple death penalty as adequate . . . (. . . Achan, Josh. 7:15, 25; certain sexual offences, Lev. 20:14; 21:9; Gen. 38:24). In behaving thus to the Edomites the Moabites treated their king as one would treat a dangerous criminal.'

not things. Let us suppose that the description of Hazael's conduct as 'threshing' Gilead does not actually mean that he used animals to drag flint-studded, weighted platforms of wood back and forth across the prostrate bodies of living Gileadites. Take it metaphorically, but ask what the metaphor means. 'Threshing' is what a man does to a thing, a grain crop, in order to extract his own profit from it. This is what Hazael did in Gilead. He treated people as things. But he found no sympathy, allowance or forgiveness in heaven.

The allied principle in this opening pair of oracles dealing with general human relationships is the priority of human welfare over commercial profit (1:6). We have moved from the battle-field to the board-room, from the camp to the counter. Gaza was a hive of commercial activity, a great trading-centre. Buying and selling was its life-blood, maintained at the cost of many a life. But then, as was well known in Gaza, no-one was in business for philanthropic reasons. Where money talked loudest it was often best to learn to hold your tongue, and where the margin between solvency and bankruptcy depended every day on making a profit-margin over your nearest rival, or finding a market for what he had thought unsaleable, why, then, best to turn a blind eye and get on with it. If life is hard, business is even harder. And, as we can well imagine, nowhere was this philosophy more thoroughly known and practised than in the emporia of the slave-trade. 'See this one here? Went down on her knees to me to let her stay with her crippled husband—said he'd die if she left him. Hard luck, sweetheart, said I, you'll fetch too good a price.'

They carried into exile a whole people—young, old, men, women, married, single, rich, poor. Only one question was asked: Will they sell? And God took notice, as He always does when things are valued more highly than people.

Brotherly relationships

Amos' analysis of the obligations into which our common humanity brings us now becomes a little more particular, and the principles arising out of the examples he offers become a little more personal. Within the human family as a whole there are some to whom we bear a closer relationship: this may be a relationship deliberately formed, and sealed with a compact (1:9), or a relationship inherited by blood (1:11).

Out of the former of these Amos brings the third of his six principles of human conduct: the inviolability of the pledged word. It is the element of 'covenant' or promise which distinguishes the accusation against Tyre from that against Gaza. Both were identically immersed in the inhuman traffic in human flesh; both were identically linked by commercial ties to Edom. But in the case of Tyre an additional factor was involved. Tyre's third transgression may well have been its greedy carelessness of human suffering, but its fourth transgression—the final item which God would not overlook—was that Tyre, in its slave-trade, acted in breach of treaty obligations. The word had been given, and the word had been broken.

This is not, of course, to say that in every case we are bound irretrievably to keep our word. Some promises can be honoured only by repenting of them. We cannot, for example, foresee the future, and it could well be that a promise might be given to take a certain action, or to support another in taking a certain action within the year, yet when the time for standing by the promise comes it is clear that the action in question involves a greater breach of honour, a more shameful and blameworthy course than to break the original promise. In such circumstances it is the action of a fanatic to insist on keeping the pledge. Did not Herod commit a greater sin by keeping his word than he would have committed by breaking it (Mk. 6:26)? A child was once asked what Herod should have done—for, after all, had he not promised up to half his kingdom? 'Oh,' she said, 'he should have replied: I'm sorry. I'm afraid John the Baptist's head is in the other half of my kingdom!' And if we, moralistically, think that such a course is an evasion, let us at least recognize that it is an evasion which sides with righteousness. The course of absolute honour for Herod, as for us, would simply be the words 'I'm sorry'. The path of abject repentance of the whole thing is often the highest moral good in a world of sinners.

All this is certainly true, and Amos is not to be thought of as advocating some unreal moralism. Yet however true it is that some promises should be honoured by repenting of them and taking the consequences, nevertheless no pledged word should be treated as negotiable simply for self-interest and self-advantage. This was what Tyre had done, and it was the fourth and unforgivable transgression.

The second aspect of brotherliness (and the fourth principle of conduct) arises in contrast to the sin of Edom. It is remarkable that Edom, already implicated twice in the abomination of slave-trading (1:6, 9), is now charged with an entirely different and new sort of transgression. Truly the Lord does not act in an arbitrary fashion towards any of His creatures. That which is the unforgivable 'fourth transgression' in one case, is only incidental evidence of sinfulness in another and a further step towards the dread point of no return when repentance, though it may well be sought, cannot ever again be found. In Edom's case, the fourth transgression was concealed in the heart. They had a long history of antagonism against the people of God[9] and it was yet to culminate in their devilish joy over Jerusalem's downfall (Ps. 137:7). Behind all this Amos discerns an *anger* which tore at Edom *perpetually* and a *wrath* guarded lest it evaporate. This hidden thing, this spring from which flowed the outward acts of aggression and spitefulness, this was seen and known to God, and it was this which He could not overlook.

By contrast to this sin of Edom what principle can be deduced for a God-pleasing life? The inadmissability of hatred nourished in the heart. If there is anything lying patently on the surface of Scripture as a candidate for being the unforgivable sin it is this, for nothing could be plainer than that in the absence of any outflow of forgiveness on the human level there can be no inflow of forgiveness from God. Edom's was an unreasoning (and as far as we know uncaused) hatred, but by whatever rationalizations it was buttressed, the Edomites could find no means of putting it aside, and it lay there poisoning the heart of their life with its bitterness and its inflaming bile. In principle God said to them through Amos what Jesus says to us: 'If you do not forgive men their trespasses, neither will your Father forgive your trespasses'

[9] *Cf.* Nu. 20:18–21; in 1 Sa. 14:47 the Edomites are among the 'enemies' of Saul, *i.e.* his wars as here mentioned were defensive, *cf.* Ps. 83:5, 6; 2 Sa. 8:13, *cf.* Jos. 15:62 which records 'the City of Salt' as within Judah's frontiers and we may thus presume the 'valley of Salt' to have been the depth of penetration of invading Edomites; 1 Ki. 11:14 ff.; 2 Ki. 8:20; 14:7; 2 Ch. 28:17, note 'again', which in the Hebrew is emphatic.

(Mt. 6:15)—and how can He? For those who cannot forgive have forgotten their own position as guilty sinners (Mt. 18:32–35): how then can they plead for forgiveness? Furthermore, those who allow old sores to fester proclaim that they are not interested in forgiving, they do not see it as having anything to contribute, it is not important to them: how then can they ask for it? Hatred maintained in the heart is a fourth transgression without peer.

The strong and the weak

We come now to the third area of human relationships from which Amos proposes to deduce principles of conduct: those relationships in which helplessness in the one party ought to elicit tenderness and compassion in the other. His chosen instances are the expectant mother and the unborn child (1:13–15) and the dead body (2:1–3).

This is a characteristically biblical and specifically Old Testament attitude. How readily Moses reacted on behalf of the helpless and afflicted,[1] a practice rendered obligatory in Israel through the law which he gave![2] The kings of Israel, mixed bunch though they were, were noted for mercy,[3] and the social conscience of the prophets on behalf of oppressed minorities and individuals was outstanding.[4] Amos stood well within this tradition.[5] It is noteworthy that in the oracle against Ammon more than in any other there is a dwelling on the detail of the exacting of punishment: we hear the shout of the in-rushing enemy (1:14), and Amos adds that even the very forces of nature (as we would call them) —*tempest* and *whirlwind*—symbolic as ever of divine antagonism, add their weight to that of the human assailant. Nothing moves God to punish so much as wanton cruelty to the helpless, for is He

[1] It is a remarkable study in divine providence that out of a royal house which could blandly decree infanticide, God brought a tender-hearted princess (Ex. 2:6) to become Moses' adoptive mother. He grew to resemble her: *cf.* Ex. 2:11 f., 16 f.

[2] *E.g.* Ex. 23:9, 12; Lv. 19:10, 13, 14, 33, 34; Dt. 15:12–15; 16:11, 12.

[3] *Cf.* 1 Ki. 20:31. A typical example of the contrast between Israel, instructed by the humane law of Moses, and pagan nations is furnished by the reaction of the Amalekite and David to the sick Egyptian slave in 1 Sa. 30:11 ff.

[4] *E.g.* 1 Ki. 21:17 ff.; Is. 1:17, 23; Je. 7:6; 22:16.

[5] *Cf.* 2:6, 7, 8; 4:1; 5:11, 12; 6:6; 8:5 6.

not rightly called the Father of the fatherless and the Defender of the widow's cause (Ps. 68:5)?

The motivation of the Ammonites was ambition, *that they might enlarge their border* (1:13) by the territorial acquisition of the neighbouring Gilead. It is in this setting that we must seek to draw out of the words of Amos the fifth principle of conduct: the limitation of personal ambition by the rights of the helpless. It is not that personal ambition is itself wrong. It is indeed necessary to life, and is part and parcel of the constitution given us by the Creator. But suppose ambition leads a man to gain a better job by conniving at the unjust dismissal of the man who at present holds that job? Suppose ambition to build up his business makes a man deprive his wife of his husbandly company and his children of their father's care? Suppose ambition acquiesces too readily or too thoughtlessly in the maxim that the weak go to the wall? Does it not matter when small traders fall before the supermarket? Does it not matter when private holdings are squeezed out, without redress, by the juggernaut of compulsory purchase? The issue may be clouded—and glorified—by much talk of progress, when the real motivation is Ammonite ambition.

The womenfolk of Gilead, and their unborn babies, had never hurt the Ammonites, and consequently the sin of the latter is crystal clear, and so is the precept against careless ambition which arises from it. But could there not be a case where retribution is involved, and the point is not wreaking senseless havoc but exacting a just revenge? This may well be the background to the charge of sacrilege levelled at Moab (2:1–3). The incident recorded in 2 Kings 3:26, 27 is most easily understood in the light of a desperate, violent enmity between the two nations. There, the king of Moab and his forces were pinned down by a coalition of Israelite, Judahite and Edomite armies. Since he could not vanquish the coalition, the king of Moab determined that at the very least the king of Edom should not get away unscathed (verse 26), and when even that proved impossible he savagely took Edom's son (possibly taken prisoner in the abortive counter-attack) and immolated him publicly (verse 27).[6] We may well believe that in

[6] This interpretation is persuasively advanced by Pusey, and provides a very satisfying understanding of an otherwise difficult passage. Consequent upon the brutal death of the crown-prince of Edom, the 'wrath' spoken of is

the context of an enmity which was capable of reaching such a fever pitch, Moab also had many scores to settle with Edom. But the vengeful spirit was such that what could not be settled while life lasted even followed the king of Edom into his grave. Could anything publicize more clearly the senseless irrationality of a nourished hatred than to see a venerable corpse dragged from its tomb to suffer pointless indignities?

Hatred is like that. It poisons the heart much more than it hurts its object. But in context, let us observe how the accusation against Moab balances the accusation against Ammon (1:13-15). Regarding Ammon, Amos taught us how to think about the future, keeping ambition within the bounds of mercy and kindness; regarding Moab, Amos teaches us how to think about the past, and we may spell out his sixth and final principle of conduct simply as the renouncing of vengeance. The day Moab opened the Edomite tomb he signed his own death warrant—*Moab shall die* (2:2). Every sin has a boomerang factor in it; none more so than to take revenge. It has no place in human behaviour, much less in the behaviour of the people of God.[7]

---

the understandable reaction of the Edomites to an alliance which had brought them such grievous loss, and the coalition broke up in dissension and disarray.

[7] The Bible contains a rich instruction on the question of 'vengeance'. The first emphasis is that vengeance belongs to God and must be left to Him, *e.g.* Dt. 32:35, 41, 43; 1 Sa. 24:12; Ps. 94:1; Is. 34:8; 35:4; 59:17; 63:4; Je. 11:20; Na. 1:2; Heb. 10:30. God sets Himself against the vengeful and forbids His people to take vengeance into their own hands, *e.g.* Lv. 19:18; *cf.* 1 Sa. 25:26, 33; Ezk. 25:12-15; Rom. 12:19, 20. When God's people are tempted to take vengeance, their proper response is rather love, kindness and compassion, *e.g.* Ex. 23:4, 5; Lv. 19:18; Dt. 23:7. In Dt. 22:1, 4 it is noteworthy that the enemy and the brother are to be treated alike; in Rom. 12:20 (*cf.* Pr. 25:21, 22) Christians are not called to act, so to say, from an ulterior motive, to be kind in order to hurt. Rather we must understand the matter thus: there is a situation in which the world would not hesitate to 'heap coals of fire', but Christians have a unique sort of coals to heap, the loading of the enemy with kindness. In Mt. 5:43-48 it ought to be noted that verse 43b is not an OT precept at all but appears to be some sort of 'logical' elaboration made by our Lord's contemporaries when they perverted OT law-court procedures into a code of personal vengeance. Care must be taken to exclude the familiar idea of 'the avenger of blood', *e.g.* Nu. 35:19, from this series of references. A different word is used. Elsewhere it signifies the Lord as redeemer, *e.g.* Is. 41:14, and the basic idea is rather that of identifying oneself with the helpless than of adopting an attitude of remorseless

The watchful eye of God

It is a constant aspect of the Bible's view of life that earthly relationships have a heavenly dimension: actions directed towards men provoke reactions from God.[8] The words of Amos which we have been following were his own, reflecting his own intense fervour for social and personal righteousness, but they come to us under the heading, six times repeated, *Thus says the Lord*. God watches the whole career of our sinfulness, the first, second and third transgressions; it is He who has annotated the six deadly sins, noting them as the fourth transgressions, so that we might avoid them and adopt on His authority the six corresponding governing precepts of life. Nothing has escaped His eye: He sees the past, the sin of Hazael (1:3) already half a century old; He sees the individual act, every single monstrosity of Gaza's slave-trading (1:6) as if He had counted the heads of their captives; He sees the broken promise (1:9) and the hidden enmity of the heart (1:11); He sees the emotions, and observes when ambition swallows up pity (1:13); He sees the memory and what it cherishes and its lurking, treasured sins (2:1).[9]

The one sin which runs like a devilish thread through the six aspects we have studied is the sin of self-pleasing: the self proudly trampling on others, intent on its own profit, sitting loose to troublesome obligations, indulging its secret motives, careless of

hostility towards the wrongdoer. In addition, the idea behind the usage is different: 'avenging blood' was an aspect of the early judicial system and one which the OT was careful to surround with safeguards like the 'cities of refuge' (*e.g.* Dt. 4:41–43); it was not a precept for personal ethics.

[8] *E.g.* Gn. 4:10; Ps. 51:3, 4 (*cf.* 2 Sa. 12:9–14); Mt. 25:40, 45; 1 Thes. 4:6–8.

[9] When I gave this material in the Keswick Bible Readings, I used here the words, 'I don't know that the Christian Church could have a greater blessing than that we should let the cleansing blood of Christ into our memories.' This (frankly unpremeditated) form of words seemed to catch the imaginations of some who heard, but without conveying a clear idea of their meaning! But surely this is what Scripture means when warning us against a 'root of bitterness' (Heb. 12:15): some grudge harboured, some grievance kept alive in memory to aggravate the present with its ill-savour. Whereas repentance, bringing cleansing, sweeps out the cobwebs of the past and liberates us to live for God now. The same line of thought could, of course, be followed in connection with all the aspects of divine observation of our lives noted above.

all so long as it has its way, and bitter to the last against all who dare to say it nay! But the particular way in which this sin has been brought to our attention is its manifestation in the context of human relationships and its origin in ignoring the voice of conscience. Thus we learn the cruciality of the ambition of the apostle—and therefore of the apostolic Christian—always to *take pains to have a clear conscience toward God and toward men* (Acts 24:16).

Amos 2:4—3:2
The Peril of Uniqueness

WE have very little positive information about the way in which the prophets actually delivered their messages: were they always open-air preachers? Or did they minister to select groups? Did they ever circulate their messages or their experiences in written form? In the majority of cases we are shut up to speculation. The one thing we need to guard ourselves from thinking is that the message was an impromptu or extemporaneous performance under pressure of a sudden inspiration from God. The clear evidence of structure in their oracles, of a deliberate building up of a case, points to careful preparation of their material.

Amos is a case in point. As we have seen, the roll-call of the nations (1:3—2:3) is by no means an unplanned ramble round Israel's borders. On the contrary, the nations are so placed in sequence as to present us with a structured review of human relationships as they appear to the divine Observer. The same evidence of planned utterance runs through the ministry of Amos.

But as to the occasion of ministry, if Amos were an open-air preacher he could not have acted with greater subtlety to gain the ear of the casual passer-by. We can hardly be wrong in guessing that a word of condemnation of Syria and Philistia, the more recent and the more ancestral enemies, would always be popular; likewise, if Tyre was living in open violation of treaty obligations, there cannot have been much love lost in that direction either. Edom would be another popular object for condemnation, and few tears would have been shed over its candidature for divine overthrow. And in respect of Ammon and Moab, we know to this day the news-value of far-off atrocities.

Moral encirclement

While Amos was thus winning his audience's attention to his message, it is probable that few of them gave attention to the fact that the review of the encircling nations was also a noose of judgment about to tighten round their own throats. The first three nations reviewed, Syria, Philistia and Tyre, belonged to Israel's political environment and nothing more. But in the biblical view of things the next three, Edom (*cf.* Gn. 25:29f.), Ammon and Moab (*cf.* Gn. 19:36–38), were 'cousins' to Israel: divine judgment was now falling, so to say, within the family.

It is appropriate to notice here that in condemning these nations—both the outright heathen and the related heathen—the ground of accusation is never simply that they have acted to the detriment of Israel. Thus the actual covenant which Tyre violated (1:9) probably was with Israel or Judah, but their names are not mentioned and the accusation remains exclusively one of promise-breaking; likewise, in the case of Edom (1:11 f.) the 'brother' in question is not named and the sin is that of unbrotherly conduct, no matter what its context. Other prophets, in reviewing the coming judgment of heathen nations, specify from time to time that the charge against them is what they have done to the people of God.[1] This, in its place, is right and proper, for the Lord is ever represented as jealous for His people's welfare (*cf.* Ze. 2:8), but it is not Amos' message as he begins to open the mind of God to Israel.

The people to whom Amos spoke had devalued the doctrine of election into a non-moral doctrine of divine favouritism: Israel was God's 'pet', surrounded by a divine imperial preference, protected, subsidized, the recipient of many unique allowances and special pleadings. The word to this people is based on the inflexible, unchanging righteousness of the Lord God, and the foundation for such a message is unobtrusively laid when Amos brings his charges against the nations. He speaks in the name of the God of righteousness, and neither here nor elsewhere in his book does the title 'God of Israel' appear. In the same way, the appeal to conscience, to common humanity, underlying his review of the

[1] *E.g.* Is. 14:1, 2; Je. 50:33, 34; 51:11, 33–37, 49; Ezk. 25:3, 4, 6–9, 12, 13, *etc.*

world is another move depriving Israel of any special ground or plea. Whatever makes Israel distinct among the nations, there is no distinction at this point, that the same moral rules operate inside as outside. Thus the noose tightens until, as we shall now see, the unique position granted by grace to the church of God, far from excusing or even ameliorating the offence, aggravates the situation so that Israel's fourth transgression is even less understandable or forgivable than that of the heathen who knew not God. The uniqueness of the church includes its unique peril.

The voice of revelation

Was there any twinge of unease among Amos' audience when he pronounced the name of Judah as the next object of divine displeasure (2:4)? Probably not. Relations between the two sundered parts of the people of God had hardly ever gone beyond the stage of peaceful co-existence, and well within living memory Jeroboam's father, Jehoash (798–782 BC), had been provoked into war by Amaziah of Judah and had carried out severe reprisals by destroying part of the wall of Jerusalem (2 Ki. 14:8-16; 2 Ch. 25:17-24) and looting the temple and royal treasuries. Likely enough, therefore, the name of Judah produced nothing but further derisory cheers, yet Judah was part of the people of God, and to Amos part of a unity established by the act of God in Egypt (*cf.* 3:1). His arrows of condemnation were at last falling within the main target area.

At once his line of attack changes: Judah's fourth transgression is that they have *rejected the law of the Lord* (2:4), and Israel's fourth transgression, first displayed in its visible acts of unrighteousness (2:6-8), is speedily traced to its root in their refusal of the voice of God in the prophets (2:12). Whatever their sins against the voice of conscience, this is no longer in the forefront. They have passed the point of no return by disregarding and silencing the voice of revelation. It was held to be their central privilege to have personal dealings with God denied to the surrounding nations, 'the lesser breeds without the law'; it now turns to be their central peril in a condemnation which cannot be averted.[2]

---

[2] Throughout these oracles, where the Hebrew says simply 'I will not

The Lord's concern for His truth

The structure of the passage now before us is as follows: Judah (2:4, 5) and Israel (2:6–16) are first addressed in separate oracles,[3] and then Amos, using the name 'Israel' in its strict sense as the title of the people of God, brings the northern and southern kingdoms under an identical and deadly condemnation (3:1, 2). Within this over-all structure, the Judah-oracle states the divine accusation in terms of principle and the Israel-oracle states it in terms of practice.

What, then, was the 'fourth transgression' with which the Lord charged His very own people? Within the broad unity of 2:4—3:2 as we have outlined it, the accusation can be studied in four sections.

First, we learn that *God's people have despised His truth* (2:4, 5). While this is specifically the sin of Judah, it is equally true of Israel, as verse 12 shows. Three contrasts are set before us in verse 4, beginning with the contrast between the divine and the human. Amos speaks of *the law of the Lord* and also of *lies . . . after which their fathers walked*. They possessed the law of the Lord but they

---

revoke it' or 'bring it back', RSV adds the explanatory word 'the punishment'. Mays interestingly suggests that 'it' may refer back to the lion's roar (1:2). For the same verb in similar usages, see Nu. 23:20; Is. 14:27b.

[3] Part of Mays' argument against the authenticity of the oracle against Judah is that the character of the indictment is out of step with all the others in the series, being a 'sweeping theological accusation'. But this is exactly the point. If it is true that 'all who have sinned without the law will also perish without the law', it is equally true that 'all who have sinned under the law will be judged by the law' (Rom. 2:12). Even when the accusations levelled against the people of God coincide with those charged against the heathen, the basis of the accusations must differ. The latter ought to have known better; the former did know better because truth had been revealed to them. The difference between Christians and 'the Gentiles' is drawn precisely in this way in Eph. 4:17–24 (NB verses 20, 21). Nevertheless the brevity of the Judah-oracle is surprising, even granting that Amos' primary call was to the northern section of the people of God. He had a firm grasp of the unity of the one people as he looked back to their common history (3:1, 2) and forward to their common destiny (9:11–15) and one might have expected a more elaborate statement of Judah's short-fall. Maybe Amos has preserved only the headings of a longer oracle preached at some time in Judah (note the four 'key-words': law, statutes, lies, fathers), here deliberately paring it down to the bone in order to state in its starkest form the actual charge of rejection of revelation.

preferred the traditions of men. The ancient people of God stood where the people of God still stand (and ever must stand), constantly assailed by competing voices saying, 'This is the way, walk in it.' Where is truth to be found? How is truth to be known? It is a problem for kings, so that they may guide national policies aright (*cf.* 1 Ki. 22:5–7); it is a problem for prophets, that they may be certain that what they preach is dictated by God and not by the preferences of their congregations (*cf.* Ezk. 2:6, 7); it is a problem for priests, lest pastoral counsel degenerate into that sort of 'partiality' or 'respect of persons' which tells people what they want to hear (*cf.* Mal 2:7–9). But the problem is not confined to the great ones of the earth. Amos makes no reference to them. It was the people themselves, and each for himself or herself, who faced the choice and chose amiss. Antiquity is no safe guide, for (as Pusey says) 'the popular error of one generation becomes the axiom of the next'. Human authority is no safe guide, for (to quote Pusey again) 'the children canonize the errors of their fathers'. Nothing affords a safe anchorage for life except the word which God Himself has spoken. The people of God possess this—in Amos' day by the written and preached deposits of their own ancient past and in the contemporary voice of prophecy; in our day by the written deposit of the completed Scriptures—and it is the hall-mark of the people of God to recognize this divine word of truth, to use it as the criterion for judging all things, and to reject all would-be competitors.[4]

In the contest between Scripture and Tradition, the Word of God and the inherited wisdom of man, it is precisely the contrast between truth and falsehood that is pin-pointed, and this is the second contrast which we must notice. The *law* stands in contrast

[4] 'Man', says Pusey, 'carries on the serpent's first fraud, "Hath God indeed said?".' The first point of attack in Gn. 3 is the first point of accusation in Am. 2:4. From Adam to Amos and from Amos until today the people of God are under the same pressure, and fall into the same perilous error: to subject the Word of God to some form of human criterion of judgment, some tradition or other, enshrined maybe in the logical processes of fallen human thought processes, or in inherited presuppositions, or in ecclesiastical systems. To make such the supreme or even the co-equal arbiter is to perpetuate the error and the doom of Eden. Our Lord Jesus has not left us unguided or unwarned: see Mt. 15:1 ff.; Mk. 7:1 ff., and the penetrating treatment of these passages by J. R. W. Stott, *Christ the Controversialist* (Tyndale Press, 1970), pp. 65 ff.

to the *lies*. Now Amos is not saying that man is incapable of ever unearthing truth. He is not even saying that unless a thing can be verified by Scripture it must be false. He is saying this: when anything other than the Word of God is given the supreme place, so that we base our lives upon it and guide our lives by it, then it becomes a lie and a source of lies. To put it at its best—*i.e.* when 'tradition' expresses a truth and not an error—when a part of the truth is taken to be the whole of the truth it becomes an untruth, simply because it is stretched beyond its limit, and becomes warped and altered. And when such a misshapen 'truth' is taken as the guide for life, what can it do but mislead?

Now, on the contrary, whereas the 'truth' deriving from man becomes a lie and a source of lies, the truth of God, accepted and persevered in, safeguards us from lies. In Amos' day the people fell into the 'lies' only when they strayed from the truth; had they remained in the truth they could not have fallen into the lies. Here is a very largely forgotten and yet most vital principle. It is certainly the case that the church is called by God to safeguard, publicize and transmit His truth (*e.g.* 2 Tim. 1:13, 14; 2:1, 2); but it is equally the case that the truth is the safeguard of the church, both in the corporate sense of preserving the whole body and in the individual sense of guarding, defending and keeping each member.[5] The life which walks in the truth is impregnable (*cf.* Jn. 8:31, 32, 34–36).

There are two sides to this security. The truth which Amos observed to have been despised was *the law of the Lord* and *his statutes*. Neither of these expressions quite conveys the correct meaning. 'Law' signifies not 'legislation' (with its related ideas of legalism, enforcement, reward and punishment) but 'instruction', with the related idea of a personal contact between teacher and pupil. The Lord's law implies His personal drawing near as teacher and the establishment of a personal relationship between Him and the one to whom He purposes to impart His truth.[6]

[5] Pusey quotes Jerome: '"They would not have been deceived by their idols unless they had first rejected the law . . . "' and adds: 'So it ever is . . . (Man) first in act despises God's law (and whoever does not keep it despises it) and then he must needs be deceived by some idol of his own.'

[6] Hammershaimb observes that the verbal root behind 'law' means 'to throw' and suggests that the movement of meaning from 'throw' to 'teach' came about *via* the revelation of the will of God through the casting of the

The other word, 'statutes', arises from a verb meaning 'to carve out, to engrave'. Its meaning in context is well illustrated by reference to the 'tables' of the commandments written in rock by the finger of God. The 'statute' is symbolic of the law of God in its aspect as unchangeable, imperishable truth. And from these two things arises the secret of the strength of the obedient life: it is a life in fellowship with the living God; it is a life resting on the rocklike foundation of the truth.

The final contrast whereby Amos describes their rejection of the Lord's truth can now be seen in its full shame: the contrast between rejection and cultivation of the truth: they *rejected* and *have not kept* God's word, but on the contrary have been *led astray* after lies in which their fathers *walked*. Both in what they have rejected and in what they adopted the whole man was involved. *Rejected* points a mental state which first despises and then dismisses; *lies* also belong to the activity of mental appraisal and (in this case) to the adoption of falsehood as truth. But in contrast *kept* and *walked* imply the sort of life which arises out of the mental decisions which have been made: once the truth has been despised it is not kept in an obedient, conformed life; once the lie has been embraced it guides the walk, the direction which life takes.

In complete consistency with the Bible's testimony on the point, Amos emphasizes the inner spring of conduct and then the outer manifestation of conduct. Life begins on the inside. Their abandonment of the fellowship with God and the foundational strength of God's truth began in the mind and nothing could then stop that rejection from appearing in the life; equally the willing adoption of the lie as authoritative issued in a life gone astray. Thus in a nutshell Amos summarizes the Bible's doctrine of the life of holiness as the life which loves and obeys the truth. But when the truth is no longer loved and is not kept by daily obedience its rejection is complete: and this is the charge levelled against Judah. God's people have despised His truth.

---

lots of Urim and Thummim. This may or may not be the case, but it serves at least to focus attention on the direct relationship implied in 'law' or 'teaching': God comes to make known His will. Both noun and verb are widely used throughout the Old Testament in the sense of 'teaching'.

The contradiction of salvation

Though he now turns to charge *Israel* (2:6) by name, Amos is in fact continuing his indictment of the people of God by exposing the breakdown of social and personal life which follows from the rejection of the truth. Perhaps we could put it this way: Amos the open-air preacher, addressing the people of the northern kingdom, has captured their attention by voicing condemnations with which they would cheerfully agree and has gradually brought his accusations nearer home until it is impossible for his audience to resist the logic which now places them also under hostile divine scrutiny. But Amos the editor, without losing this sense of the inevitability of judgment beginning at the house of God, does something else as well: he links the Judah and Israel oracles so that they stand together as an analysis of the sins of the church.

We may thus move on from the basic charge of rejecting God's truth to the second, and consequential, charge that *God's people have contradicted His salvation* (2:6-12). The point here is that when God comes near to His people in revelation of Himself, He not only makes His truth known, and not only points to a new sort of life but also, as we shall see, works to make that life possible. This is His salvation, fully accomplished by Him, fully contradicted by His people.[7]

Amos opens his case against Israel by a sweeping exposure of the sins of God's people. He sees them from three points of vantage: sins against others, against revelation and against grace (2:6-8).

The person-to-person aspect of their sin is treated in verses 6, 7a, and while there is some possibility of doubt in individual points of interpretation, and at one place even regarding the proper translation,[8] RSV is more than adequate to expose the general

[7] The passage pivots on the opening words of verses 9 (*Yet I*) and 12 (*But you*). The element of contradiction can be seen by observing the structure of the verses: Israel's deeds (6-8) contradict the Lord's deeds (9,10); the Lord's words (11) were contradicted by Israel's words (12).

[8] 'Righteous' (2:6) can mean 'in the right in a law suit' (*i.e.* innocent of the charge) as well as the more general sense of 'the one who has right on his side' and the particular sense of being 'right with God'. Maybe, therefore, verse 6a points to bribing the magistrate to swing the verdict, and verse 6b to taking a person to court for as small a debt as a pair of shoes. Some commentators take both halves of the verse as referring to bribing the authorities; others take both halves as referring to the prosecution of debtors. In verse 7,

trends of life as it was then lived. Three principles were held and acted upon: the primary importance of seeking material possessions (the sin of covetousness), the irrelevance of the rights of other people (the sin of indifference and oppression)[9] and the unrestricted promotion of self-advantage (the sin of self-importance).

The absolutely devastating thing about all this is that these are precisely the sins discovered and condemned in the heathen. It was for this that Damascus, Gaza, Tyre, Edom, Ammon and Moab fell before the wrath of God, and the charge, as we saw, was their failure to be and to act as human beings. But now these very things are the sins of the church! There are lessons here to ponder. When the grace of God reaches out to man its purpose is to make him truly human: as we would say, the purpose of God's saving work is to make us like Jesus, the perfect Man. It is a perversion, indeed a denial, of this grace when we become wrongly isolated from the world and its needs and when we (perhaps unwittingly) restrict our awareness of sin to those offences which we commit against the first and great commandment and dismiss as even immaterial the sins against the second. When the Lord levels against His people the charge of rejecting His law (2:4, 5) He finds the evidence supporting the charge in their social misdemeanours.

The second aspect of Israel's sin is disobedience to specific divine commands: sins against revelation. *A man and his father go in to the same maiden, so that my holy name is profaned* (2:7b). To be fair to the Hebrew two changes must be made here: first, we should read not 'so that' but 'in order to'. In other words, when people do that which they know to be offensive to God, the Bible

---

RSV represents a small alteration in the Hebrew text, which is widely adopted by the commentators. It reveals a general attitude of oppressiveness against the helpless. The Hebrew, more literally rendered, reads 'that pant after the dust of the earth on the head of the poor' (so RV), suggesting such a lust for real estate as to grudge the ousted former owner the earth he daubs on his head as a sign of mourning.

[9] 'Needy' (6b) signifies those who can offer no resistance, 'poor' (7a) means 'weak' rather than poverty-stricken, and 'afflicted' is much what we mean by the 'under-dog'. On 'turning aside the way' *cf.* the similar expressions in Ex. 23:6; Dt. 24:17; 27:19; 1 Sa. 8:3; Pr. 17:23; 18:5; Is. 10:2, pointing to the meaning here of 'depriving the under-dog of his rights'.

bluntly insists that they do it in order to offend Him. Behind all deliberate, witting sin there is this careless affrontery towards God. God and His law, God and His word cannot be separated. When the word is rejected, God is rejected (cf. 1 Sa. 15:23), and when the word is knowingly, deliberately rejected there can be no evasion of the charge of wanting to be shut of God.

The other adjustment of the translation is to omit the word 'same'. The charge is not of some curious perversion but rather (if we may use a somewhat outdated expression) that 'every adult male without exception is a womanizer'. Without a doubt this is what Amos meant, though he was putting his own construction on what the people concerned would have explained rather differently. To them their sexual activities had a religious significance, and they would have described the women involved, not as prostitutes, but as 'holy', women who dedicated themselves to Baal by making themselves available for this aspect of his worship.[1] But Amos was not addressing Canaanites, but people who had been given a clear statement of the divine will for life and who had allowed Canaanite principles and practices to erode the distinctive standards and practices of their holy religion. They may smoothly talk, if they will, of visiting the holy women at the religious shrine, but Amos will describe them as running after girls, and he sees the whole adult male population involved, 'father and son'. The father was untrue to his marriage vow and committed the sin of adultery; the son contravened the law of God against fornication; both alike transgressed the divine prohibition of the use of 'holy'

[1] We find it very difficult to accommodate ourselves to this aspect of Canaanite religion and a silly illustration may help. Small children must be taught to blow their noses long before parent and child have sufficient vocabulary in common to make the teaching task easy. So what most parents do is to hold a handkerchief to the child's nose and make nose-blowing noises! The theory is that if we do something more or less like what we want the child to do it will catch on to the idea and act accordingly. Communication between Baal-worshippers and their god was chiefly along this line. When, therefore, they wished him to perform his acts of fertilizing land, animals and man, they could only perform the human acts of fertility and hope that he would be prompted to perform his equivalent function. Baal was a non-moral force. His 'holiness' was a mere 'difference' or 'separatedness' from men. Yahweh's holiness was from the start 'moral' or 'ethical'. Hence, in Israel, fertility or prosperity was linked with moral obedience. Cf. Dt. 28:1-14.

women in the worship of Yahweh.[2] They sinned against revelation.

Thus it was not only in the social manifestation of their sins that the people of God had become like the heathen, but also in their assiduous cultivation of the principle of self-pleasing. Sexual gratification had replaced the *holy name* of God as the guiding principle of life; even divine revelation had to bow to the superior demands of insistent self-centredness. (*Cf.* 1 Thes. 4:3-8.)

In his exposure of the sins of God's people Amos has adopted the pattern of working from the circumference to the centre. He began with the observer's point of view, the evidence of the social life, the person-to-person relationships, of Israel. Next he adopted a more interior standard of assessment, judging them in the light of specific revealed rules. Now finally he brings them into the very secret place of God's presence, the *altar* and *the house of their God* (2:8), to see how they are faring in the enjoyment of what they would undoubtedly have claimed to be the height of their distinctiveness as God's people. Thus we are brought to consider their sins against grace.

The central reality in the religion of Israel was the dwelling of God in the midst of His people. It was at this point that the whole work of God, redeeming His people from Egypt, reached its climax. This had been His aim throughout it all (Ex. 29:43-46). The *house of God* was the outward and visible sign of that indwelling; the *altar* was God reaching out to draw people into His presence through the virtue of the shed blood of sacrifice. God in His grace condescends to dwell among sinners; God in His mercy makes it possible for them to dwell with Him.

But what was happening in Amos' Israel? Mercy was being destroyed by the abandonment of mercy (2:8a), and fellowship was corrupted into carousal (2:8b). The fundamental law shines through: it is impossible to be right with God if we are wrong with men, or, to put it another way, if our attitudes and actions

[2] IB catches the spirit of Amos' denunciation exactly in the comment, 'Young and old frequent the shrine together . . . as if taking part in a kind of outing.' Hammershaimb points out that the verb 'go in' is not that customarily used for sexual intercourse (*e.g.* Gn. 16:2) and suggests 'betake themselves openly': they had lost all sense of disobeying the commandments and the implications of the law of their God. *Cf.* Ex. 20:14; Dt. 22:13-29; 23:17 ('cult prostitute' is literally 'holy woman').

towards men are not patterned on the attitudes and actions of God to us, then we cannot in reality claim to belong to Him. As Amos watched the men of his day, he saw them draw near to the altar of God, into the place of mercy, but they brought with them garments taken in pledge and unmercifully kept back from those who had pledged them. The law in Exodus 22:26, 27 is plain as to the fact that a cloak might be taken as security against a loan but could be held only by day and must be returned for the night; and it is plain as to its motivation: the cloak was used by night as a blanket; to deprive its owner of this necessary protection was an act of unfeeling thoughtlessness, the essence of the pitilessness of covetousness for money, and (note it well) it offended the compassionate God. In other words, when the divine compassion finds no reflection in human compassion then the altar is visited in vain. Those who are not interested in mercy when it lies within their own sphere cannot in sincerity concern themselves in mercy or sue for it from God, nor will He extend mercy to those who hate it (Mt. 18:32–35).

Furthermore, it was not fellowship with God which they sought or enjoyed. The Hebrew does not say 'they lay themselves down' (2:8a) but 'they take (them) aside',[3] the reference being to the 'temple girls'. Another aspect of their carousal was liquor, condemned not for itself but because of its source in ill-gotten wealth. According to the biblical laws, fines were not paid to the 'state' but to the 'injured party'. We are left to assume (in the light of verse 6) that the forms of the law were open to financial manipulation and provided a source of income worth celebrating. But the basic issue is more important than the contemporary form it assumed: if fellowship on the human level is contrary to the law of God, impure, oppressive, then all possibility of fellowship on the divine level has been destroyed. We cannot be right with God and wrong with man; we cannot be right with God unless what He is to us provides the pattern for what we are to others. It is possible to sin against grace and this is the way in which it is done.

[3] There does not seem to be any occasion in the Hebrew Bible where this form of the verb supports a reflexive meaning. It is always transitive, and according to regular Hebrew practice we ought to supply the pronominal object as above.

The contrasting God

Verses 6–8 resound with the sinful acts of Israel; verses 9–11 with the redeeming acts of God: the first person singular verb occurs five times, and twice it is reinforced (at the opening of verses 9, 10) with the personal pronoun. Salvation is all of God; man has contributed neither power nor merit.

We will see these two aspects worked out step by step as we follow through the work of God as Amos sets it out.[4] In detail, the Lord, by His sole power and activity, gave His people victory over their enemies by His 'root and branch' destruction of the then population of the promised land, the Amorites (2:9). But before that He had already accomplished their redemption by bringing them out of the land of Egypt (*cf.* Ex. 6:6, 7), giving them not a mere possibility of becoming His redeemed but the actual gift of a ready-made salvation which they could not refuse (*cf.* Ex. 12:33) and which the power of man could not undo (*cf.* Ex. 14:13, 14, 30, 31). He had, furthermore, introduced them into a fellowship of grace (2:10b). The reference to the *forty years* recalls the sin of rebellion against God for which the sojourn in the wilderness was a divine discipline (*cf.* Nu. 14:26–35), yet we read 'I *led you*': the Lord did not forsake His sinful people but, by His leadership of them even while they were subject to His displeasure, declared that the fellowship which they enjoyed with Himself had its basis in grace. And when the forty years were ended, He brought His people into their promised inheritance, their actual possession of the land of the Amorites (2:10b). But the acts of God were not ended. Divine guidance by word and deed such as had been experienced in the Exodus and in the wilderness was continued in the voice of the prophets and the demonstration of consecrated living by the Nazirites (*cf.* Nu. 6:1 ff.). The God of revelation maintained His revealed truth by word and good example.

[4] The order in which Amos retells the historical events is unusual: Conquest, Exodus, Wilderness, Possession. It is, happily, no longer the fashion with commentators to suggest re-organizing the verses here but to recognize that 'this unusual order has its own logic' (Mays). See NBCR, p. 731 for a demonstration of the way 2:9–12 is integrally related to 2:6–8.

Full salvation

Let us notice three things in order, which belong to us as much as to the people in Amos' day. First, the object of divine saving outreach is a company of helpless slaves, guilty sinners, frail mortals. They can neither deliver themselves from Egypt, maintain their walk with God, nor overthrow the power of their Amorite opponents. Left to themselves they are finished. This not only high-lights that salvation is all of God, who brings His chosen ones into a non-contributory benefit, but also it illuminates the theme that the human relationships of the redeemed are to reflect what their God has done for them. Consequently if, as in Israel of old, there is insistent self-seeking, carelessness of the welfare of the other man, readiness to climb over his prostrated hopes to self-aggrandizement—in a word, heedlessness of our brother's person, dignity, need and claim on our compassion—how can a credible claim be made out that we have experienced the saving grace of God in truth?

Secondly, and in direct relation to this, comes the observation that what the Lord did for His people was to furnish them with a full salvation, thus depriving them (and us) of every excuse for failing to be like their God. They had been redeemed by the blood of the Passover lamb and effectively brought out of bondage; they had been nourished and provided for in a fellowship of divine grace; they had been given the victory over their foes and made partakers of the inheritance of the people of God; they had been instructed throughout, and continued under the divine instruction of word and deed.[5] This is full salvation. It left them, as it leaves us, inexcusable if we fail to become like God.

The emphasized sin

But, thirdly, in all this catalogue of divine grief, one thing stands out for special astonishment—rightly reflected in RSV by the

[5] *Cf.* Pusey, *in loc.* 'The Nazirite was a fruit of the grace of God in its moral and religious workings . . . as the prophets were of that same grace, conferring superhuman wisdom and knowledge . . . The life of the Nazirites was . . . a life above nature . . . They had no special office except to live that life . . . (There was) nothing to distinguish them from ordinary men except extraordinary grace . . . an evidence of what all might be and do if they used the grace of God.'

allocating of a separate paragraph to verse 12. If there is one thing which (dare we say it?) amazes God more than anything else in the life of His people, it is that He should make His way plain to them, in word and deed, and that they should reject and deny it. Israel wanted neither the example of holy living nor the declaration of divine truth.

Amos has come full circle. True indeed it is that the outward sins of the people of God lie in parallel to the sins of the heathen, but behind this similarity there is a most appalling difference. To Israel, to His own people, God had spoken and they had said 'No'. The deepest sin of the people of God, the sin from which all sin springs, the sin which, through His prophet, the Lord singles out for final reaffirmation, is the sin of possessing revelation from God and ignoring it.[6] This is the 'fourth transgression' of the people of God.

The same God, but how different

Of the four sections which compose Amos' charge against the people of God, the third, to which we now come (2:13-16), is rather different from the other three, though vitally related to them. The first (2:4, 5), second (2:6-12) and fourth (3:1, 2) sections deal with errors and transgressions of God's people: their rejection of His truth, their contradiction in life of the salvation He had worked for them, and (as we shall see in 3:1, 2) their misunderstanding of the status conferred on them by His love for them. The third charge stands in contrast to all this, for it outlines the stern reaction of the Lord: *God's people have forfeited His favour.*

This title expresses the plain truth of the verses in their context. Three times Amos not only speaks in the first person singular of the voice of God but adds additional emphasis by using a separate personal pronoun: '*I* destroyed (2:9) . . . *I* brought you up (2:10) . . . *I* will press you down (2:13) . . .': the God of victory and of redemption is the God of hostility. The sequence of pronouns proclaims the actions of one and the same God, and the

---

[6] For opposition to the prophets see, *e.g.*, 1 Ki. 13:4; 18:10-12; 19:2, 3; 22:26, 27; 2 Ki. 1:9-13; 6:31; 2 Ch. 16:7, 10; 24:20, 21; 25:15, 16; Is. 30:10, 11; Mi. 2:6.

more Israel exalts the divine power which could drive out the Amorite and loose the iron grip of Egypt, the more certainly Israel must become aware that if that God turns to become an enemy then there can be no hope of escape.

Israel had comfortably forgotten 'the vengeance of the covenant', the jealousy of God at work within the confines of His chosen people to punish transgression, to discipline unto greater holiness and to purge out evil. The words 'the vengeance of the covenant' (RSV 'vengeance for . . .') occur in Leviticus 26:25 and the 'whole picture' is given in verses 14–45 of the same chapter, the broad truth being that God's saving work, bringing people into His covenant of grace, is not intended to induce a spirit of moral complacency but of moral ambition after holiness through obedience to the divine commands. Disobedience will be visited with punishment, even to the point of apparent destruction of all that God had built up, yet in the end, since salvation depends on the will of God and not of man, divine faithfulness will never break the covenant. This is a key passage for understanding life within the covenant as the Bible depicts it. A 'covenant theologian' like Amos could never have been guilty of proclaiming the end of the covenant relation between the Lord and His people. Passages such as Leviticus 26:31–38; Deuteronomy 28:58–68; Amos 2:13–16 and others may appear to destroy the entire covenant relationship between the Lord and His people, but if they are held within their own contexts (Lv. 26:14–45; Dt. 28:1—30:10; *etc.*) as well as within the context of the whole Bible's teaching on the covenant, it becomes clear that these fearful destructions are to be accounted among the covenant-keeping (not the covenant-breaking) acts of God. They purge out pretended members and purify true members. 'The vengeance of the covenant' warns us never to allow our membership to give house-room to moral complacency, for though the promises of God can never change, the reality of our possession or inheritance of those promises must ever be subject to scrutiny so that our assurance may be well and not falsely founded.[7]

The idea, therefore, of the 'vengeance of the covenant' has much to say to us as individuals, but it equally addresses us as the church. For we are as prone as any earlier age—back to and including the

[7] *Cf.* 1 Cor. 10:1–13; 2 Pet. 1:10, 11.

days when Amos addressed the nation–church of Israel—to lean on natural abilities and acquired skills, to blame our misfortunes on the adversity of our circumstances and the peculiar difficulties of the age in which we live, and to discount the opposition and alienation of God. Put those three items in the reverse order and they summarize the contents of 2:13–16: God has turned to afflict His people (13);[8] He proposes to do so by means of an enemy much too strong for them, before whom neither native ability (14) nor acquired skill (15) nor outstanding qualities (16) will avail anything.

The point at issue here can be very well illustrated by recalling a complaint often made about the way in which the Bible tells, for example, the story of king Jeroboam in whose reign Amos prophesied. It was a reign of forty-one years (2 Ki. 14:23 ff.) but it merits only seven verses of text; it was a time of enormous political, military and commercial advancement for the kingdom of Israel, but the Bible tells nothing of this at all in anything but the barest outline, its sole comment on Jeroboam being that he did what the Lord considered evil and continued in the sins of his earlier namesake. No modern historian would even begin to think that this was satisfactory history-writing, but the Bible is simply being faithful to its own axiom that 'righteousness exalts a nation, but sin is a reproach to any people' (Pr. 14:34). We are conditioned by our whole inherited cast of mind and our education to look for political, social and economic causes of the rise and fall of nations and empires; the Bible would have us reform our thinking and seek the cause of things in the moral and spiritual realm upon which all else is consequent. Sin is the hinge upon which destiny turns, effecting a downfall which good policies could never in themselves avert nor policies, however mistaken, could quite so fully accomplish. To the Bible, history is the arena of moral decisions, moral conflicts and moral consequences.

[8] Verse 13 is peculiarly difficult to translate because of the uncertainty which surrounds the verb which RSV translates 'press . . . presses'. RSV, NEB, JB give the most generally considered possibilities, though it is frankly hard to see what JB means or why, as in RSV, it should in particular be the heavy downward pressure of a harvest waggon which is selected to typify the divine oppression of the people. Some relief is gained if we understand 'cart' as a threshing device (cf. Is. 28:28) and take 'sheaves' as the object of the verb: 'as a weighted threshing cart presses the sheaves'. Cf. NBCR, pp. 731 f.

In effect therefore these four verses, in which Amos asserts that God's people have forfeited His favour, are profoundly significant in their message to us. They speak of our first practical duty and our continuing basic concern: are we right with God? Can we with credibility believe that He is on our side? Everything hinges on the answer to these questions.

The discipline of love

We have now reviewed three of the four charges which Amos levelled against the people of God: that they had rejected His law (2:4, 5), contradicted His salvation (2:6-12) and (consequently) forfeited His favour (2:13-16). The fourth charge traces this sequence back to its root: it is their very status as the people of God which makes them liable to such vengeance. To a people steeped in spiritual complacency because of ancestrally-bestowed privileges, Amos urges that *they have misunderstood God's love* (3:1, 2).

A small retranslation will, perhaps, help us the more readily to feel the amazement and surprise which Amos' words in these verses would have caused. Instead of *against* (verse 1) read 'about'.[9] The neutral word 'about' has a matter-of-factness which makes the ensuing sentences all the more telling.

The Lord has five truths to assert about His people: four are descriptive and the fifth consequential. The address to *Israel* recalls that this is the people of election and adoption. They were God's elect in that He had covenanted to Abraham to be God to him and to his descendants after him (Gn. 17:7); they became collectively God's adopted son at and in the historical event of the Exodus (Ex. 4:22). They were, thirdly, His redeemed, being *the whole family*[1] *which I*[2] *brought up out of the land of Egypt* (3:1).

---

[9] This is in fact the proper translation in by far the majority of places where the verb 'to speak' occurs with this preposition ('al). Cf. BDB, p. 181b. It is only the over-all sense of divine hostility in the passage which has beguiled all the translators in this place.

[1] JB correctly observes in a footnote that Amos is 'apparently addressing all twelve tribes'. Thus the whole section commencing at 2:4 is unified: the oracle against Judah states the sin of the whole people in principle (2:4, 5), that against Israel (2:6-16) states their sins in detail, and 3:1, 2 rounds off the sequence with a common conclusion, their particularity and its surprising consequences.

Fourthly, they possessed these privileges in a unique covenantal intimacy[3] as the only one *known of all the families of the earth* (3:2a). To elaborate these four facets of relationship further would require a wholesale retelling of the Bible story, yet a deep sense of wonder, love and praise forbids haste, for here is the whole amazing love of God for His people. Uncompelled except by His own heart (*cf.* Dt. 7:7 f.), He chose, yet not as a man chooses a tool nor as an employer a slave. The choice issued in family ties, sonship of God, and when that relationship was threatened by earthly hostility (Ex. 1:22) the Lord stood by it, entering Egypt in pursuance of covenant loyalty (Ex. 2:24 f.) and redeeming (Ex. 6:6), as the event showed, by the blood of the lamb (Ex. 12:13). Now let all human history be searched: as far back as records go, and beyond; among the great peoples who have won empires and changed the world and among obscure tribes living and dying in remote isolation—no time, no place, no people except this can register the claim. God has said 'You only', and we reply 'Only us'.

Therefore, says Amos, *I will punish you for all your iniquities* (3:2b). Sin is desperately serious among the people of God. The heathen come under condemnation for violating conscience; the people of God must therefore be trebly under condemnation for

---

[2] The change from the third person to the first person ('the Lord has spoken ... I brought up ...') is noted, *e.g.*, by IB as indicating that a 'later hand' inserted the second phrase ('against the whole family ...'). It ought surely to be felt necessary to explain why the 'later hand' thought such an addition necessary and why it was so stupid as to make it syntactically discordant with its context! Hammershaimb is much more perceptive in saying that quibbles about the change of person here make 'the unreasonable demand that the prophets ... should attain the precision that we would expect in a carefully revised literary account'. Such changes are, however, commonplace in the style of a vigorous preacher and the fact that they remain in the books of the prophets is rather an indication of the care which was taken to preserve the forms of the spoken original.

[3] Mays and Hammershaimb point out that 'to know' has many shades of significance, including 'to choose' (*cf.* Je. 1:5), 'to watch over' (*cf.* Ps. 1:6), and that in the Hittite Treaties it is used in the sense 'to recognize by covenant'. The supreme use of the verb 'to know' in a relational rather than a cognitive sense is Gn. 4:1, where it is in no way a sexual euphemism but a proper expression of the deepest possible communion in love and oneness. All this is expressed in the use of 'known' to describe the Lord's relation to Israel.

they violate conscience, revelation and the love which has made them what they are. And yet nothing is easier: if His love is so great, does His holiness after all matter? Since He chose, will He not keep, come what may? So it goes on, the voice of complacency eroding spiritual reality. But love has brought us near to the Holy One; the blood of the Lamb has redeemed us for obedience. 'To be chosen is to be put under judgment.'[4] 'The nearer God places anyone to His own light, the more malignant is the choice of darkness.'[5]

It is not, of course, that the Lord chooses and then reverses His choice, makes folk His sons and then unmakes them. Amos is not at variance with the rest of Scripture and for him as much as for Paul 'God never takes back his gifts or revokes his choice' (Rom. 11:29, JB). Amos is declaring the vengeance which falls within the covenant; there is no such thing as a divine vengeance nullifying a covenant once made or revoking a promise once bestowed. Within the covenant, vengeance purges, removing from among the covenant people those who claim to be members but are not (cf. Jn. 15:2, 6), and vengeance chastises, disciplining those who are true members but who as sons need the Father's loving punishment (cf. Heb. 12:7 ff.). It is of these things that Amos speaks. To walk with God in the covenant of sonship is not a soft option (cf. Phil. 2:12; 1 Pet. 1:17). The Father requires His children to be perfect as He is perfect; the Son who alone knows the Father (cf. Mt. 11:27) has said so (Mt. 5:48).

It is part of our tendency to constrict the teaching of the Bible that we differentiate between true believers and mere professors by the content of their verbal testimony to their experience of God. But Jesus says (and did Amos say any different in the passage we have now reviewed?) that it is of no significance to say 'Lord, Lord' and then to turn from doing the will of His heavenly Father (Mt. 7:21).

Special privileges, special obligations; special grace, special holiness; special revelation, special scrutiny; special love, special responsiveness . . . the church of God cannot ever escape the perils of its uniqueness.

[4] Mays, *ad loc.*   [5] Pusey, *ad loc.*

Amos 3:3-8
Appeal and Apologia

THERE is a 'before' and an 'after' to everything in life, a time of opportunity and a time when opportunity has gone, a time for saying 'I must and I can' and a time when all that is left is 'I cannot'. In the formation of habits, there is a moment or period when mind, emotions and will are sufficiently disengaged to make a complete change; there is also the point of no return after which a whole area of liberty has died and, for good or ill, life has taken on another bond. There is, every day, some 'now' of fading or dying opportunity.

The significant 'now'

It is to this crucial moment that Amos appears to address himself in the concluding passage of the first section of his book. The Lion is still roaring (3:8), therefore the prey has not yet been seized. There is still a chance to come to terms. Hope has not yet vanished.

A 'before and after' pattern appears throughout the central verses (3:4–6). In 4a the lion roars its pouncing roar (*cf.* on 1:2), but in 4b the prey has been taken and the growl of the beast is heard from the den to which the carcase has been taken for food;[1] in 5a the bird falls into the snare but in 5b the snare has snapped shut;[2] in 6a the trumpet advertises a coming danger, but in 6b

---

[1] RSV *cry out* fails to represent the Hebrew 'give (forth) his voice'. We might say 'give tongue' or, as NEB, JB, 'growl', which, in context, is exactly right.

[2] In 5a *trap* should rather be 'bait'. The word is used of the snare or trap but its stricter use is of that which ensnares, the thing which entices rather than the place into which it entices. The picture is therefore of a bird hastening to a self-chosen doom.

the blow has fallen. This movement of the verses from threat to execution constitutes a powerful concluding appeal to the message Amos has just preached. Consider what the illustrations, taken in turn, are saying. First, threats are not idle (verse 4): to single out Samson was an unfortunate error of judgment, but ordinarily, once the lion has roared and pounced, that is the end of the matter. Certainly it is not safe to assume otherwise. David noted it as a signal instance of divine aid that he rescued his flock from a lion (1 Sa. 17:34 ff.). And when the divine Lion roars, then let the people shake off their complacency. The Lord is bent on action. Secondly, judgment is not uninvited (verse 5). The bird is in the trap through no fault but its own. Therefore let the people examine themselves, their chosen course, their desires and ambitions, for it is nothing but their own hearts which has led them astray. Thirdly, God is not mocked (verse 6). There is a divine and wholly just providence controlling world history. Calamity[3] never falls without the directive hand of God.[4] The translation offered in JB is excellent: 'Does misfortune come to a city if Yahweh has not sent it?' He is no absentee landlord in relation to the world He created; He has neither abdicated nor delegated His powers. He rules and He executes judgment and justice. The people must not presume otherwise or think that any special plea will be heard. This is the God with whom they have to do. But at this particular moment, as the passage shows, they can seize the opportunity to have dealings with Him other than in terms of judgment and overthrow.

The moment, the man and the message

We must now consider the meaning of verse 3. Reading through from the opening verses of the chapter it has a plain significance. Two people do not 'keep company' except by making an arrange-

---

[3] 'Evil' (6b) is a word used about 640 times in the Old Testament. Its main uses are of moral evil, whether against the law of God, an affront against God or man (about 350 times) and physical calamity, disaster, hurt of body or loss of goods (about 270 times). It must always be interpreted according to context. Here (as in the often disputed Is. 45:7) it refers to historical calamity or overthrow in war.

[4] The doctrine of divine providence indicated here will occupy us more fully in dealing with 4:6 ff.

ment.⁵ Just such an arrangement was made between the Lord and His people at the Exodus and they began to 'keep company' (*cf.* Je. 2:2, 3 where *followed* is 'walked (the same verb) after'), but now they have proved false and must be disciplined.

But when we read forward from verse 3 something wonderfully unexpected happens. We have already noticed the 'before and after' pattern of verses 4-6, but where is the 'second half' of verse 3 which would make it conform to this pattern? It would not be difficult to propose a question which would fill the gap:

> Do two walk together,
> unless they have come to an arrangement?
> Can a marriage be restored
> if the certificate of divorce has been written?

But there is no such second, final question asked. The first question stands awaiting an answer. While it waits, we are shown three times over that inevitably things pass through the interim period to a conclusion: the moment of hope does not tarry indefinitely. After the illustrations, verses 7, 8 explain why verse 3 was left incomplete: again the roaring lion is heard (3:8a), but it is not followed by the lion growling over its prey. The roaring lion has provoked the voice of prophecy (3:8b). The completed message then is this: the 'arrangement' between the Lord and His people is threatened, it is deeply and seriously at risk. Unless action is taken the 'punishment' (3:2, lit., 'visitation') cannot but come: the roar will be followed by the growl (3:4). But in the interim

---

⁵ The meaning of this verse often proposed, that in the open spaces of Tekoa where Amos lived meetings took place only by appointment, will hardly do. Amos is here (presumably) preaching in Bethel (*cf.* 7:13) and is asking a question of his hearers. There is no indication that he expects them to transport themselves imaginatively out of their own crowded streets into his deserted countryside before answering! Cripps rightly suggests taking the verb *walk* in a continuous sense: 'keep going about together'. Regarding *made an appointment* he prefers the slight emendation suggested by LXX, 'are known to each other' (even though the reciprocal sense of this form of the verb 'to know' appears to be unexemplified in the OT). D. W. Thomas (*Journal of Theological Studies*, 1956) proposes that the meaning for the emended form should be, not 'to know', but 'to be still, quiet', *i.e.* 'are at peace with each other'. But without emending the text at all, the sense of 'come to an arrangement with each other' is well exemplified in Jos. 11:5; Jb. 2:11; Ps. 48:4 and this does very well in the present passage.

(that precious, crucial moment when, however belated, a decision may still be taken) the incompleteness of the structure of verse 3 leaves the future open, and the voice of the prophet (3:7, 8) calls the people to renew their 'arrangement' with the Lord and to act promptly, for even as he speaks to them the Lion is roaring.

The decisive word

This, then, was the high task Amos was called to perform. He had to step forward in the interim of grace between warning and disaster and make his message clear to the people. It is the task every preacher has in relation to his congregation; it is the task the Word of God has to the church and to the world: the sirens have sounded, the end of all things is at hand, here is the way of salvation, the way back to God, the message of reconciliation.

Verses 7 and 8 are rich in their teaching about prophecy (and by implication about the whole Bible). We shall glance at the message, the inspiration and the self-awareness of the prophet.

The task of the Old Testament prophet was to address the present in the light of the future. We have seen throughout how Amos labours to make his message relevant to his hearers, rehearsing their history, their sins and their characters to them. In this sense, his message arose from the circumstances of those to whom he spoke, it partook of the nature of current political, social and personal comment. But it also arose from an awareness of the future for, throughout, the present only possessed seriousness or urgency because of what was going to happen next. What would the crimes of Damascus matter except that the Lord was going to send fire in punishment for them? Apart from this ultimate sanction of divine wrath and impending divine overthrow, it would only be a matter of the relative weight of the humanitarian opinion of Amos as against the unconcerned self-seeking of Damascus and the others. This particular integration of present and future, this grasp upon prediction as belonging to the essence of the prophet's task, could hardly be stated better than in the penetrating comments of Emil Brunner: 'the idea that permeates Old Testament prophecy is that of the coming God and the coming kingdom of God. The prophet is the herald of God's advent . . . His whole proclamation is to be understood only from the side of this future.

For in this future his message has its meaning, its goal, its necessity ... The thing that makes the historical moment into a moment of decision in such an unprecedented manner is simply this eschatological reference ... The historical Now receives its seriousness from the viewpoint of the end of all things.'[6]

To such an extent did Amos hold that prediction belonged to the essence of the prophetic office that he was ready to commit himself to the general principle that *surely the Lord God does nothing, without revealing his secret to his servants the prophets* (3:7).[7] But there is also an aspect of this saying which leads into our discussion of the inspiration of the prophet. The future which was the subject of his prediction was not merely 'coming events', an exercise in crystal-gazing or fortune-telling; it was 'God's future', the coming acts of God as arising out of the nature of God and His reaction to affairs on earth. Brunner expressed this admirably in calling the prophet the 'herald of God's advent'. The point is that it is not correct to speak of a prophetic gift of prognostication but of a prophetic privilege of knowing God. Prediction came about as part of the prophet's conscious fellowship with the Lord.

Looking now at verses 7 and 8, there is first of all a declaration of divine policy: it is God's general plan to anticipate coming events by informing His servants the prophets of what He intends to do. Secondly, this information comes to them by means of a fellowship with God into which they are admitted: the words *revealing his secret* equally mean 'opening his fellowship'. Jeremiah expresses the same thought (and uses the same word) when he describes the prophet as one who has *stood in the council of the Lord to perceive and to hear his word* (Je. 23:18; *cf.* verse 22). Micaiah allows us to understand the matter pictorially when he alludes to a heavenly consultative body into which he was incorporated and from which

---

[6] In the essay 'The Significance of the Old Testament for our Faith' in *The Old Testament and Christian Faith*, edited by B. W. Anderson (SCM Press, 1964), p. 259. The same idea runs through the whole Bible. John the Baptist's message was not 'Repent in order that the kingdom may come' but 'Repent because the kingdom is coming': it was the settled and searching future fact which gave him a present, urgent message. Equally, New Testament ethics customarily have an eschatological frame of reference: *e.g.* Rom. 13:11-14; 2 Pet. 3:11.

[7] *Cf.* Elisha's astonishment when something germane to his ministry was not made a matter of prior divine revelation, 2 Ki. 4:27.

he was commissioned to report back to earth (1 Ki. 22:19-23). Thirdly, the outcome of this fellowship was the unique task of speaking on earth the very words of God: *The Lord God has spoken; who can but prophesy?* [8] We need to be careful that we understand what is being claimed and the ground on which the claim rests. Amos is his own interpreter when he describes his book thus: *The words of Amos ... Thus says the Lord* (1:1, 3). He made each claim equally: the words were his—and we may fully understand that all the study, deliberation and choice of alternative wording, which ordinarily belong with sermon preparation, lie behind the claim; the words were the Lord's, in the unique, affirmative sense that Amos (or any of the prophets or Bible writers) said neither 'I think this is what God means', nor 'I know this is what he means and I will say it as best I can', but 'Here is God's message in God's words'. That they were *the words of Amos* forbids us to think in any quasi-mechanical terms, as that Amos became God's typewriter or animated tape-recorder: he was there in the fullness of his individual personality, temperament and humanity; that they were *the words of the Lord* forbids us to allow that as originally given they partook of or were in the least infected by human sin or error. We are dealing with a unique thing and these are the dimensions of the uniqueness.

It is at this point that the doctrines of inspiration and revelation need to be kept in the context of fellowship with God, as Amos does in the present passage. The nearer a man is brought to God, the more truly human he becomes; the more he reflects the likeness of God, the more he is man. It is because Jesus is Son of God that He can be Son of man. For the purposes of communicating His message, God gave to His servants the prophets a unique fellowship with Himself. This very experience which brought them into knowledge of God and His ways, His plans for the future and His message for now, also brought them to a fuller, truer, finer flowering of their humanity. Thus (so to speak) the Amos who spoke the very words of God was not (typewriter-fashion) less human than before, devalued from being fully a person, but was 'more

---

[8] *Cf.* Ex. 4:15, 16; 7:1, 2 as describing exactly this relationship between the prophetic message and the words of God; and Je. 1:9; Ezk. 2:7 (NB 'words' in each case, the actual verbalized form of the message), *etc.*, as registering the same claim.

Amos' than ever, a truer, fuller, greater human being. This accounts for the 'larger than life' impression which the prophets (and indeed all the Bible writers) make on us: they make this impression because it is simply and plainly the truth about them.

Finally, Amos was fully aware of all this concerning himself and the office to which he was called. We will do no injustice to his words if we cast them into the first person singular: 'You know that the Lord forewarns through His servants the prophets before He acts. He has made me one of that company, and seeing that He has spoken to me, how can I help bringing the prophetic message to you?' Courage, urgency and authority all arise from this point. It was on this ground that he was able later to outface the authority of the High Priest and courageously to stand his ground in the face of a charge of treason (7:10-17). It is the ground of his courage here as he enforces on the people the unpalatable truth that they are in danger of losing an inheritance which they had been brought up to think of as their automatic and inalienable birthright. Note how the claim in verse 8 comes as a climax to a series of verses which proclaim that there is no effect without a cause: the sight of prey stimulates the lion to pounce; the tasty morsel provokes the contented, mouth-watering growl (3:4); the dropping flight of the bird bespeaks the baited trap (3:5); the fear of the people arises from the trumpet blast of warning (3:6); and the message of the prophet is caused by the voice of God (3:8). Amos is self-aware of his God-given privilege, position, message and ministry.[9]

'Is there an Amos in the house?'

Are we involved here in a merely antiquarian study of certain unique men and unique phenomena of the ancient world? In one sense Amos and the prophets are as unrepeatable as Paul and the apostles, and the Word of God will never again come to the church

[9] In the light of all this is it not less than realistic ever to have doubted whether Amos could or would have committed his prophecies to paper and arranged them so as to reflect accurately his God-given message? As a well-read man in a literate age it is to the highest extent unreasonable to think that he knew his words to be God's words and then let them disappear into thin air once the message was delivered. The ground of written prophecy is in the self-awareness of the individual prophet.

in the same precise quality as it was preached and written by them. But in another sense, the invigorating truths of this study belong to every Christian, both as a statement of fact and as a summons to ministry.

Consider the church in Amos' day: it was desperately needy and (though all unconscious of the fact) was threatened by the imminent displeasure of its God; it lacked true knowledge, true spirituality, true repentance; it was full of corruption; it had departed from the truth; it was proud, complacent and self-satisfied; it set itself on a pedestal and despised the world. It could produce all the evidence which today makes people cry out to God for revival, being convinced that nothing can stop this rot and rebuild the ruins but some over-mastering spiritual effusion from on high which will bring the faithful remnant into proper trim for service, cast the unbeliever down in a deep sense of the incurable guiltiness of sin, and say to the world that there is a God who lives and reigns.

What, however, did God do? He sent a man who had been in His fellowship to preach His Word.

We cannot be in actuality what Amos (or Paul) was; but we can be like them in principle. Thanks to the unique inspiration and revelation granted to them we possess the Word of God; thanks to the reconciling work of Jesus we have, in Him and by one Spirit, our access to the Father (Eph. 2:18). In that precious fellowship, centred on His holy Word, the book of the Scriptures, we—even we—can become those who will meet and face the church of our day with courage and authority, buying up the opportunity afforded to us in the interim of grace between the Lion's roar and the onset of judgment.

Part Two
THE ENCIRCLING FOE
Amos 3:9—6:14

General Introduction

AS in the first part of his book, Amos marks off the limits of this section by returning at the end to the thoughts which occupied him at the beginning. In this case the key idea is stated in 3:11, *An adversary shall surround the land* with consequent overthrow especially of the *houses* (3:15) which even in themselves symbolize the luxury-loving spirit of their builders; the same two thoughts in reverse order conclude the section: the overthrow of every sort of house (6:11) and the enemy advancing from Hamath in the north and the Arabah Brook in the south (6:14).

Thus, whereas Part One was full of threat, indicating what the Lord would do in punishing His people and analysing the grounds on which they merited His punitive action, and Amos was able to cast himself into the role of one leaping into the breach to set the divine Word before the people as the means of their escape and salvation, now the die has been cast and it is only a matter of time before the overthrow actually takes place. Amos reveals calls which have gone unheeded (*e.g.* 4:6–11; 5:4, 6, 14). He even laments as if at the funeral of Israel (5:1, 2). The majesty (4:13; 5:8, 9) and the alienation of God (5:21; 6:8) are set forth. But, as ever, the Bible has no appetite for mere denunciation, bare announcement of imminent, inescapable doom. The section is a reasoned argument why these things must be so: it therefore exposes the sins of the people of God, the areas of life in which evidence will show itself that they are not living in harmony with their God, the things which (however unimportant they may be to the unaided human gaze) make Him mourn, the reasons why the church is powerless in the face of the world. It is along these lines that what would otherwise have been the tale of a by-gone tragedy remains the voice of the living God speaking to us and to His whole people today.

For simplicity the section may be viewed in three divisions, with two passages of diagnosis (3:9—4:5; 6:1-14) sandwiching a passage of appeal (4:6-13; 5:1-27). The first diagnosis covers the social (3:9-11), personal (3:12) and religious (3:13-15) aspects of life and the basic sin of self-indulgence or self-pleasing is exposed (4:1-5). But the Lord has not been idle: He has addressed His people through circumstances (4:6-13) and through the intelligible voice of prophecy (5:1-27), calling them back to Himself (4:6, 8, 9, 10, 11; 5:4, 5, 14, 22-24); His call to repentance (4:6, *etc.*) focused on the spiritual (5:4-13), moral (5:14-20) and religious (5:21-25) aspects of their life, but it was all to no avail. And indeed why should they turn to Him when they were so completely self-sufficient? The concluding diagnosis reveals man's proud self-satisfaction (6:1-7) and God's hatred of it leading to its complete, imminent overthrow (6:8-14).

Amos 3:9-15
'He turned to be their enemy'

EVERY biblical truth has, in turn, been proclaimed as the truth which the church has forgotten and needs desperately to recover! Has it not been so with the truth about the Second Coming, or Revival, or the Holy Spirit? But to begin this study by saying that here is a forgotten truth which must be recovered is not to employ a threadbare preaching formula. We have forgotten that our God can turn and become our enemy (Is. 63:10) and with all our talk of taking care not to fall into the power of Satan we have become blind to the much more dangerous possibility of falling out of the power of God. We dismiss it, ignore it or forget it to our peril. Why ever is the individual believer powerless against his foes, or why is the whole church powerless? Is it because God has lost His power? No, but because we have lost His power. *Behold, the Lord's hand is not shortened, that it cannot save, or his ear dull, that it cannot hear; but your iniquities have made a separation between you and your God, and your sins have hid his face from you so that he does not hear* (Is. 59:1, 2). The Scripture abounds with examples of the divine alienation,[1] but we must focus on this passage in Amos where it is the leading thought.

Amos depicts for us a powerless nation and a powerless church. Nationally they can point to their *strongholds* (3:10), but when the enemy surrounds the land *your strongholds shall be plundered* (3:11). Ecclesiastically they are equally defenceless. Verse 14 reflects the pagan supposition that to cling to *the horns of the altar*[2] gave a

---

[1] *E.g.* Gn. 3:24; Jos. 7:11, 12, 26; Jdg. 3:7, 8, 12; Ps. 78:58-64.
[2] There was no 'altar-asylum' among the people of God. Verses sometimes quoted in favour of such a practice (Ex. 21:12 ff.; 1 Ki. 1:49 ff.; 2:28 ff.) reveal on examination that the horns of the altar offered no refuge. The

79

person (whatever and whoever he may have previously been) sacrosanctity, but in the day when such asylum is most grievously needed they will find that even the imagined refuge has failed them: the altar will have no horns.[3] With the neatest possible touch Amos exposes the wholesale failure of their religion as a protection against disaster. If we translate *Bethel* in verse 14 we get the following interesting sequence: '... house of God ... winter house ... summer house ... houses of ivory ... great houses. ...' Where religion is powerless everything is powerless; when the house of God falls no house can stand.

But in all this powerlessness, it is the Lord who is their enemy. They are powerless because they have lost Him. The encircling foe of verse 11 is followed by an illustrative use of attack by a lion (12). Amos draws no conclusion but leaves us to make our own comparison with Part One of his book. The encircling foe speaks of the enmity of their Lion-God. In verses 14 and 15 the wording is direct: *I punish ... I will punish ... I will smite ...* The vengeance of the covenant is a reality,[4] and we would do well to ponder what it is which alienates God from His people and renders them helpless before their foes.

Social relationships

This is a particularly easy passage to analyse for it includes three distinct introductory sayings: *Proclaim* (3:9) ... *Thus says the Lord* (12) ... *Hear* (13). Each calls attention to a specific aspect

'horns' were projections from the four corners of the altar and are specially mentioned in connection with the sprinkling of the blood: Ex. 29:12; Lv. 4:7, 18, 25, 34.

[3] IB wonders if the oracle contained in 3:13–15 ought not to be considered an insertion by a later editor in that it 'interrupts the sequence of oracles directly concerned with Samaria'. But this fails to take note of the fact that in this series of oracles as it stands Samaria (the political capital) and Bethel (the religious capital) alternate: see 3:9 and 4:1 for Samaria, 3:13, 14 and 4:4 for Bethel. This interweaving bears witness to Amos' stress that religion and society belong together: false religion begets false social values. The crimes of society cannot be exposed unless they are seen as sins against God (on this see NBCR, pp. 732 f.). Therefore Samaria cannot be diagnosed without Bethel.

[4] Nothing which has taken place in Christ renders this truth void. We are God's covenant people, subject to His covenant blessings or His covenant curses. A study of the Letters of Jesus to the Seven Churches (Rev. 2:1 ff.) is particularly revealing in this connection (*e.g.* 2:5, 16, 23; 3:3, 16).

of the life of the people of God in respect to which they fall under condemnation and experience the divine alienation. The first (9–11) delves into their society and emerges with the principle that the Lord turns to be their enemy when His people live below the level of grace in the matter of their social relationships.

Their sins are specified in the words *tumults . . . oppressions* (9) *. . . violence and robbery* (10). The first and fourth point to disregard for the proper order and fabric of society, the second and third are concerned with oppressive, unjust and self-regarding behaviour towards other people. Considered from the point of view of the state, it did not concern them that a course of action would inevitably disrupt the good order of social life. Law and order in this sense was not important to them. From the point of view of the church, it seemed no hindrance that some contemplated line of speech or conduct would breach the fellowship. Social cohesion, church harmony were not operative factors. All that mattered was some new acquisition for the self, something to *store up* (10). And the same was true person-to-person. If other folk were 'downed' as the self ascended the scale of importance and wealth, so much the worse for them. Does it help us to identify with what Amos is saying to note that he is talking of conduct opposite to that which *in humility counts others better than yourselves*, looks *to the interests of others* and displays *the mind . . . which is yours in Christ Jesus* (Phil. 2:3–5)? So often the things which Amos condemns openly and Paul condemns by contrast are the things which fail to be categorized as sins at all in the general run of life, but they are first on the list here and the Lord roundly condemns them as *not . . . right* (10).[5]

This is one of four notes of condemnation which Amos sounds here against conduct which disrespects society and fellowship and devalues other people. He says also that such deeds induce spiritual blindness: *They do not know how to do right* (10). 'It is part', says Pusey, 'of the miserable blindness of sin, that while the soul acquires a quick insight into evil, it becomes at last, not paralysed

---

[5] Mays says that Amos uses here 'a normative term by which actions can be measured'. He offers the following analysis of meaning: what is straightforward, honest, right in contrast to what is deceptive and false (Is. 30:10); the right/good as opposed to the bad/evil; synonymous with justice, righteousness, faithfulness (Is. 59:14); that which is 'in the right' in a legal suit (2 Sa. 15:3); acceptable practice in court and commerce.

only to *do* good, but unable to perceive it.'[6] Furthermore, this line of conduct is inherently destructive. A *therefore* links verses 10 and 11. A logic binds *violence and robbery* to their just recompense in an enemy who destroys all and takes all. Indeed the form of words Amos uses insists that it must be so. He does not say (what some commentators limit him to meaning and which of course, in part, he does mean) that they *store up* that which they have gained through *violence and robbery*. In terms of the bank balance or the strong room this is of course so. But Amos actually says that they are putting by *violence and robbery* themselves, storing, treasuring, preserving, guarding the very means of their own destruction. The Bible often represents sin as possessing this boomerang quality, but nowhere more clearly than here, and in relation to sins which we often gloss over as insignificant.

But his greatest condemnation of this line of conduct comes at the outset of the passage (9) in the address to *Ashdod*[7] and *Egypt*. What a particular sting there would be for the proud northerners of Amos' day in making these hated, ancestral enemies the ones who could sit in judgment on them! To be judged by those who are known and despised as graceless and spiritually ignorant runs far beyond the indignity of being subjected to the judgment of the great but remote Assyria. Yet even this is not precisely the point Amos is making in calling on Ashdod and Egypt. Ashdod has already been before our attention, summoned by God for the very same crimes of social injustice and inhumanity now charged against Israel (1:6–8): clearly the less guilty is being made the judge of the more guilty. But at that point, Ashdod was numbered among the nations to whom special revelation from God had never come, and yet Ashdod can be judge of the people who possess the truth! In the same way Egypt was the oppressive enslaver of others—as Israel, more than most, had the opportunity

[6] *Cf.* Is. 5:12, 13, 18, 19; Je. 4:22, *etc.*

[7] RSV, JB, IB, *etc.* prefer to read 'Assyria' here following LXX. As RSV mg. and JB footnote make clear the Hebrew reads *Ashdod*. J. L. Mays says that 'LXX reads "Assyria" probably because Ashdod seemed to make an inappropriate pair with Egypt.' He (and Hammershaimb) prefer to retain *Ashdod*. Amos, as a matter of fact, nowhere else refers to Assyria by name: the place of exile is darkly referred to as *beyond Damascus* (5:27) and Gwynn (*The Book of Amos*, Cambridge, 1927) is probably correct in saying that Amos 'deliberately keeps Assyria an unnamed terror'

to know—yet, though guilty of social injustice and oppression, it could judge the people of God as being more obviously guilty than itself. Furthermore, in Egypt Israel had experienced a particular redemption, wrought by God, denied to the Egyptians, and yet, again, the unprivileged can be the judge of the privileged.

Here is the real thrust of Amos' condemnation. Those who had no special revelation and who had never experienced special redemption can rise up and judge the social misdemeanours of those who were uniquely privileged towards God but seemed to think nothing of despising, abusing and oppressing their fellow members of the family of grace. And he offers them a fair trial: the *strongholds* of Ashdod and Egypt (9) to judge the *strongholds* of Samaria (10). In this sense like judges like, but otherwise how unequal are the participants! Here are people with no revelation and no redemption; here are others full of grace and light from God, and the former can judge the latter for disrupting the fellowship of good social order and despising and devaluing their fellow men and women!

This is the heart of the first explanation of God's alienation from His people: they live below the level of grace in the matter of personal relationships and social concern. Certainly they flock to church (4:4, 5), but the very heathen can be their teachers when it comes to a proper regard for the welfare and dignity of their fellow men. The accusation cuts very deep. Their God defined His name and nature to them by His concern for them in their slavery, oppression, humiliation and hopelessness in Egypt. Can He do other than stand aloof from people who claim to know His name but refuse to imitate in life the very things the name stands for— human and humanitarian concern, good social order, even-handed justice, the dignity and well-being of men and women?[8]

---

[8] Pusey recalls the imaginative way in which Cyprian, commenting on this passage, calls on 'Jews, Turks and all Hagarenes' to behold the sins of Christendom: '". . . a world reeking with mutual slaughter; and homicide, a crime in individuals, called virtue when wrought by nations" . . . immortal man glued to passing, perishable things! Men, redeemed by the blood of Jesus Christ, for lucre wrong their brethren, redeemed by the same price, the same Blood! No marvel then that the Church is afflicted, and encompassed by unseen enemies and her strength drawn down from her spoiled houses.' The only way in which this striking comment needs to be made appropriate to the present day of the church is that our enemies are no longer unseen.

Personal spirituality

The clear division of the text in RSV helps us to see that the illustration used in verse 12 is a separate oracle and therefore brings before us a distinct truth. It is wholly ironic. The law (Ex. 22:12 f.) required an under-shepherd to furnish proof that an animal had been snatched from the flock: he must retrieve enough to show that it had been torn as prey by a marauding beast; otherwise he would be assumed to have appropriated the animal for himself and must pay compensation in full. Such a *rescue* was no rescue at all; it was only the evidence of what once was but now is no more.

Here, then, is the irony. The remains of the people of God, the rescue which is no rescue, the surviving proof of what once was, consists of *the corner of a couch and part of a bed*. We may pose the question: if *two legs, or a piece of an ear* point to the former existence of a sheep, what sort of people are represented by the rescued evidence of parts of beds and couches?[9] Imagine that these are the vestiges of the people of God! In spite of the abundance of their religion (4:4, 5) it is not in temple ruins or shattered altar-stones that Amos finds evidence of the character and concerns of the people who once lived there. Beds, couches, pillows summarize their life and habits. Sensuality, luxury, idleness, bodily care—but no evidence of religion, never mind spirituality. Amos writes no 'therefore'; he leaves us to draw our own conclusions. Why would God withdraw from such a people? Because there was nothing in their lives corresponding to a heart-concern for spiritual things; their character-reference could be written without mentioning

[9] The words *the corner of a couch and part of a bed* should either be associated with the verb *dwell* ('who dwell in Samaria. . . . on . . .') or be treated as parallel to *two legs, or a piece of an ear* ('so shall . . . Israel . . . be rescued—the corner of a couch and part of a bed!'). In either case (and the latter is to be preferred) there is reference to a luxury-loving, sensual and indolent people. *Cf.* 6:4–6. The key phrase, however, is as hard to translate in one of its details as it is clear in its general significance. The Hebrew reads 'the corner of a bed and the *d^emešeq* of a couch'. There are as many explanations of the disputed word as there are commentaries and translations. Over them all Hammershaimb rightly writes the word 'dubious'. Some have related *d^emešeq* (but impossibly) to the word 'damask', but it at least provides a vigorous and pointed rendering: 'the leg of a settee and a silken pillow'. Pillows and bed-legs leave us in no doubt of the interests and occupations of the former residents.

God, or prayer, or holiness; their legacy to the future was wholly a testimony to a life lived for the body. And these claimed to be the people of God! Here then is the second reason for the alienation of God, the second reason why His people lose touch with Him and His power: personal spirituality had disappeared from their lives. Sleep and ease, luxuriousness and body-care, indolence and indulgence—but not prayer and the Word of God, no self-mortification, no dying to sin, no armour of God, no discipline or battle for holiness! Thus God departs and the people of God go down in defeat.

In moving on to the next section of his penetrating diagnosis of the ills of the church of his day, Amos takes a backward glance at the two things which he has already said move God to displeasure: falling below the level of grace in relationships and social concern, and losing the spiritual dimensions of personal life. The day of punishment for these things is described as *the day I punish Israel for his transgressions* (3:14): *transgressions,* wilful disobediences to the known will of God! We need to be open-eyed about what this means. When the people of God behave towards each other as though the seamless robe of fellowship in Christ did not matter, when they are careless about social justice and welfare, when they lord it, insensitively, over others in things great or small, when they forget about a personal walk with God, Bible-reading, prayer, the fellowship of other believers, the Lord's Table, testimony to Jesus—these are rebellions, disobediences, contradictions of the known will of God for our lives. And there is no point in expecting anything but powerlessness and the adversity of an alienated God as long as we tarry in the place of rebellion.

Religious declension

The third area in which Amos diagnoses the people of God and exposes a cause for the divine alienation is brought before us in the words *altars of Bethel.* He turns (3:13–15) to review the religion which they so assiduously practise and finds that they have departed from divinely-given ordinances and norms into theological and religious compromise. For this also the Lord turns away from His people.

The religion of Bethel had its origin (1 Ki. 12:25–33) in the attempts of Jeroboam to wean people's affections away from the Jerusalem temple and the dynasty of David. Politically he acted astutely, for if his newly-rebellious people continued to attend the religious festivals at Jerusalem he could not hope to consolidate the national sovereignty of the Northern Kingdom and the position of his own royal house. In turn, therefore, he became a political rebel (against the house of David), a religious schismatic (against the Jerusalem Cult) and a theological heretic (against the truth of God). He was moved by political expediency, but he chose to extend his rebellion into the religious and theological fields.

In bringing in these accusations Amos first addresses the people as *the house of Jacob*. He uses these ancestral titles[1] as reminders of who they really are, their true position, privileges and obligations. Were they simply the people of Jeroboam (whether the first Jeroboam of 1 Ki. 12 or the last Jeroboam who reigned in Amos' day is no matter), they could believe and worship as they chose. But if they are the people of Jacob, Isaac and Joseph, then they have inherited traditions, truth received by revelation. Their religious and theological position is entirely different. They have no liberty to invent and innovate; they can do so only by rebellion with consequent forfeiture of privileges.

Here also, for the first time, Amos elaborates the titles of God: *The Lord* GOD, *the God of hosts* (3:13), the Sovereign Yahweh, God the Omnipotent. Implicit here is a rebuke of the diminished god of the religion of Jeroboam, who, though he might still bear the name 'Yahweh' in the mouths of worshippers, had become utterly debased from the God of Moses, the Exodus and the Law. When Jeroboam set up his golden calves (1 Ki. 12:28) he succeeded in confusing the visible and the Invisible. Without a doubt he intended the calves, not as representations of the divine nature, but as a visible pedestal on which God sat invisibly enthroned. But in the mind of man a visible object inevitably projects its nature on to the nature of the being who adopts it even as part of his outward manifestation. So Yahweh became identified with the bull-calf, the Creator with the creature.

In Canaanite practice the bull-calf was the symbol of fertility,

[1] *Cf.* 5:15; 6:8; 7:2, 5, 9, 16; 8:7.

and the god (Baal) identified with the bull-calf was sought because of his supposed capacity to bring fertility and therefore prosperity to the nation. In this the moral (or holy) became exchanged for the non-moral (or natural). When Israel entered the promised land they brought with them a 'fertility religion' (if we may so speak): that is to say, they were guaranteed fertility, prosperity on the basis of obedience to the holy law of their holy God (*cf.* Dt. 28; 29). Their religion was a religion for this world, catering for its adherents in the actual, material needs of life on earth. The Lord promised plenty. But, under Jeroboam, His people finally chose a non-moral way of prosperity, the way of Baal, whereby, in order to prompt Baal to perform his fertilizing functions, they resorted to the public performance of human acts of procreation as a religious ceremonial, and the holy was corrupted into the unholy.

The visible replaced the invisible, the creature the Creator and the unholy the holy. And it all happened so easily, so sensibly, so in accord with sound national policy! In other words, religiously and theologically the mind of man had taken the place of the mind of God. Revelation was adapted, distorted and trimmed until it matched human wisdom.[2]

Heresy, furthermore, never stands idle. Jeroboam I built an altar in Bethel (1 Ki. 12:32 ff.) but Amos speaks of *altars* (3:14). True religion became lost in formalism, ritualism for its own sake, performance to the point of nonsense. There is another way also in which heresy never stands idle: false religion produces false society and a religion of bricks and outward display produces a materialistic and ostentatious people with winter and summer houses, houses of ivory—even Solomon in all his glory had only a throne of ivory!—and great houses (3:15). What goes up like a rocket comes down like a stick: the false religion with all its display ends in total collapse of shrine and society alike. The hand of God goes out against religion which has adapted revelation to its own likes and dislikes and made the truth of God into its own sort of lie. But the God of Scripture has to be taken whole, or else

---

[2] The parallel between all this and Romans 1:18-32 is astonishing and ought to be studied. Note especially the emphasis throughout on knowledge which has been rejected, and on theological corruption precisely at the points of invisibility, creatorship and holiness.

He will be estranged from us and we shall know nothing of His power.

The passage we have now traversed resounds with words of impressiveness and power: strongholds (3:9, 10), defences, strongholds (11), houses of all sorts and great houses (15). But it was all hollow. The glory had departed, banished along with social sensitivity and concern, personal spirituality and a religion conformed to the revealed mind of God. These are the points of living and dying for the church.

Amos 4:1-13
Alternatives

HOLINESS is the quality which makes God what He is. It is first that which makes Him God, and secondly that which makes Him a particular sort of God, in distinction from any other possible claimants.

Oddly enough, we can most easily accustom our minds to thinking correctly about holiness if we turn first to a discreditable story about the patriarch Judah, recorded in Genesis 38. Some time after he had been bereaved of his wife, Judah left home to oversee his sheep-shearing. By the way he met a woman whom he took to be a prostitute, but who, in the delicious subtlety of the narrative, turns out to be his daughter-in-law whom he had earlier deceived.[1] Later he sends a friend to pay his immoral debts. When the woman is nowhere to be found, the friend asks (verse 21), 'Where is the harlot?' The interesting point for us is that he uses a different word, 'the holy woman'.[2] How, we may well ask, could such a woman be called 'holy'?

Basically the word translated 'holy' throughout the Old Testament seems to have the meaning 'separate', or 'different'. Unfortunately these are both comparative words. They provoke us

---

[1] This story ought to stress for us the absolute honesty and veracity of holy Scripture. Not even the sins of David's forefather (and ultimately the ancestor of the Lord Jesus) are hidden. But it also has a significant role to play in the developing narrative of Genesis. Without this incident, culminating in the public disgrace and open confession of Judah, there is no way of explaining how the callous and self-confident man of Gn. 37:26 ff. became the sensitive, diffident and self-sacrificing man who made one of the most moving speeches recorded in Scripture, Gn. 44:18 ff.

[2] NEB translates 'temple-prostitute' and RSV mg. 'cult prostitute'. With its customary preciseness RV provides the marginal note: 'Heb. *kedeshah*, that is, a woman dedicated to impure heathen worship.'

to ask 'separate from what? different from what? other than what?' But 'holy' is not comparative. It expresses that distinct, positive 'something' which makes the gods belong to their own class of being. We, for example, would find it inadequate to try to define 'man' in terms of what makes him different from 'dog'. We would want to say that there is much more to it than comparisons can express, that there is a whole realm of positive, unique distinctiveness which comparisons cannot catch. In the same way, 'holy' is not a word for the way in which God or the gods are different from men but is a word for that basic uniqueness, that positive speciality, which is the ground of all actual differences. And the 'holy woman' earned her title by the fact that her 'dedication' (see RV mg.) had brought her to belong to that other, different, special sphere of things.

Thus 'holiness' is that which makes God what He is. It is 'not a word that expresses any attribute of Deity but deity itself'.[3] In the Old Testament God's 'name' is referred to about thirty-six times with a qualifying adjective. Of these the expression 'holy name' is found in twenty-one occurrences and the remaining fifteen occurrences are distributed over a variety of adjectives. When we consider that the 'name' is not a mere label but 'is the expression of the Being itself',[4] this concentrated association of being and holiness is most impressive.

But there is holiness and holiness. There is the sort of god whose 'holiness', i.e. his uniqueness as god, is served by the dedication of girls to prostitution (Gn. 38:21) and there is the sort of God who repudiates such worship and service as an 'abomination' (cf. Dt. 23:17, 18). In other words, just as the bare notion of the 'holy' distinguishes the category 'god' from all other categories of being, so different sorts of holiness distinguish one sort of God from another, and 'in the faith of Israel a moral content was given to the term'.[5] The place where the Lord dwelt in isolation was called 'the holy of holies' (e.g. Ex. 26:33, 34), lit., 'the holiness of holinesses'. But in the tabernacle and temple theology this isolation of the Lord was not caused by the bare or neutral 'otherness' of God.

---

[3] A. B. Davidson, The Theology of the Old Testament (T. and T. Clark, 1925), p. 151.

[4] T. C. Vriezen, An Outline of Old Testament Theology (Blackwell, 1960), p. 198.

[5] H. H. Rowley, The Faith of Israel (SCM Press, 1956), p. 66.

It was a product of His moral holiness: the distinctive furnishing of 'the holiness of holinesses' was the tables of the moral law, the perfect code for holy being and holy living, and the mercy seat where was sprinkled the blood which reconciled the holy One to sinners and constituted them as His redeemed. This distinctive moral holiness of the God of Israel pervades the Old Testament. Why does man tremble for his life when he sees or stands before God? 'What makes him tremble', says Rowley,[6] 'is not the consciousness of his humanity in the presence of divine power, but the consciousness of his sin in the presence of moral purity.' This was Adam's experience: he had no fear before his God until he became a sinner (Gn. 3:8). Only then did he hide.[7] The testimony of Isaiah comprehends all that the Old Testament has to say on this point. The 'Holy, Holy, Holy' of the seraphim (Is. 6:3) is most fittingly understood by realizing that Hebrew commonly expresses superlatives and completeness by means of repetition.[8] Rarely is the repetition given triadic expression and seemingly nowhere else is a personal quality 'raised to the power of three' except in the seraphim's song. Its meaning therefore is that the Lord is 'completely and utterly holy': holy not only describes the totality of His nature but also the holiness He possesses is the perfection of Holiness. The consequence of this revelation of God is Isaiah's sense of desolation and exclusion as a sinner (Is. 6:5) until he is brought near to God by the seraph's ministry from the altar (6:6, 7), imparting cleansing and redemption.

The oath of the Holy One

Holiness therefore both makes the Lord what He is (God) and also what He distinctively is (the God of utter moral perfection). In both these ways, and in every way, it is His inmost, utmost and uppermost being. It is what makes Him uniquely distinct from

[6] *Ibid.*, p. 66.

[7] On this fear before God, *cf.* Jdg. 6:22, 23; 13:22.

[8] For completeness, *e.g.* Gn. 14:10 (lit., 'pits, pits', *i.e.* 'full of pits'); Ex. 17:16 (lit., 'generation, generation', *i.e.* 'all generations without exception'); Ezk. 21:27 (Heb. 21:32) is specially notable in that it is one of the few 'triads': 'ruin, ruin, ruin' means 'complete and utter ruin'. For perfection, *e.g.* 2 Ki. 25:15 ('of gold ... as gold' is lit., 'gold, gold', meaning 'fine gold'); Is. 57:19 ('peace, peace', *i.e.* perfect peace).

man, and what marks Him out from all other claimants to be God.[9]

Now in the passage of Amos which lies before us we read that *the Lord God has sworn by his holiness* (4:2). The point, of course, of swearing 'by' something is to add the note of assurance to the oath. It is equivalent to saying: 'The oath I make is as certain as is the existence of that by which I make it.' This consideration alone gives tremendous weight to the passage in which such an oath formula is embedded. It must be something of great intrinsic weight and urgency to suggest that the very nature of God Himself must be invoked to support it. But Amos does not simply say that the Lord has sworn 'by himself' (*cf.* Is. 45:23), but by His holiness. We are bound to ask what there is in this passage which specially affronts Him as the Holy One, the divine One who in the totality of His nature is unutterably and perfectly moral. It is a violent oath. It appeals to that which is inmost, highest and most all-pervasive about God. What can it be that so moves Him? A society and a religion organized on the basis of human self-pleasing.

Reader and writer will do well to pause and reflect. It is surely anticlimactic to have traversed all this ground in pursuit of a biblical understanding of divine holiness in order to come at last to something as commonplace as human self-pleasing. That may very well be so, and in so far as it is so it reveals how gravely our sense of proportion and of values has strayed from that which is current in heaven. When we discover that our thoughts are not His, nor His ways ours, then let us take note and be ready to re-form our thoughts and our ways of thinking, our values and our canons of appraisal. Where it is natural to scoff (at worst) or turn complacently aside (at best), we need to goad ourselves into repentance and bow before the Lord our God. When human self-sufficiency takes the stage, the Lord God vents a great oath for its destruction.

The relationship between 3:9-15 and 4:1-5 is that of narrowing the enquiry from the gathering of broad impressions to a focus on the one thing which occupies the centre. There is nothing new in 4:1-5; what has been diffuse is now gathered to a point. Under-

---

[9] *Cf.* Is. 40:25. The force of the otherwise unexpected description 'says the Holy One' is to deny *a priori* the possibility of any other being coming forward to claim equality or likeness with the God of Israel.

lying 3:10, with its description of people storing up treasures in strongholds, is the twin thought of self-seeking and self-preservation; 3:12 points openly to a society devoted to self-indulgence; 3:14, 15, centring on the house of God and the houses of men, exposes a self-taught religion issuing in a society proud of its wealth and possessions. Amos has gathered his facts; he now allows them to assemble into sharply focused pictures, the first in a wealthy Samaritan home (4:1–3) and the second in the well-attended shrines at Bethel and Gilgal (4:4, 5). The point in each case is the same: all is organized by self for self.

Women are the trend-setters in society. They have ever been the final guardians of morals, fashions and standards. Consequently Amos (as Isaiah after him, *cf.* Is. 3:16 ff.) can isolate the heart-beat of society by examing its typical women. He starts by noting in such typical Samaritan society two of the features already exposed. First, a way of life which excludes all personal spiritual dimensions: the womenfolk are just like so many prime head of cattle (4:1), content with a purely animal existence, wanting nothing more. In their kind they were champions—Bashan was noted for its cattle (Dt. 32:14; Ps. 22:12)—but it was a wholly body-centred, flesh-and-bones contest in which they had excelled. Maybe some of the fine ladies were more concerned to lose weight than to gain it, but none the less it was the body and not the soul which occupied their waking hours. Secondly, Amos notes again that the society of which they were the trend-setters was an 'I'm all right, Jack' outfit thriving on the miseries suffered by and the indignities loaded upon the defenceless. The *poor* and *needy* were fleeced and squeezed without qualm of conscience.

But now Amos brings these two lines of diagnosis to their root. The *cows of Bashan* are described in three parallel participial phrases, which, after the manner of the participle in Hebrew, offer an unchanging picture of abiding situations: 'oppressing the needy, crushing the poor, saying to your husbands, "Bring us something to drink!" ' (JB). If we are to find a distinct emphasis in each of these descriptions, the first points to self-concern, whereby even the poor must lose their little all to satisfy the needs of the lady of the manor; the second points to self-importance, whereby everyone of lower rank must accept a conscript's place in the army serving the cause of the 'big house'; and the third (how Amos must have enjoyed the irony of calling the husbands of these matriarchs 'their lords'—as the word literally is, see RV. It is clear who lorded it in these marriages!) points to self-determination, whereby no-one can side-step the mandate of the mistress.[1] And all is done so that there may be drink in the house: not done for necessity but for luxury; not done for life but for kicks.

In his great oath the Lord, specified as 'the sovereign Yahweh', commits the whole unique resource of His nature to the complete reversal and destruction of this order of things. It seems that there is no room in His world for life organized on a self-basis. Status will be lost in subjugation, for *they shall take you away* (4:2), bodily comfort lost in the excruciating *hooks* and cords of the captive (2), security lost in the downfall of the city whereby it will no longer be necessary to go out by the gate, for everyone can walk confidently straight ahead knowing that the wall has been breached into non-existence (3).[2]

Of the three aspects of national life examined in 3:9-15 Amos has now traced two—social malpractice and personal self-indulgence—back to their root in self-pleasing. One other matter remains: religion. Is the broad hint at the Bethelite heresy of self-

[1] The analysis offered here arises out of the usage of the key-words as they occur in the Bible. *Poor* is used 22 times of those of lower social rank, but 16 times of the financially poor; *needy* is rooted in the verb 'to be willing' and is used basically of those who 'go along with' something or someone else—voluntarily or under compulsion. It thus has a 'good' use of those who will to do the will of God and are ready to be bent to His will; its 'bad' use refers to the uninfluential in society, those who are open to be 'leaned on' by the boss-classes, those who are fair game to be cheated because they have no redress, *etc.* It is used 28 times of those in the lower strata of social influence and importance and only five times of the financially poor as such. It seems best, therefore, to allow *poor* to tend to mean those who are without worldly resources and are therefore fair game to be exploited, and to allow *needy* to tend to mean 'the small man' who can so easily be swallowed by the super-market, *etc.*, and who may, in given cases, be 'small' because of lack of capital.

[2] *You shall be cast forth into Harmon* has called forth as many conjectures as there are commentators. If it is a place-name, it is so far unidentified. NBC (first edition) may well have spoken the last and wisest word in saying that 'in any case, some unpleasant fate is indicated'! The simple emendation from Harmon to Hermon (*cf.* JB) has more to commend it than first sight suggests. Hermon is in the Bashan range. There is irony in the cows of Bashan going home: did not their whole way of life in Samaria suggest that they would be happier as free-range heifers in Bashan? But even so there seems no good reason why in all Bashan Hermon should be singled out.

made religion a true description of what all this national religious enthusiasm was really about? The answer in 4:4, 5 is in the affirmative. The tone of the two verses is that of taunt and irony without sparing. Amos mocks the invitation to pilgrimage, the song which the pilgrims sang as they went: *Come to Bethel*;[3] he mocks their purpose, telling them that the outcome of the exercise will be only transgression multiplied by transgression; he mocks their ritualistic punctiliousness over *sacrifices* and *tithes*.[4]

In verse 5, however, things take a much more pointed turn. He underscores their self-invented regulations governing the use of leaven, which was strictly forbidden in the law of Moses[5] but which, for motives unspecified here, had apparently been introduced in Northern Israel; he points to the ostentation with which individuals made a public fuss of *freewill offerings*, essentially private matters between the individual and God; and he exposes the inner motivation prompting all: *for so you love to do*—'this is what makes you happy' (JB). It is all for self. He has spoken of religious privileges: to have the house of God to visit and the atoning *sacrifice* to offer; religious duties, the presentation of the *tithe*; religious joys, the *sacrifice of thanksgiving*; religious devotion, the *freewill offering*; religious pointlessness! For all was unreal in the sight of God, and more than unreal, positively harmful to the

[3] This splendid suggestion comes from Hammershaimb. For such pilgrim summonses, *cf.* Is. 2:3; Ps. 122:1.

[4] Some find here a reflection of a custom whereby the pilgrim sacrificed on the day of arrival and brought his tithe on the third day: *cf.* NEB. In this case Amos' mockery is of punctiliousness as such, concentration on the minutiae of doing the thing exactly in the approved and traditional way. Others hold that his mockery runs thus: if benefit accrues from the doing of ritualisitc practices, then the more the ritual the greater the blessing. So why not have a sacrifice every day (instead of once a year) and a tithe payment every three days (instead of once in three years)? *Cf.* 1 Sa. 1:3, 7, 21; Dt. 14:28. It is hard to decide on the correct interpretation: the former is slightly less than striking; the latter more than a bit overdone. Even so, the latter is surely preferable.

[5] Leaven was prohibited in an offering to the Lord made by fire: Lv. 2:11; 6:17; 10:12. It was commanded in the case of that part of the thank offering shared with worshipper and priest in the fellowship meal (Lv. 7:12, 13) and in the 'wave offering' given 'to the Lord for the priest' (Lv. 23:15-20). If the 'corruption' symbolism of leaven is followed out, these regulations point to the need for absolute purity in the Lord's offering and to the continuance of impurity in the human offerer and priest. Amos makes his case here by joining together the words 'offer (lit. "burn") that which is leavened', the very thing the law forbade. *Cf.* E. W. Bullinger, *Leaven* (Longmans, 1907).

practitioner, a cause of yet more sin: for it was all in one way or another a manifestation of that heart of self-pleasing which offends the holiness of God.

But if the Lord, in this outburst of His holiness, reveals that in us which most grieves and provokes Him, He also shows that His holiness is completely consistent with His mercy and pity. He does not leave His people alone, no matter how much they have fallen in love with themselves. His mercies are age-long, and He reveals the antidote which He would willingly and patiently apply for the healing of our souls.

The purposes of a Sovereign God

The passage which commences with Amos 4:6 opens with a first-person singular verb and contains eight further first-person actions before it concludes in verse 11. The first verb (6) is also emphatic in that the pronoun 'I' is used to reinforce the verbal form. The ensuing forceful 'Now I for my part . . .' makes a vivid comparison between the Lord and His people. To be sure they had been busy, busy making money, putting by in store for the future, being exceedingly religious. He, on His side, had been busy too, with the odd busy-ness of sending famine (6) and drought (7),[6] blight and locust plague (9), epidemic (10a),[7] war (10b) and earthquake (11). A busy God indeed, but a decidedly odd busy-ness!

Every Bible reader has to decide sooner or later whether he is ready to conform himself to the way the Bible thinks, and it is remarkably easy to sit loose to Bible modes of thought. Tracing lines of cause and effect comes as naturally to us as breathing: it is

---

[6] Hammershaimb's note on the rainfall of Palestine is helpful: 'In the latter half of October the rain begins to fall again after the dry period . . . This rain . . . marks the beginning of the rainy season (and) lasts until the beginning of December. (It) is called "the former rain" . . . After this the rain falls at intervals until the end of February . . . Then, in the spring, in March and April, there are heavy showers again . . . the latter rain . . . which determines the final growth and ripening of the corn. The corn harvest (comes) at the end of April and in May.' He describes the situation as Amos put it: 'The winter rains stopped too soon, and the latter rain failed . . . the cisterns stood empty and the corn suffered serious loss.'

[7] On *after the manner of Egypt*, cf. Ex. 15:26; Dt. 7:15; 28:60. The reference in Amos may, of course, simply be to the fact of divine plagues on Egypt, but it is much more likely to be to the notoriously unhealthy nature of Egypt.

part of the fabric of our educational tradition. The Bible does not exercise itself to deny chains of causation, but equally it is not accustomed to clog up its reasoning by giving them undue prominence. It leaps back directly to the divine Agent from whom come all things and by whose will they happen.

The troubles of life are spread before us here by Amos: troubles caused by deprivation (famine and drought), troubles caused by infliction (blight and epidemic), troubles caused by opposition (war and earthquake)—all the troubles of life are there in principle, falling into one category or the other. Right at the centre is one of the things that worries us most of all: troubles apparently falling by chance—rain here, drought there, seemingly haphazard, luck for one, ill-luck for the other (4:7b, 8). But over them all the first person singular of divine decision and action. Everything on earth comes from a God who rules and reigns in heaven.

If we are at all sensitive we rebel. Our emotions rebel: we feel sick to think of a God like that; our minds rebel, for we want a workable logic on which to base our lives; our wills rebel, for we desperately want to leave room in our world-view for the beloved freedom of human causation. But the Bible marches steadily on: Amos, *Does evil befall a city, unless the Lord has done it?* (3:6); Isaiah, *I form light and create darkness, I make weal and create woe, I am the Lord, who do all these things* (45:7); Jesus, *Not one of them will fall to the ground without your Father's will* (Mt. 10:29); Paul, *For from him and through him and to him are all things. To him be glory for ever. Amen* (Rom. 11:36). The list could be prolonged and the testimony would not be altered. This is the biblical view of the sovereignty of God over the history and experiences of man. Words could not be plainer, and unless we wish to trim Him down to the poor limits of a God nice enough to suit our emotions, small enough to fit within our logic and effete enough to leave room for our wills, we shall bow before the Sovereign revealed in this passage and throughout the rest of the Bible.

We do ourselves an immense disservice and we weaken our ministry to each other as soon as we dismiss or diminish this great doctrine. Amos writes of catastrophes small and great, of things as chancy as rainfall (to us at least), things as indiscriminate as the death toll in battle, but none of these things separates us from God. His will reigns even there. He has even created the destroyer to destroy and no weapon forged against His people can prosper (Is. 54:16, 17). If only we stopped to think about it, this is *why* nothing can separate us from the love of Christ! For everything is a manifestation of His will, controlling, directing, appointing. As the Bible sees it, this affirms human responsibility. Isaiah uses the image of the horse and the rider (37:29) and it is as far as either illustration or reason will take us: all the immense power and vitality belong to the horse; all the purpose and direction belong to the rider. Isaiah used it in a battle situation in which his king, Hezekiah, suffered loss. He knew the rigour of what he was saying. Sennacherib, proud in his unassailable strength, came with confidence in himself as the world's emperor, to take Jerusalem. Was it not his right to do so? And in so doing, he was moved entirely by his own sinful, imperialistic impulses. But there was a divine Rider on his back; heavenly purposes were being wrought out. The Lord was at no point the author of pride and sin—all that belonged to Sennacherib; but the Lord was at no point absent from His post of direction and control.

A God absent from life's troubles, a God away elsewhere when most needed, a God who was too preoccupied to take note of a four-year-old walking in front of oncoming traffic—what good is a God like that in *this* world? The name for such a god is Baal (1 Ki. 18:27). No, no, what we need is to be able to look into the teeth of the storm and discern our Father. That is the God for today.

But we must return to the track Amos is following. If we were to share his vision of God's sovereign working we had to pause and even go a little aside from what he is saying in this precise place—though not astray, please God, from what he believed and would approve of. But having seen God's sovereign working, here now is God's purposeful working.

'I have been busy too': that is the divine word of verse 6. You have been busy being religious (4, 5); I have been busy seeking to bring you to repentance (6, 8, 9, 10, 11). It is surely significant that in all the catalogue of their religious works and rituals there is no reference to the sin offering. Self-pleasing, self-satisfaction is the death-knell of repentance; and the absence of repentance is the death-knell of true religion. What did they want? A religion which pleased their own tastes—doubtless, as they would have said, 'a religion we find helpful'! What did the Lord want? A religion which brought His people all the way back to Him,[8] a beautiful metaphor for true, full, unremitting repentance. And there was enough in the working of God to open the blind eyes of His people. First, He did exactly what He said He would do. Had they looked candidly at their misfortunes, they would have discerned the hand behind them: the Covenant God implementing the curses of the covenant.[9] Again, they devoted themselves to the false Bethel cult, a religion for this world if ever there was one: no nonsense about heaven, practical, dealing with crops and harvests, bank balances and prosperity. And the Lord laboured to open their eyes to the fact that it was bogus and phoney, promising much, bringing nothing. Where were their gods of rainfall when there was no rain, their gods of harvest when the crops were blighted?

'It is a great gift of God', says Pusey, 'that He should care for us so as to chasten us.' But much more, it is a great gift of God that He should care for us so as to chasten us because He will not be satisfied until we come all the way back to Himself. He looks for repentance, not through sadistic delight in seeing us grovel, but because there is no other way back to the fellowship which delights Him. He looks for repentance, not because He wants us to live amid the ruination wrought by sin, but because repentance is the gateway to recreation. Think of *a brand plucked out of the burning* (4:11), dead, charred, black and ugly, helpless in itself, unusable, unsalvable by man. But even it could 'return right up to where I am'. Religion without repentance kills; religion centred on repentance makes alive. May that God never cease to be busy with us!

The great appeal

In the light of this divine insistence on repentance, we must surely interpret the *therefore* of verse 12 as introducing a continuation and conclusion of the same theme: on the basis of a grim reassertion of His threats (*thus will I do to you*, i.e. continue the destructive

---

[8] The phrase Amos uses (*šaḇtem 'āḏay*) signifies a return which reaches right up to (and does not stop short of) its mark. Pusey aptly comments that since 'God does not half-forgive, so neither must man half-repent'!

[9] *Cf.* Dt. 28:15—29:28. *E.g.* Am. 4:9; Dt. 28:22. See also the discussion of 'the vengeance of the covenant', pp. 64 f. above.

judgments of verses 6–11 and implement the predicted disaster of 3:9–15), He issues a final, great call to the repentance He has long sought to achieve.

There are five indications in these verses that it is allowable and proper to hear in them the notes of encouragement, grace and welcome.[1] First we may note the words *prepare to meet your God* (4:12). Wherever the idea of meeting God is found in the Bible it has a connotation of grace. The nearest parallel to this verse in Amos is Exodus 19:17 where Moses leads out the people from the camp 'to meet God'. The situation was one of immense, condescending grace: God descending, clothed in the majesty of His holy law, yet purposing to speak to the people on the ground that He is their Saviour and Redeemer. Amos' language at this point, therefore, points to grace rather than wrath.[2]

Secondly, the words *your God* are most striking on the lips of Amos. We have noted that he never speaks of the Lord as 'God of Israel'. He found that the covenant terminology of a 'special relationship' between God and Israel has become a debased coinage in his day, an invitation to moral and spiritual complacency, as

[1] The fact that in the popular mind the words 'Prepare to meet thy God' are the supposed stock-in-trade of the 'hell-fire' preacher, the words on the poster carried by the prophet of doom, aptly reflects the almost unbroken opinion of the commentators—including my own opinion in NBCR (p. 733). Calvin appears to come down on the side of 'a simple and serious exhortation to repentance'. Unfortunately Calvin was often wretchedly served by his translators who confused dignified wording with extreme archaism, yet the sense of the thing is here: 'thou canst yet mitigate God's wrath, provided thou preparest to meet him.' Pusey likewise notes that 'God never, in this life, bids people or individuals "prepare to meet Him" without a purpose of good to those who do prepare . . . He saith not "come and hear your doom" but "Prepare to meet thy God".' Undoubtedly the verses can with complete exegetical legitimacy be understood as a final denunciation; it is the accepted view and the statement of it in NBCR is reasonably 'main line', except that not all agree that verse 13 can be soundly attributed to Amos. On this, however, Hammershaimb sensibly gives priority to the exegetical argument: 'The concluding doxology . . . serves to assure the hearers that he will also be able to carry out what he threatens. It is therefore a complete misunderstanding . . . to explain both this doxology and the two in 5:8 f. and 9:5 f. as secondary because they do not fit the style of the context.'

[2] *Cf.* Gn. 18:2; 19:1; Ex. 5:3; Nu. 23:3; Zc. 2:3. Where the verb 'to meet' occurs with hostile significance it is the enemy or the assailant who comes 'to meet' his victim. On this ground Amos would be inviting the people to attack their God. Ex. 4:24 uses a different verb (*pāgaš*, not *qārā*) of divine hostile assault.

we shall see again when dealing with 5:18–20. It is hardly too much to say that he appears to have avoided anything which could have been construed as making Israel seem unconditionally God's 'favourite'. Yet here he breaks his own custom: *your God*. Certainly when for the only other time he uses this expression, in 9:15, it is a word of intense comfort and assurance, and it stands to reason that it should be so here. The personal possessive pronoun is inexplicable unless it speaks of hope.

Thirdly, references to the Lord's status and power as Creator are often intended to reinforce the truth that He controls all for the welfare of His people and will yet intervene on their behalf.[3] The reference to the doctrine of God the Creator is not by itself decisive (as the footnote shows), but adds its due weight to the testimony of the four other facts adduced.

The fourth feature of these verses suggesting a hopeful interpretation in a way partakes of the same ambivalence as the third: the words translated *who makes the morning darkness* (4:13) could at least equally well mean 'who makes darkness into the morning' or 'who makes morning out of darkness'. Symbolically there is a total difference in the objective of the divine work, but it is decidedly possible that here Amos is depicting the God who allows weeping to endure for a night but brings joy in the morning (Ps. 30:5).[4]

[3] *E.g.* Ps. 74:12 ff.; Is. 40:27 ff.; 50:2, 3. References to God as Creator are also used to reinforce His threatened judgments, as indeed in Am. 5:8 f.; 9:5 f. The implication of the reference must be decided as each case requires. It tells slightly, though not, of course, decisively, against a hopeful interpretation of the present passage that the other two similar passages in the same book are entirely devoted to inescapable overthrow.

[4] The Hebrew of this disputed phrase simply places two nouns side by side: 'maker of dawn, darkness'. Sensing the need to express the relationship, LXX inserted 'and' in some MSS and this reading is adopted in BHS. Hammershaimb is certainly not correct in saying that the Hebrew 'must be translated "he who makes the dawn darkness"'. It is not, of course, possible to be certain that one has collected all the evidence on such constructions, but enough has been done to show that it is at least equally possible that the connecting link between 'dawn' and 'darkness' is 'out of' and not 'into'. S. R. Driver, *Hebrew Tenses* (OUP, 1892), paras. 194 f., ought to be consulted. He contends that the principle of apposition in Hebrew or the use of the 'accusative' of limitation requires that the word expressing that 'out of which' something is composed should come second. *E.g.* Gn. 2:7; 18:6; Ex. 20:25; 1 Ki. 7:15; Ps. 104:4. That Amos' thought would not resist the idea of 'making the dawn out of the darkness' is shown in 5:8.

Finally, Amos speaks in the name of *the Lord* (Yahweh), *the God of hosts*, 'Yahweh, the omnipotent God' (4:13). In using the divine name, Yahweh, Amos automatically puts mercy and redeeming grace in the forefront of the picture. Yahweh is chiefly and prominently the God who went to Egypt to redeem a hopeless, graceless and thankless people. Coupled with his surprising use of the description *your God* (verse 12), we cannot but feel that it is this same Yahweh (who redeems the undeserving) who in His omnipotence[5] calls for their eleventh-hour return. But the matter is delicately balanced. The call to *prepare* is issued against the background of an affirmed judgment, *I will do this to you*. Mercy and wrath look each other in the eyes. A phrase here, a phrase there now flash hope, now warning. Amos stabs the conscience with his ambiguities: is the darkness to become dawn or the dawn darkness? Will the Creator leap in to save or to destroy? Yet there is in abundance that on which faith can rest: He calls to a meeting, not a confrontation; He speaks as *your God*; He names Himself by the name of sovereign grace, *Yahweh*. The way lies wide open for the penitent; they can still flee from the wrath to come.

A sure stronghold

Strongholds were the passion of the day (3:9, 10, 11). Thought about security must have been in the air. Therefore the God who is never irrelevant to His people's needs, nor out of touch with their fears, does not propose repentance as a spiritual exercise unrelated to life's needs and anxieties. Repentance is the door into safety. As this passage has unfolded before us, it has passed through three main points of emphasis: first (3:9—4:5) the total collapse of all that man erects for his own safety because it is vitiated at centre by self-seeking and comes under divine animosity; secondly, the prolonged work of God to recall His people from religion to repentance (4:6–11), culminating, thirdly, in the final, great appeal (4:12, 13). It is therefore the lynch-pin of Amos' argument to show in conclusion that by going along with God, by listening

---

[5] 'Of hosts' most likely signifies 'who is in Himself a whole host of potentialities and powers'. This is well reflected in the suggested translation 'the omnipotent'.

to His call to repent and coming to the meeting with *your God* to which He invites, all the security which man could never achieve is to be found in the reconciled God. The passage which opened with *strongholds* (3:9) ends with omnipotence, *the God of hosts* (4:13).

This is, first, the omnipotence of complete power (13a). There are three areas of divine capability: the visible, *he . . . forms the mountains*; the invisible, *he . . . creates the wind*; the personal and rational, *he . . . declares to man what is his thought.*[6] The mass of the world is in His hands, *the mountains*; the powers of the world, symbolized by *the wind*, are His; and that wonder of all wonders in the world, the mind of man, is subservient and open to Him. His power is complete.

Secondly, His power is transforming power (13b). It takes the blackness of night and makes it into the brightness of dawn. This is the power that looks on the black, charred *brand plucked out of the burning* and knows not even a passing second of despair or doubt that it can be renewed.

Thirdly, His power is down to earth (13c): He *treads on the heights of the earth*. The picture is one of triumph (*cf.* Hab. 3:19), but it is triumph here, in this world. It is here that He is sovereign, not only in heaven. Therefore by the way of repentance the people of God come within the sphere of almighty, transforming and ever-present power. What a tragedy that the people of Amos' day failed to hear the call! And are we any better?

[6] *His thought* refers to *man*, not God. The truth here is not revelation (God revealing His mind), but the power of omniscience (God knowing man's mind). *Cf.* Je. 11:20; Ps. 139:2; *etc.*

Amos 5:1-5
A Tale of Three Shrines

THE centre-piece of Amos 5 is his striking call to the people to give up their festival pilgrimages to the three great shrines of Bethel, Beer-sheba and Gilgal. As we shall see, it is round these shrines that the message of the chapter is constructed. If we are to appreciate the force of what Amos is saying, we must try to understand what motivated the people to journey (presumably annually) to these places—involving in the case of Gilgal a journey as far as Jericho in the extreme south-east of their land,[1] and in the case of Beer-sheba a journey which took them over fifty miles deep into the south of Judah. That these shrines were hallowed by their association with Abraham, Isaac and Jacob would in itself constitute a call to visit them, and not least to a schismatic people like those of the north, anxious to demonstrate the legitimacy with which they could lay claim to ancestral titles. But there is more to it than that.

Bethel

In Genesis, Bethel is specially associated with the patriarch Jacob, which would, of course, make it specially significant to the people who had taken 'Israel' as their national name. There are two main points in Jacob's life when he comes to Bethel. On the first

[1] Hammershaimb notes that it used to be held that there was a shrine, Gilgal, in the neighbourhood of Bethel, where Elisha dwelt (2 Ki. 2:1; 4:38), 'but it is now the general view that there was only one Gilgal, near Jericho.' NBD, art. 'Gilgal', concurs in general but thinks that another Gilgal may conceivably be mentioned in Jos. 12:23. This could have no bearing on the place mentioned in Amos, which may be confidently taken as Gilgal by Jericho.

occasion (Gn. 28:10–22), Jacob came there all unwittingly as a homeless wanderer without any certain future. It was there that he slept and dreamt and awoke with the consciousness that *the Lord is in this place* (Gn. 28:16). The second time Jacob came to Bethel, it was on his return from Paddan-aram (Gn. 35:1–15). He looked back to his earlier experience and remembered that there *God had revealed himself to him* (35:7), but while he was there he had a fresh experience (35:15): *God had spoken with him*. Bethel took its name from its spiritual reality: God was there, revealing Himself, speaking to His people.

But there was more to a Bethel experience than the vision and voice of God present there. On his first visit Jacob arrived as the man with a past and left as the man with a future (28:13–15); on his second visit, he arrived as Jacob but left as Israel (35:10), that is to say with a new assurance that in reality he had received a new name from God and was therefore a new man.[2] In other words, according to these Bethel traditions the presence of God was experienced there in renewing, re-orientating power. This being so, let us sense the surprise and hurt with which Amos' words would be greeted: *Seek me and live; but do not seek Bethel* (5:4, 5). There was something about the whole Bethel syndrome which inhibited the pilgrims from experiencing the reality which Bethel was supposed to be all about, the life-giving presence of the Lord.

Beer-sheba

Turn now to the second of these popular shrines, Beer-sheba. In Genesis it is associated with every member of the great trio, Abraham, Isaac and Jacob. Abraham paid his first call there— and indeed it was the occasion on which it received its name— in Genesis 21:22–33, and it was there, from the lips of a pagan king, that he heard the words which were to become the Beer-sheba theme: *God is with you in all that you do*. In Genesis 26:23, 24 Isaac

---

[2] Documentary Analysis allocates the naming account in Gn. 35 to the source P, and that in Gn. 32:24 ff. to J. Adhering to this schema, von Rad (*Genesis*, SCM Press, 1961) urges that 'the word "again" in v. 9 is a redactional addition in view of the preceding Bethel story'. But there is no reason for treating it as redactional except that the documentary schema requires it to be so. As the text stands, 35:9 ff. is self-confessedly the story of a re-affirmation of earlier promises.

came to Beer-sheba. It is interesting to read through the stories of Isaac on the supposition that he meditated much on what his father had passed on to him. At any rate, at Beer-sheba he experienced a night-vision of the Lord who announced Himself as the God of Abraham and pronounced the promise: *Fear not, for I am with you.* Years later (Gn. 46:1-4), Jacob was heading for Egypt, responding to the invitation of his long-lost son, Joseph. Journeying south he arrived at Beer-sheba, and once more the sojourn there was marked by *visions of the night* (verse 2) and a communication from *the God of your father: Do not be afraid.* ... *I will go down with you* (3, 4). Thus at Beer-sheba each of the three patriarchs in turn received the assurance of the companionship of God with them, 'I am with you.' With what horror and disbelief, then, did the people of Amos' day hear him say: *Do not* ... *cross over to Beer-sheba* (5:5), amplifying the thought later in verse 14 by saying that it is on entirely other conditions that *the Lord, the God of hosts, will be with you, as you have said.* Clearly they had claimed the certainty of divine companionship—doubtless on the ground of their Beer-sheba pilgrimage—but for Amos it was not so. Like Bethel, Beer-sheba was the repository of promises, but somehow it could not bestow what it expressed, the living companionship of the Lord.

Gilgal

Gilgal first entered the history of the people of God when they invaded the promised land under Joshua. It was the site of their first encampment (Jos. 4:19) and the place where they erected a twelve-stone commemorative monument to the miraculous crossing of the Jordan whereby they had been enabled to set foot in Canaan (Jos. 4:20). It was at Gilgal that they were reconstituted as the people of the covenant by means of circumcision and the passover (Jos. 5:2-12); there also they experienced the firstfruits of possession of the land as the manna ceased and they *ate the fruit of the land of Canaan* (Jos. 5:12). From Gilgal as his headquarters Joshua pushed out west, south and north in his wars of conquest (Jos. 9:6; 10:6, 7, 9, 15, 43; 14:6), and at Gilgal Saul, the first king, was confirmed in his kingship (1 Sa. 11:14, 15), a fact which would have made the shrine even more appealing to the ten tribes of the north with their special loyalty (*cf.* 2 Sa. 2:8–10; *etc.*) to Saul's house. Clearly, then, Gilgal was the shrine which proclaimed the inheritance and possession of the promised land according to the will of God.

Once more, then, we can appreciate the disbelieving horror in the minds of Amos' hearers at the words *Gilgal shall surely go into exile* (5:5) and *I will take you into exile beyond Damascus* (5:27). Gilgal, like the other shrines, made a promise but could not keep it; it spoke of an inheritance but could not make that inheritance a sure possession—rather the reverse, for, in spite of much veneration at the shrine, banishment (and that by the same divine hand which once bestowed the land) is to be their experience.

This, then, is the tale of three shrines in outline. Amos devotes the remainder of chapter 5 to a more detailed examination of each of them (Bethel, verses 6–13; Beer-sheba, 14–20; and Gilgal, 21–27) and we shall turn to this presently, but first we must see the grim seriousness and solemnity with which he invests his message.

Preaching at the funeral

The first five verses of Amos 5 consist of lamentation (1, 2),[3] application (3, the 'death' of Israel will be by military decimation) and explanation (4, 5): it has all happened because the shrines were trusted to fulfil their promises and they could not do so, as we have just seen. In all the seeking after the shrines, the Lord Himself got left out.

But having looked at the message of the shrines we are in a position to understand the message of the dirge. It speaks of death where there should have been life: *Fallen, no more to rise* (2a). Here is the failure of Bethel: the house of God, the location of the promise 'God is in this place' as the giver of hope and new life, the one who can make the name 'Israel' a reality. Secondly, the dirge speaks of abandonment where there should have been

---

[3] The poetical metre in the Hebrew of verse 2 is that typically used in dirges. We can best imagine the effect this literary device would have on Amos' hearers by recalling our own somewhat heavier heart-beat on hearing the Dead March in 'Saul'. Pusey suggests that it would be 'as if a living man . . . could see his own funeral procession, and hear over himself the "earth to earth. . . ."'. Mays perceptively notes that the choice of this metre 'testifies to the prophet's own grief at what his words foretell'.

companionship: *the virgin Israel; forsaken . . . , with none to raise her up* (2b). Here is the failure of the Beer-sheba promise 'God is with you'. Israel has been carried off in death as a virgin who has never known the joys of married companionship and who, even in her virgin state, could find none to befriend her in the hour of need. Thirdly, the dirge speaks of dispossession where there should have been inheritance: *Fallen, . . . forsaken on her land, with none to raise her up*, the failure of the Gilgal promise, the people of God lying in defeat, dead, where in the heyday of Joshua's Gilgal they had shouted in triumph over dispossessed foes.

For sure it was a grim sermon which Amos preached at the funeral, but it was not mistaken. 'As a people, he says, she should be restored no more; nor was she' (Pusey). The last twenty years of the kingdom of Israel saw its domestic policies in ruins, one political coup after another until in 722 BC Sargon II of Assyria put an end to the kingdom of Israel for ever, deporting the remnant who survived siege and slaughter and sowing the land with an alien population. It is against this background of realism—the realism of historical fulfilment—that we read the words of Amos. He was not mistaken in his forecast; nor was he mistaken in his analysis of cause and effect. Events vindicated the words, so that we can say that, like Moses, *he received living oracles to give to us* (Acts 7:38).

Confirm your call and election

We cannot be wrong in supposing that at any rate the majority of those who flocked to Bethel, Beer-sheba and Gilgal thought that they were legitimate partakers of the promises of God. Amos and history unite to proclaim that of these the majority was wholly mistaken. In the bitter event they discovered that it was one thing to know a promise but quite another to be an inheritor of it; it was one thing to be around to hear the promise proclaimed but quite another to be able to register a valid claim to possess it for oneself.

And the promises of which the shrines spoke were not irrelevant to the people of God then, nor are they irrelevant to us now. Life, peace and security are precious things, all the more so when we speak of life from God, peace with God and security in God. As we have seen, when the Bethel priests proclaimed 'God is here' the tradition taught that He was there as the giver of hope and life; Beer-sheba stated 'God is with you', nothing stands between Him and you, you have peace with God; and Gilgal pointed to a God-given and inalienable inheritance. These are the very promises of God in Christ. Hearing and knowing them is not enough. Inheritance alone will suffice. Can we be certain that we possess them? The question is directly addressed to us. Nothing is more certain in Scripture than that when once the Lord has actually bestowed His promises on anyone He will never withdraw them, allow them to be withdrawn or in any way do or tolerate anything other than bring that person into eternal glory. But who can claim and sense this assurance?

It is false humility and needless hesitancy to reply that no-one could presume to be certain of these things and least of all sinners like us. To Amos the people had only themselves to blame that they failed to inherit. Scripture requires us to believe that there is such a thing as assurance and that in God's ordinary providences it is intended to be the common experience of His people.

As we proceed to the remaining studies[4] in Amos 5 may our prayer be that we shall see clearly there the grounds of humble assurance, take our stand upon them and thus confirm our call and election as the people of God.

[4] To some extent the treatment of chapter 5 as analysing in turn the parts played by Bethel, Beer-sheba and Gilgal in the religious life of Israel must remain hypothetical and dependent on the comparison between what Amos says and what Genesis tells us about the traditions of these holy places. In the interests of following out the hypothesis, the ensuing three chapters will work on the assumption that Amos addresses the devotees of each of these three shrines in turn.

Amos 5:6-13
God Makes a Difference

WHEN Jacob dreamt at Bethel (Gn. 28:12 ff.) he saw a ladder linking earth and heaven. Its purpose, surprisingly, was not to provide man with a means of ascent but God with a means of descent. The ladder brought God to Bethel so that ever after its name meant 'God is here'.[1] But where God comes He makes a difference. At Bethel He touched Jacob's circumstances, giving him promises and hopes (Gn. 28:13-15), and in the end He changed Jacob himself, confirming all that was inherent in the gift of the new name, Israel (Gn. 35:9 ff.). Bethel was the place where the old life became the new life and the old man the new man.

The great Transformer

The heart of Amos' oracle about Bethel is occupied with the Hymn to the Transforming God (5:8, 9). It is an attractive conjecture—though, of course, no more than a conjecture—that Amos quotes here to the Bethelite pilgrims one of the hymns from their own hymn-book. Where better than at Bethel to sing to the God who makes a difference?

He makes the seasonal changes. This (8a) appears to be the force of the reference to *the Pleiades and Orion*, constellations which were used in the ancient world to mark the turn of the seasons (*cf.*

---

[1] In Gn. 28:13 read with RSV mg. 'beside him'; *cf.* NEB, JB. If the Lord was standing 'over it'—*i.e.* on top of the ladder, Jacob could not have said 'The Lord is in this place. . . . this is the house of God'. Jacob, the great opportunist, saw at once that logically speaking Bethel must also be 'the gate of heaven', but only because it had first brought God to him.

NBCR, p. 734). He also makes the daily changes, when *deep darkness*[2] becomes *morning* and subsequently *day* yields to *night*. He makes the occasional changes (8b), as when the sea wall is breached and the land is inundated,[3] and the historical changes, when *the strong* and *the fortress* fall before the destroyer (9).

But this fine hymn is bracketed about with references to a people who resist change. They come to Bethel (7) and they go from Bethel (10–12) totally unaltered. The failure, therefore, lay not in the Bethel promises, nor in the God of Bethel, but in the wilfulness which would not be transformed from lawlessness and transgression.[4] Amos' exposure of a religion which leaves life untouched could not have been more brilliantly accomplished. They go, they sing, they come away, and nothing, simply nothing has changed. Justice is still turned sour (7a, 12c) and righteousness is still overthrown (7b, 12b). It is an argument against those who wish to insert verse 7 immediately before verse 10 that in that position it becomes otiose. It adds nothing to the contents of verses 10–12. It is a supreme argument for the verse order as it is that it enables us to follow the worshipper through what was (if this hymn is a sample) a superb spiritual experience and see him emerge on the other side exactly the same person.

[2] The emotive quality of the old translation 'shadow of death', especially in the light of its occurrence in Ps. 23:4, makes it worth while to indicate the general use of this word in the Old Testament. It is used of physical darkness (Jb. 12:22, 24:17; 28:3; 34:22), of that which is threatening, gloomy, the blighting effects of grief, disappointment, trouble (Jb. 3:5; 16:16; Pss. 44:19 (Heb. 20); 107:10, 14; Is. 9:2; Je. 2:6; 13:16), and of the darkness of death itself (Jb. 10:21, 22; 38:17). In the present context we are hardly warranted in giving prominence to any metaphorical use. The passage seems to emphasize creatorial changes.

[3] This interpretation is to be preferred to that which sees here a reference to rainfall and the circulation of the waters, *cf.* Ec. 1:7.

[4] NEB and JB both follow the conjecture of some commentators that verse 7 ought to follow verse 9. It is a regrettable and unjustifiable feature of these two translations (which are otherwise so often fine and helpful) that they tinker with verse order even though there is no objective warrant in the MSS for doing so. It is all very well for commentators to 'fly kites', but to admit such fancies into public versions of the Bible gives them a colour of authority which they do not possess and removes the task of interpreting the Bible one stage further from the ordinary reader. The case for the changed verse order is argued by Mays and Hammershaimb; a defence of the Hebrew verse order is attempted in NBCR.

What might have been

The truth comes home to us straight away. A new life is primary evidence for having had credible dealings with God. Where there is no change, then we are saying that God makes no difference! The Transformer has not transformed!

The first mark of the transformed person, by contrast with verse 10, is that he loves the voice of God's law. As things were the worshippers returned from Bethel to their old resentment of the voice of justice in the gate. They wanted neither the judge who pronounced a correct verdict, *who reproves in the gate*, nor a witness who tells the facts as they happened, *who speaks the truth*. The point at issue is not the social injustice involved, that comes later, but the refusal to allow life to be governed by truth. Amos puts this first. The evidence of having come into personal contact with the transforming God is that from then on a person longs to have life changed according to the dictates, principles and examples of His Word. The God of Bethel was not just a vision, there to be admired; He was a God who speaks (Gn. 35:13–15). Yet they came away as those who had heard nothing. Not for them the passionate cry, 'Oh, how I love thy law!' (Ps. 119:97), but it is the cry which arises from real touch with God and which gives assurance that the relationship is real. Was not Isaac Watts expressing the very heart of Amos' doctrine when he wrote:

> Thy noblest wonders here we view,
> In souls renewed and sins forgiven:
> Lord, cleanse my sins, my soul renew,
> And make Thy Word my guide to heaven![5]

The second evidence of transformation under the hand of God we deduce from verse 11a: self-submission within the fellowship of God's people. Amos turns from their relationship to truth to their relationship to other people. The *poor* man is the one without resource and therefore without redress. He is weak in every sense. He can be mistreated with impunity. We might translate *exactions* with the rather double-edged word 'tributes'. It appears as 'tax' in 2 Chronicles 24:6, 9 and is used there in a perfectly good sense. We seem to need a word, therefore, which is capable of looking

[5] From the hymn 'The heavens declare Thy glory, Lord'.

right but involving wrong! They leaned so heavily on the defenceless man (was this an early 'protection' racket?) that to him the payment was as compulsory as a lawful tax demand, but to any who questioned the receiver it was 'just a tribute from a friend'. The principle on which life was lived was that other people are there to be milked. Certainly the great Transformer would have laid His hand on this at Bethel had He been sought, for when at length He Himself came to visit His people did He not say 'I am among you as one who serves' (Lk. 22:27)?

As we continue to delineate the true by contrast with the false, the third point at which life would change on the basis of veritable dealings with God is that there would be a new concern to have His approval (12a). The introduction of the vocabulary of *transgressions* and *sins* comes as no surprise in Amos (or anywhere else in the Bible). Nothing can be done against the truth or against people that is not done directly against God. They left Bethel bearing abundant rebellions on their consciences and still gripped by 'strong' (RSV *great*) sins, but unconcerned to be transformed. He who changed Jacob to Israel could have dealt with this situation, but unfortunately He alone worried about it; they were unconcerned. Outwardly they sinned; in their inner motivations there was a heart of rebellion (so the words in verse 12a balance each other in significance). But there was no concern to be different. There can obviously be no assurance of sins forgiven where there is no concern about sins as such! It must surely be a mark of the person who has done business with God that from that moment onwards he is concerned to have the divine approval, to love what He loves and to hate what He hates.

Verse 12b pursues the delineation of the person who has met with the transforming God—or, at least, by implication we may understand it so. It brings before us the feature of moral integrity.

The picture in verse 12b is of a man who sides with people not because of what they are but because of what they have got and are prepared to give. He weighs the bribe in his hand, but he does not weigh moral values in his head, heart and conscience. This, Amos suggests, ought to have come under the transforming influence of the God of Bethel. Indeed so, for did not that God care for the isolated, helpless Jacob when he strayed accidentally into His house? But these 'set themselves in opposition to the man who is in the right . . . and side-track the uninfluential when he comes seeking justice in the gate—but when they see the colour of a man's gold, ah, that's a different story'. And this (not very elaborated) paraphrase helps us to see what is at issue: the intangible moral values versus the tangible monetary values. By contrast, there is a moral determination about the person who has sought the Lord.

Finally, in verse 13 Amos implies that, had they been effectively in the presence of the God of Bethel, they would have sought to achieve a social order favourable to righteousness, but instead the social climate of the day threatened anyone who voiced an opinion contrary to its unrighteous and self-seeking ethos. Such was the rule of lawlessness (*cf.* on 6:3) that a person feared to open his mouth to protest: prudence dictated otherwise. There may be a little more to it than just that, the silence of prudence. The word translated *prudent* could well mean 'anyone who wants to get on' or 'succeed'.[6] In this light we can easily see the sort of pressures society at that day was exerting: 'You wouldn't want to spoil your prospects, now, would you?' It both silenced protests which might have been made for others who had been wronged and placed severe adverse pressures on the person who wished to steer a straight course for himself. It was a society which encouraged wrong-doing and discouraged standing for principle. When grace transforms a person it brings this aspect of life into focus: a determination to create a society in which righteousness dwells.

Perils and empowerings

It must be clear by now that the Bethel pilgrimage was a Bank Holiday outing devoid of serious religious or spiritual intent. It was playing with God, and as such, according to Amos, came under the double peril of fire and frustration. *Fire* stands for the ultimate display of divine rejection of this non-serious way of life (5:6). The verse sets out the two sides of such a situation: first, the reality of the wrath of God against a religion devoid of renewal, a play-group and not a church (6b); and secondly the total incapacity of such a religion to offer any palliative in the day when God acts (6b). This is precisely what Jesus taught in

6 It is so translated in Jos. 1:8.

Matthew 7:21-23. He faces people who have a testimony to religion (*says to me, 'Lord, Lord'*), to communication of the truth (*prophesy in your name*) and to supernatural ministry (*cast out demons . . . do many mighty works*) and, in His assessment, it all adds up to a non-event because it lacks the reality of a credible relationship with God (*I never knew you*) and the evidence of a life transformed by obedience (*does the will of my Father*). Jesus emphatically places this confrontation *on that day*. It is the final judgment, the downfall of a religion which produced much display but no renewal.

The frustration is described in verse 11b. Under the façade of the pilgrimage game the real 'name of the game' was acquisitiveness (11a, 12b). But it would prove to be a life without either stability (houses built but not inhabited) or enjoyment (vineyards planted but their wine never sampled). This is not the threat that others will possess their labours, but that such labours will not bring the expected rewards to those who have done them. This is frustration, the cramping, non-productiveness of a life apart from God.

There is an impressive timelessness about these strictures of the prophet. Stability and satisfaction—to achieve that which will endure and to enjoy the benefits of having achieved it—have ever been the objectives of man. But they cannot be brought to pass apart from a living and life-giving relationship with God.

This brings us, at the end, to the point at which Amos started his oracle. Take again the five points at which true religion manifests its reality in life: love of God's truth, submission within the fellowship, concern for God's approval, moral integrity and social order. These are not five rungs of a ladder up to heaven, five superlative good works meriting God's approval in the bestowal of eternal glory. They are the five parallel evidences that a person has met the God of Bethel at the bottom of the ladder, whither He has come to reveal Himself, to speak and to bless. True religion is not a way to God but a way from God! It springs out of union and communion with God and seals its veracity in the display of a fivefold transformation. Therefore the great, opening call from Amos is this: *Seek the Lord and live* (5:6). Make Him your place of pilgrimage. You have had to set time aside to go to Bethel; set time aside for God. You have had to organize your life to be able to make the pilgrimage; organize your life round God. Your pilgrimage has involved you in prayer and praise and hearing God's Word; maintain these things but focus them on Him. *Do not seek Bethel . . . Seek the Lord* (5, 6). For this is the way of life. Otherwise you walk the way of fire (6b) and frustration (11b); this is the way of life: *Seek the Lord and live.*

In the Hebrew of this phrase *live* is an imperative, yet here according to the idiom it is more a promise than a command. Of course it must be a command, for the whole thrust of the fivefold transformation is that we must deliberately set ourselves to live in this way. But, nevertheless, it is really a promise. When Hebrew wants to express emphatically that something will really, truly, automatically and inevitably follow from something else, it expresses the consequential thing by an imperative. When God says through the prophet 'Live' He is promising life, indeed He is donating life. It is as when Jesus called Lazarus from the tomb: the command carried the enabling. So the God of Bethel says 'Live' because it belongs to His nature to transform by His own patience and power the lives of those who have been brought into communion with Him.

Amos 5:14-20
Seeds of Uncertainty, Harvest of Assurance

IT can be the faithful pastor's task to sow doubts in the minds of those in his care. It is a thing which requires wisdom. It was a true pastoral heart, for example, which spoke in Psalm 73:15: *If I had said, 'I will speak thus,' I would have been untrue to the generation of thy children.* Every stage of Christian experience confronts its own problems; it is no part of a pastor's duty (or of the duty of any Christian towards another) to implant the problems of a mature experience in the mind of an immature believer. But on the other hand, at every stage of experience we may very easily become deeply committed to propositions and suppositions which our more fully instructed and matured brothers and sisters know well to be mistaken. Frontal assault only stimulates pride to build stronger entrenchments. What does the pastor do then? He gently sows doubts. In one way or another the tendency of his ministry is to leave the mind enquiring, 'Can it be as I have thought?'

It is in such a task that we find Amos occupied here. He is probing an entrenched position. He does not batter; he seeks to insert a 'may be' in the hope that it will grow into a 'cannot be'. If this conflicts with a traditional picture of Amos, incessantly roaring like one of his own lion metaphors, it just goes to show how much our impression of Bible men is dependent on the tone of voice in which we read their words. Certainly Amos was 'the prophet who feared no man',[1] but this does not mean that he

[1] I am happy to acknowledge the source of the words quoted. In the early 1940s it was my privilege as a very young Christian to belong to St Kevin's Church, Dublin, and to profit from the ministry of the then Rector, the Rev. Martin Parsons. For this I have never ceased to thank God. In the course of a

went round shaking his fist in people's faces or behaving in a needlessly provocative manner. We noted above the suggestion of J. L. Mays that Amos' choice of the lamentation-form for 5:2 evidenced the sorrow of his own heart and the depth of his feeling for his countrymen. It would be a salutary exercise (not least for those who write commentaries) to read the oracles of Amos in the quiet tone of one presenting well-thought-out rational arguments and especially to read the passages of judgment in the voice of a man who can only with difficulty hold back his tears.

At any rate, here Amos probes his way forward, if by sowing doubts he can pierce hard and self-assured (but wrongly assured) hearts. The problem is that they have assumed themselves to be the inheritors of the Beer-sheba promise, 'The Lord is with you.' They believe that in the present tense of their contemporary life they can say 'The Lord is with us' (5:14) and they look forward with complete equanimity to the time when He will be with them in the particular and dramatic sense conveyed by the words *the day of the Lord* (18). The inner heart of the idea, 'The Lord is with you', is peace with God. Between man and God there is no barrier, no constraint; all is well; harmony reigns; the two can walk together because they have come to an understanding. The test of such a belief is to cast it forward in time to the *day* when the Lord will be present, not as now invisibly and with Self-imposed constraints, but visibly, wholly, gloriously. Will there still be peace then? Will we then be able to *endure the day of his coming* (Mal. 3:2)? It is this consideration which prompted the hymn-writer[2] to ask

> O, how shall I, whose native sphere
>   Is dark, whose mind is dim,
> Before the Ineffable appear,
> And on my naked spirit bear
>   The uncreated beam?

But no such doubts assailed the people of Amos' day who felt able to *desire the day of the Lord* (18).

---

series of sermons on the Minor Prophets, he preached on Amos under the title 'The Prophet who feared no man' and this was my first and one of my most fruitful introductions to this portion of God's Word.

[2] T. Binney, 'Eternal Light!'.

Unready but unaware

Why could not Amos share in their happy optimism? Why does he feel it incumbent upon him to sow doubts?

It seems fair to begin to interpret his thought this way: Can one claim to walk with God and at the same time be unaware of His greatness and majesty? Their light assumption of peace with God spoke to the prophet of an imperfect perception of the God of whom they spoke. At any rate, he appears to have addressed himself to precisely this state of affairs. If we take the oracles of Amos one by one, the passage before us is unique in its stress on the greatness of God. Nowhere else do we find in three successive verses *The* LORD, *the God of hosts . . . the* LORD, *the God of hosts . . . The* LORD, *the God of hosts, the Lord* (14, 15, 16). Does it not create the impression of someone trying to make a point without putting it in so many words? 'Yahweh, the omnipotent God . . . Yahweh, the omnipotent God . . . Yahweh, the omnipotent God, the Sovereign'—such is the delineation of God. Maybe one would unthinkingly speak of walking with God—but with such a God of sovereign omnipotence? Is there not here a corrective to all such complacency, namely that whatever I might think of walking with Him, He might have doubts about walking with me? Adam would happily have remained in the garden provided he could hide; it was God who knew that he must be banished and who drove him out (Gn. 3:8, 23 f.).

Amos proceeds to amplify the point (16-20). Following on from the most complete of his majestic entitlements of God (16) he describes, as a message from that God, a situation of complete despair: wailing everywhere, in the towns (*squares . . . streets*) and in the country (*farmers . . . vineyards*), wailing by everyone, those to whom tears came possibly less easily (*farmers*) and those who could turn on the tap with professional alacrity (*skilled in lamentation*), wailing preoccupying the whole of life so that the business of life is halted in *squares* and *streets*, the work of life is halted as the *farmer* leaves his task and the joys of life are superseded as wailing fills those traditionally happy places, the *vineyards*. He presses the matter further: complete despair arises from a judgment of self-condemnation passed by everyone and the recognition that there is no escape. It is, says Amos (19—restoring

the 'and' of the Hebrew where RSV inexplicably reads *or*[3]) as if
(*per impossibile*) a man evaded a pursuing *lion* only to run slap into a
bear, yet at the crucial moment found a door offering him an
asylum; he slams the door in the bear's face and, safe at last, leans
on the *wall* for breath only to be bitten by a *serpent*. The picture
has its grim humour! But we need to take particular notice when
Amos reverts to the lion-imagery! The lion is an unexpected,
startling danger. It was no part of the planned country walk. When
all was peace, suddenly all was danger and such a danger as to
demand a verdict of hopelessness. (And the Lion is roaring from
Zion . . .) To escape at all is a miracle, yet each successive escape
turns out to be no escape until, as the verdict turns from hopelessness to 'peace at last', the serpent inflicts the mortal wound.

But the message from the majestic God is not finished yet.
Wailing and inescapable judgment are followed by total darkness
(20). Complacency had been telling the people, with irreproachable
logic, that when the Lord comes it will be to side with His people.
That day will be their crown of glory; all who despised them will
see how wrong they were; everything that had ever plagued them
will be over for ever; all will be gladness and light. No, says Amos,
darkness . . . not light, and gloom with no brightness (20). In other
words, they have been feeding themselves on false hopes. In the
day when God comes He will turn out to be their enemy! It will be
their worst day by far, without even a flicker (*brightness*) of hope.

And what is the cause of all this despair (16, 17), inescapable
doom (18-19) and darkness (20)? Nothing spectacular, just that
I will pass through the midst of you, says the Lord (17). The Lord does
not do anything; He just quietly walks through the midst—the
very thing they were taking for granted in their casual assumption
of the Beer-sheba promise of the divine companionship! And as
He (unspectacularly!) presences Himself among them there is
that about Him, His glory, His Person, His greatness, His
majesty, His Godhead, whatever, which causes all without
exception to wail inconsolably and to acknowledge themselves
lost.

[3] Also NEB and (incredibly) RV. See however RV mg. and JB which, however, like J. B. Phillips' rendering, appear nevertheless to separate the verse
into two distinct illustrations.

Moral aspirations

So Amos sows the seed of doubt in their assumption of peace with God: do they know the God they say they are at peace with? But there is a second question: do they know what peace means? It is a state of shared objectives among other things, and (if we read Amos aright) no-one can walk with God except he is giving himself to a determined pursuit of the good. Amos says, *Seek good, and not evil, that you may live; and so the Lord, the God of hosts, will be with you* (14).[4] This call to genuine moral aspiration has four aspects to which we may allude briefly.

First, commitment to holy living is both positive and negative (14a). There is a 'seeking' and also a 'shunning': *Seek good, and not evil.* Secondly, holiness is concerned with both actions and emotions: *Seek good, and not evil . . . Hate evil, and love good* (14a, 15a). It is this which saves holiness from being some sort of face worn by the people of God. There is a profound truth, however, in the fact that Amos puts the action before the emotion, *seek* (*i.e.* settle upon it as the target of your daily life) before *love.* Ordinarily the Bible represents holiness as starting in the 'inner man' and working outwards. Proverbs 4:23 calls for a special guardianship of the *heart* on the ground that all life springs out of it; Romans 12:2 looks to *the renewal of your mind* as basic to the

---

[4] IB holds that verses 14, 15 (and also 6) must be inserted by a later hand because they contain a note of hope at variance with the stern message of judgment preached by Amos. In verse 6 the word 'lest' suggests that by repentance the final blow may at least be softened if not wholly averted, and in verses 14, 15 there is a remnant doctrine. The insertion is to be explained on the supposition that a later author took seriously the doctrine of judgment as Amos preached it and sought by his insertions to impress on his own people that they were 'confronted with the necessity of making a momentous life-and-death decision'. It never seems to be observed by commentators who propose this sort of insertion in Amos that, if they are right in saying that Amos was wholly a prophet of doom, then the insertions are not 'adaptations' but contradictions, and that if at some later date there remained a people of God for whom Amos (who supposedly foretold the total end of the people of God) is thus 'adapted', then Amos proved in the event to be a false prophet who, therefore, ought not to be heeded, then or now. Even Mays, who finally denies the hopeful ending (9:13 ff.) to Amos, finds 'exhortation' as 'a marginal feature of Amos' prophecy (which) offers an alternative to those who will hear its instruction'. He rightly roots this view in Amos' theology: 'Yahweh remains the life of his people even in a situation in which they deserve the sentence of death.'

required positive (*transformed*) and negative (*not . . . conformed*)
differences in outward living. Such references could be repeated
over and over. But there is also this truth, that many, many times,
if we were to wait for emotion to prompt action, we should wait
in vain and long lists of Christian duties would rot in the pipe-line
because we did not 'feel' any stimulus to perform them. It is
therefore a salutary jolt to our tendency to exalt emotion over duty,
to think that it is more godly to 'feel led' than do something
because 'I ought', when Amos puts 'seeking' before 'loving'. It
turns to practical account that to which we pay lip service in our
better moments: that emotions are a fickle and false guide. As far
as holiness is concerned emotions may be nothing but a rational-
ization of moral idleness. But there is more to Amos' emphasis
than shocking us into action. It is abundantly true that to act
lovingly towards a brother or sister Christian will bring in its
wake the emotion of Christian love for that one, and that if we give
ourselves to obeying, God will graciously add the bonus of
prompting in us the corresponding feeling. But more than that:
even if we were never to feel the emotion we are still bound by the
duty; therefore Amos is simply putting first things where they
belong, at the head of the list. Right must be done because it is
right and not because there is emotional satisfaction in doing it.

Thirdly, holiness must be pursued both for self and for society:
Hate evil, and love good, and establish justice in the gate (15). This is no
'fugitive and cloistered virtue' interior to the heart or wrought out
solely in a one-to-one relationship between the individual and
God. Its outflow is in terms of a society founded and run on
principles of justice backed by sanctions for the punishment of
evildoers and the praise of them that do well. The *gate* is the court
of justice; behind it lies the law of the land, enshrined then as now
in principle and precedent, before it lies a particular cry for
justice and beyond it lies the good order of society. The *gate*
safeguards, applies and actualizes justice, that which is good for
all. When he calls the people of God to be concerned with *justice
in the gate*, Amos makes it their duty to be concerned basically with
social ethics, social welfare, the amelioration of conditions, the
protection of and provision for the poor, the weak, the potentially
exploited. But the call to *establish justice in the gate* is given to those
who are committed in their own persons to seeking good, and

not evil, hating evil and loving good: that is to say, they are to seek to enshrine at the heart of society that same distinction between good and evil, right and wrong by which they live and to establish a society wherein the good will be sought and the evil rejected.

What a call this constitutes to Bible Christians to rediscover the moral and social teaching of Holy Scripture! How often our contributions on social and socio-ethical questions are small, insignificant, inhibited because we simply have not laboured to acquire biblical definitions of the issues involved! If we do not labour to *establish justice in the gate*, we shall be accused from this passage in Amos of a one-sided morality stopping short of the biblical concern for society, we shall be exposed, according to Amos 3:9—4:5, of playing around with a useless religion while society rots, and we shall find, according to Amos 6:3, that, while we have been unconcerned, other and sinister forces have been at work to enthrone violence and disorder.

Finally, the pursuit of holiness is a means of life—not just a way of life or a rule of life, but a means of life: *Seek good, and not evil, that you may live; and so the Lord, the God of hosts, will be with you* . . . *Hate evil, and love good, and establish justice in the gate; it may be that the Lord . . . will be gracious* . . . (14, 15). The teaching is that when the people of God set themselves in the way of holiness, the way which accords with the will and heart of God, they come into possession of life (14a), of the reality of the presence of the omnipotent Yahweh with them (14b) and, hopefully, of a fresh experience of His grace (15b). Grace must never be a matter of presumption. If it can be commanded or taken for granted, then it ceases to be grace. Amos would teach us to walk humbly with our God! But see how he reverses what we often hear said: that by means of a new 'blessing' from heaven we are enabled to walk in holiness. We ever want the blessing first and the duty second, but Amos says that it is those who set themselves in the way that delights their God who receive life, power and grace from and in Him. Jesus put things the same way when He promised that those who hunger and thirst after righteousness would be filled (Mt. 5:6). We would rather have it in reverse: Lord, fill me and then I will aspire after righteousness with my whole heart. But no, first the aspiration and then the satisfaction. Peter followed the same line of teaching (Acts 5:32) when he referred to *the Holy Spirit whom God has given to those who obey him*. The way of holiness is a means of life. Let us get on with obeying and God will get on with blessing!

Grace all the way

As we have traced the teaching of Amos in these verses we have watched him probe the defences of his complacent people. Their casual assumption that it is a light and easy thing to keep company with God has been gently challenged by exposing their inadequate awareness of both parties to the supposed companionship: how great God is, and how far they fall short of the essential commitment to that holiness without which no man can see God. But there is a final major feature of this passage which makes its total thrust an exhortation to rest on the sufficiency of omnipotent grace.

We noted that this oracle contains an assemblage of divine entitlements unique in Amos, but we took the observation only half way. In the seven verses (14–20) only one fails to refer in some way to God by name or title (19). Three different addresses are used: *the God of hosts* occurs three times (14, 15, 16), *the Lord* (Sovereign) once (16) and *the* LORD (Yahweh) seven times, nearly twice as often as the other two together. How is it possible to say that Amos is the prophet who preaches without a note of hope when he is so prominently a preacher of Yahweh? Whatever one would judge about the psychology of such a prophet, one would have to find his theology the product of an ignorant, bigoted and unrealistic mind. The question at base is not 'Has Amos a message of hope?' but 'Has Yahweh forgotten to be gracious?'—He whose name reached definition for the first time when, in covenant faithfulness to a miserable, lost and thankless people, He came down to Egypt because he had identified Himself with their sorrows (Ex. 2:24—3:8). So in this oracle, the divine name drops again and again from the lips of the prophet, a continual dropping to wear away hearts of stone. The 'may be' of grace (15) rightly rebukes complacent human hearts, but in the divine heart there is no 'may be'. The God of grace cannot forget to be gracious.

Surely it is for this reason that He here addresses His people as *the remnant of Joseph* (15). Amos is very interesting in his use of the patriarchal names, applying them to the people of his day. Why *Joseph* here? Joseph was the man about whom the Beer-sheba promise was asserted to be true, even when every evidence available suggested that it had been forgotten. When he was first sold as a slave, *the Lord was with Joseph* (Gn. 39:2); when things went from bad to worse and he was imprisoned, *the Lord was with Joseph* (Gn. 39:21) and as the days of imprisonment went by *the Lord was with him* (Gn. 39:23). Finally, when hope had sunk beyond the horizon, Joseph was taken from the prison house to the throne room in one astonishing leap because Pharaoh looked at him and said, *Can we find such a man as this, in whom is the Spirit of God?* (Gn. 41:38)—the Lord was with him!

No matter how much our hearts speak to us of failure, failure to discern the greatness and wonder of our God, failure to walk in the way of holiness, crass complacency, self-satisfaction, whatever it may be, 'Grace has brought us safe thus far, and grace will lead us home.'

Amos 5:21-27
Religion in a Box

IT is time to do a little stock-taking before launching into this
final study in Amos 5. What in fact has Amos been teaching?
Has he been saying 'saved today, lost tomorrow'? It would certainly look like that. He has clearly defined his congregation as
those whom God redeemed (3:2), but he has come to the point
where he has held over their heads the prospect of unrelieved
sorrow (5:16, 17), inescapable sentence of death (5:18, 19), and
the darkness of hopelessness (5:20) in the day when God comes.
And, as we have noted, some hold that this was the characteristic
message of Amos: a message without hope for a people without
reprieve. It makes us wonder, however, if this can be a correct interpretation of Amos when it must be maintained by the
application of surgical excision to those parts of the book which
fail to match the theory!

But to whom was Amos speaking? Even the most casual reading
of his book reveals his hearers as a church which had confused
assurance with complacency. They not only professed salvation
but also an unworried certainty of salvation (cf. 5:14, 18). As Amos
looked at them, however, he saw a people who not only professed
salvation but who *exhibited a total lack of the sort of evidence which
would make their profession credible.* Theirs was a groundless confidence which would not bear the weight of the divine majesty
in the day of the Lord's coming.

Of course, it would be unreasonable to suppose that there was
no other side to church life in Amos' day than baseless complacency. The sword would decimate but a tenth would remain
(5:3), and even in the unspeakable horror of 5:14-20 it was
open to any to identify themselves with *the remnant of Joseph*

(5:15) and with the ever-present God of grace in the day of grace.

We shall see more of this out-shining of grace before we are finished with the book of Amos, but in the meantime the concluding passage of chapter 5 focuses attention on the shrine at Gilgal, where the sacred traditions proclaimed the Lord's gift of the land as the inheritance of His people for ever. In verses 21–27 we see the outworking of the threat expressed in verse 5, *Gilgal shall surely go into exile* (*cf.* verse 27).[1]

Eternal security

Gilgal poses the third of three questions as vital today as when Amos raised them. In relation to Bethel the question is this: what is the proof that people have had dealings with the life-giving, life-changing God who is present there? What makes their testimony on this point a certainty? In relation to Beer-sheba the question was, If a person is really walking in the divine companionship, how will it show? What proves his claim to be real? And, now, in relation to Gilgal there is the third question: On what grounds can a person be certain of his inheritance of the promised land? What is the evidence that lease-hold has become free-hold?

Now for us the 'promised land' has modulated into its permanent biblical significance of the eternal inheritance of the saints of God. How can we know that we have eternal life? It is a precious possession. Who would not desire it? Furthermore, once the inheritance is bestowed it cannot be forfeited and will not be withdrawn (Jn. 10:28). But how can I be certain that it is mine? What is the evidence? What proves the matter beyond all question?

Gilgal religion

There is a wealth of religion in verses 21–23: festivals, sacrifices and music are all evidenced in abundance. There is no doubt that

---

[1] Amos does not, of course, say explicitly that he is here addressing himself to the Gilgal pilgrims. The reasons for so understanding these verses are set out on pp. 107, 108 above. See especially footnote 4, p. 110.

they went in for religion in a big way at Gilgal. They took their religious duties seriously, the *feasts* at which attendance was by law obligatory, and the *solemn assemblies*, 'red letter' days on the church calendar which must be observed (21); they entered fully into their religious privileges, bringing *burnt offerings, cereal offerings* and *peace offerings* symbolic of their status as God's people and their fellowship with Him and with each other (22); they gave full expression to their religious joys, singing *songs* to the accompaniment of *harps* (23). Somehow the vivacity of it all and the thrill of it all communicates itself. One can almost hear the singing. But God could not! All He heard was noise!

There cannot be a passage in the Bible more deliberate in expressing divine distaste than this : *I hate ... despise ... take no delight ... will not accept ... will not look upon ... Take away from me the noise ... I will not listen.* Their religion was dutiful, exceedingly costly—think of the outlay on animals for sacrifice— apparently whole-hearted, emotionally satisfying, but if religion does not get through to God it has failed centrally.

Wherein did it fail? Verses 23 and 24 are rightly connected by the word *but*. Amos brings to our attention the neglected factor. The word *roll* is interesting. It derives from the same Hebrew verb which gave Gilgal its name. According to Joshua 5:9 the circumcision ceremony was followed by a divine comment: '*I have rolled away the reproach of Egypt from you.*' *And so the name of that place is called Gilgal* .... ('the rolling'). It is as if, in Amos 5:24, the Lord were saying, Yes, you have been to Gilgal, but there is a rolling you have forgotten, the rolling of justice and righteousness.[2] Here again is the picture of a religion that is going nowhere. They went to Gilgal to be religious, but they left religion behind when they returned home. Pilgrims rolled in to the festivals, but justice and righteousness failed to roll out into the irrigation channels of daily life and relationships. Therefore their religion stank as far as God was concerned. In verse 21 *I take no delight* is, literally, 'I will not breathe in the odour of' (*cf.* Gn. 8:21).

[2] While the derivative noun *gal* is used of 'waves', as in the English 'rollers', the verb itself *gālal* is nowhere else used in the Bible of waters 'rolling'. *Cf.* Pss. 78:16; 105:41; 124:4, 5; 147:18; *etc.*, in all of which places some part of *gālal* could well have been chosen instead of the verb actually used. We may well hold that Amos chose *gālal* for the present passage in order to use the pun to enforce his message.

What are *justice* and *righteousness*? In 5:7 the turning of *justice* to *wormwood* indicates that justice is a word involving the treatment of other people: wormwood has to be tasted before it is known for the bitter thing it is. Justice, therefore, is right behaviour in relation to others, whereby they 'taste' or experience what is good and pleasant. We may compare 5:15, where loving good leads on to the establishment of justice. The good man wants the good for his neighbours as a guaranteed element in social life, and equally his hatred of evil means that he wants society to guarantee the purging out of evil through the due processes of the law. Returning to 5:7, *righteousness* is depicted as an upright (thing or person) thrown to the ground, suggesting a standard or norm rejected. This matches the evidence of 6:12b, where two expressions lie in parallel, *justice* turned *into poison*, (*i.e.*) *the fruit of righteousness into wormwood*. According to this, justice is the fruit of righteousness. Broadly, therefore, justice is correct moral practice in daily personal and social life, and righteousness is the cultivation of correct moral principle (both for self and for society); justice is mainly outward, righteousness inward. Of course, for the Bible righteousness always has the connotation 'right with God', 'what God thinks right', and therefore when the Lord desires that the outflow of religion should be justice and righteousness, He is calling for the establishment of principles and practices of daily living which conform to His word and law.

Jeremiah spoke an unanswerable word which we may use as a final comment on this particular aspect of Amos' teaching. *Has this house, which is called by my name, become a den of robbers in your eyes?* (Je. 7:11). What does he mean? A robbers' den is a place to which they go for safety and from which they come back morally unchanged. Jeremiah saw the Jerusalem temple subjected to this abuse: people confessedly finding peace with God and all manner of religious helpfulness there, but coming back unchanged, praying on their knees in the temple and preying on their neighbours everywhere else! So it was with Gilgal as Amos observed the thronged pilgrimages, the punctilious sacrifices, the joyous singing, with choir and orchestra—but no intention to commit themselves deliberately or in any new way to righteousness and justice.

'Do not enter box unless exit is clear'

The expressions Amos uses in verse 24 speak of abundance (*roll . . . like waters*) and perpetuity (*an ever-flowing stream*). Sometimes the figure of pouring out water is used in the Bible for the consecration of life to God (*e.g.* 1 Sa. 7:6; 2 Sa. 23:16). It is as though the pouring water symbolized the direction in which, henceforth, all life's energies would be channelled. If we allow this idea to contribute to the interpretation of Amos, then the Lord is looking for lives whose energies, abundantly and perpetually, are flowing out in righteousness and justice: the cultivation and holding of sound moral principles of life, and the practice of these principles in personal and social behaviour. And religion is pointless unless this is its outflow.

The trouble with Gilgal was that they kept their religion in a box, a sealed compartment with no communicating exit. It made no difference to life before or after, and therefore it had no significance before God.

But this was never God's intention for His people. The significance of the *but* linking verses 23 and 24 is to say that, if only they will restore the forgotten factor and orientate their religion towards those things which are its proper and God-intended fruits, then He will withdraw His displeasure and make their religious observances meaningful by His acceptance of and delight in them.[3]

Returning for a moment to Amos' account of Gilgal festivals,

---

[3] I do not propose to detail here the opposing views of the interpretation of verses 24, 25. The broad lines of discussion and my own conclusions are given in NBCR, p. 727. Regarding verse 24 it seems to me at least equally sensible to consider the 'but' with which it opens to introduce something to be added to verse 23 (*i.e.* 'but if only you would also . . .') as to understand it as proposing an exclusive alternative. Regarding verse 25, and remembering that it is a question which Amos invites his hearers to answer, there seems to me no possibility but that he would have received the answer 'Yes'. Mays holds that Amos here reflects a tradition irreconcilable with extant Pentateuchal sources, a tradition of the wilderness period in which there were no sacrifices. But this will not do: Amos is not expressing his own opinion, he is inviting the opinion of his hearers. On any and every view of the Pentateuch they could only have replied affirmatively. Therefore Amos is saying 'yes' to sacrifices; they accord with God's will for His people. The synthesis of the passage offered above seeks to take this reasoning into account.

we note again the absence of any reference to sin-offerings. This basic defect in self-awareness and in theology vitiates all. Had they been aware of themselves as sinners there would surely have been a sharp realization that religion, if it means anything, commits them to a reformed way of life. Had they been aware of the holy God, surely, again, they would have found a pressure to amend their lives according to His revealed character and will. But even so, the offerings which held the centre of the stage ought to have spoken equally loudly. The essential meaning of the burnt-offering is total consecration to God: the attitude which holds nothing back (*cf.* Gn. 22:12 f.). The essential meaning of the peace-offering is fellowship, upward to God and outward to other folk (*cf.* Dt. 16:10–12), with special reference to the help-less, the uncared for. What was the use of consecration offerings which did not issue in the consecration of the life to righteousness, or of fellowship offerings which did not issue in a fellowship of justice? It was all pointless because it stopped short at the gate of the sanctuary; it did not come back into the home; it did not enter the place of business (*cf.* 8:4–6).

But this does not mean that Amos is suggesting a straight swap: give up religion and take up ethics. If this was his intention he made a cardinal mistake in addressing a question to his hearers: *Did you bring me sacrifices and offerings . . . in the wilderness?* (25). Every head in the congregation nodded an affirmative; the bolder spirits shouted 'yes'; for this was the unanimous tradition they had inherited and they knew no other.[4] Moses had received a ritual law from the Lord and they were living in obedience to it. But there is a little more to Amos' question. 'Was it sacrifices and offerings you brought to me . . . ?' Why does he ask the question in this inverted way, throwing 'sacrifices and offerings' into prominence? Remembering that in this passage he is attacking a false departmentalism which kept 'religion in a box', the force of his question is this, 'Was that what you brought—that and nothing more?'

In the Exodus narrative, Mount Sinai is not a casual halt in the

[4] For a question of this formation expecting the answer 'yes' see 1 Sa. 2:27, where RSV has adopted LXX (why?) but RSV mg. records Hebrew. To achieve the same answer, English usage would require 'Did I not. . . .?' but clearly Hebrew usage does not.

desert itinerary but the primary goal of the travellers from Egypt. It was offered as a 'sign' to Moses that he had been divinely commissioned for the task of leading the people out, that they would *serve God upon this mountain* (Ex. 3:12). The coming of the people to Sinai was the immediate climax of the Exodus. They came to the mountain as God's redeemed people (Ex. 6:6) and without a doubt, as Exodus represents it, the Passover was the moment and means of that redemption. They came from Egypt because, as the Lord's first-born son (Ex. 4:22), they had been kept safe by the blood of the lamb (Ex. 12:13) on the night when the first-born of Egypt perished under the divine wrath. Blood-sacrifice was thus a foundational necessity.

Mount Sinai added another dimension to their experience: the redeemed heard, assented to and received the law of their redeemer-God (Ex. 20:1 ff.). The law, therefore, was given, not as a ladder by which the unsaved might meritoriously mount to heaven on the rungs of their own good works, but as a pattern of life for those already the children of God by redemption through blood. There were thus two sides to the experience of the people of God, redemption and blood-sacrifice on the one hand, law and obedience on the other. These two were completely synthesized when the Mosaic system reached its full expression in the subsequent revelations vouchsafed at Sinai, of which the tabernacle was the symbolic climax. In itself it embodied the purposes of God in redemption (Ex. 29:43-46), and especially in its inner sanctum, the holiest of all, which was occupied by the tables of the law over which the blood was sprinkled once a year. Now consider the message of that symbolism. That which is permanent is the law, the nature of God written out in a series of precepts in the keeping of which His people show their likeness to Him (*cf.* Lv. 19:2 ff.). This is the perpetual requirement of God, in response to which the abiding obligation of the people is obedience. But then, as occasion demands, lapses in obedience are catered for by the shed blood of atonement.

Just as in the New Testament the outcome of the saving work of God in Christ is *that you may not sin; but if any one does sin, we have an advocate* (1 Jn. 2:1), so in the Old Testament (for the Bible is one book) the upshot of redemption was the life of obedience, but at the same time the blood of atonement lay to hand to hold a disobedient people in the fellowship of a holy God. It is to this biblical wholeness of religion that Amos bears witness and to which he recalls the people. Certainly there were sacrifices and offerings in the wilderness, but in the Mosaic ideal they had their *raison d'être* in the summons of the law to obedience and holiness. Deprive them of that context, and they become a religion-game played at Gilgal.

God is not a game

Having brought the people thus far, Amos faces them starkly with critical issues. There is a way of guaranteeing their inheritance of the land: to return to the biblical synthesis which makes up true religion—on the one hand, commitment to a life of obedience, the life of righteousness and justice (verse 24), and on the other hand, the glad appropriation of all the benefits and blessings of the shed blood of the sacrifices to cater for disobediences and to keep those who love His law in fellowship with the God who gave it. The Bible knows no other prescription for eternal security. But failing this, dispossession and banishment.

A purely ceremonial religion can never safeguard the truth or hold the people to the truth. They had been punctilious in the ceremonies of the shrines but careless of the truth of God. Now, when Amos so unexpectedly lifts the lid off the total religious life of the nation, what do we find? Equal punctiliousness in the religious ceremonies of other gods (26)! The gods of Assyria occupied the hearts of Israel long before the armies of Assyria occupied its streets and towns. *Sakkuth*, the Assyrian god of war, identified with the planet Saturn, called *Kaiwan*,[5] was right there, in Israel, cultivated by the very people who so assiduously flocked to Bethel, Beer-sheba and Gilgal. What blasphemy (26a) to exchange 'Yahweh, God the omnipotent, the Sovereign' (*cf.* verse 16) for 'king Sakkuth'! What folly to worship a star in the place of the Creator of the stars (26b; *cf.* verse 8)! What stupidity to exalt as God that *which you made for yourselves* (26b)! But there it all was, and the ritual of the shrines, divorced from the Word of God, heard,

[5] The textual details of verse 26 are not altogether certain. RSV would appear to make best sense on the basis of minimal change. See the commentaries.

loved and obeyed, was no safeguard. Is anything so perilous or so fickle as religious experience isolated from the intelligible message of God addressed to mind, heart and will?

So the issue was joined. A people who had never really held the title-deeds of inheritance—however much they fancied they did—must either come into the place of blessing or forfeit the blessings of the place. An ironic justice will carry them off *beyond Damascus* (27), whither in heart and mind they had already strayed after false gods. But *the Lord, whose name is the God of hosts*, 'Yahweh, God the omnipotent', will not be mocked.

The evidence of true religion is that it touches all life with the holiness of obedience to His Word and command. He will not endlessly live with the stench of false religion in His nostrils and its noise in His ears.

Amos 6:1-14
The Enemy of the People

ONE of the major problems in studying the books of the prophets is the difficulty, often, of seeing the wood for the trees. Individual verses and whole sections are plain enough in their meaning, but why does one thing follow on from another? Is there any plan or pattern discernible in the whole?

Every book ought to be studied on the assumption that there is a plan, simply because it is unreasonable to believe that a man conscious that he had a message (as distinct from mere individual utterances) from God for the times would not be concerned to put his 'messages' in such an order as to unfold the totality of truth entrusted to him. At the same time we must be ready humbly to recognize our own feeble powers of understanding and therefore refuse to say that there is no pattern or connection simply because at that moment we cannot see one.

At this point in our study of the second part of Amos' book there is profit in reviewing the ground we have covered and in trying to see the message in its wholeness. In 3:9-15 Amos was seeking to introduce the characteristic theme of this section: the invading foe. In true, biblical fashion, he is not concerned to act as a prognosticator but much more as an acute commentator on his own times. Therefore he shows this coming event in the light of and as caused by the existing social (3:9-11), personal (3:12) and religious (3:13-15) conditions. Further analysis (4:1-5) laid bare the inner motivation of self-pleasing as that which made them, socially, personally and religiously, what they were and exposed them to the whole-hearted opposition of the Lord. Each of these sections (3:9-15; 4:1-5) reached its climax on the question of religion (3:14, 15; 4:4, 5). Amos now proceeds to take this enquiry further—as indeed pressure from friend and foe alike must have compelled him to do, for what is more incredible to a religious people than that their religion exposes them to the wrath of God? In consequence he teaches that religion as they had organized it on the basis of self-pleasing is defective godward (4:6–13), lacking the vital component of 'returning right the way to Me', *i.e.* true repentance, and defective manward (5:7, 10–13, 14, 15, 24), lacking the fruits of righteousness in the worshipper and of justice towards others.

Amos now sets himself to round off the section. He is moving towards his climactic declaration of the incoming foe (6:14), and he shows this as the inescapable implication of what has immediately preceded. It is not just that (as we shall see) he is addressing the same self-pleasing, self-satisfied people, but that on the purely literary level he binds the central section and the concluding sections of his message together. Thus the address 'Woe!' in 5:18 is re-echoed at 6:1, giving the impression that the same preacher is moving on to the next point in his address to the same congregation; 5:27 announces the punishment of exile, and the oracle in chapter 6 repeats this at the half-way mark (6:7) and amplifies it in the threat of invasion at the end (6:14); and the terrible 'day of the Lord' (5:18–20) is clearly recalled in *the evil day* (6:3) and in the fearful catastrophe indicated in 6:9, 10 with its inbuilt and belated realization that the Lord is not on their side.

'An eye for an eye'

The oracle in 6:1–14 therefore comes before us as a final reminder in this part of the book of Amos of the fearful solemnity of religious error. Their particular error was to isolate two components within the true religion which had been revealed to them and to act as if there was nothing else to the question of being religious: sincerity and ceremony. Why should we suppose that these people were less than sincere in their seeking of God at the shrines? But it was a sincerity out of step with the truth about God; it was sincere belief in a God of their own devising. Furthermore, their ceremonies were ninety-nine per cent that which God had commanded as far as their performance was concerned: Amos can fault them only on the matter of leaven (4:5), and they covered two-thirds of the decreed material of sacrifice, omitting only the sin offering. But they treated the ceremonies as an end in themselves, done in and for the inherent, automatic benefits achieved by the ceremonial act, and they divorced them from their God-intended context in a life of moral obedience, righteous principle and just conduct. Thus sincerity over-rode theology (*i.e.* in the interests of what they would like God to be, they modified the revealed teaching of what He in fact is) and ceremony obscured ethics. Their religion was devoid of creed and conduct. It did not arise from what God is, nor did it take account of what man is. It lived alone by the principle of individual self-pleasing. Upon this religion and these people the Lord will bring a condign judgment of exact retribution.

Retribution, exact reward for deed, is the central theme of 6:1-14.[1] The oracle opens on the note of complacent security, and the proud assumption of belonging to *the first of the nations* (1); it ends with the arrival on the scene of a nation even 'more superior', before whose invasion the 'first of the nations' will enter a period of affliction (14).[2] The voice of propaganda is heard in verses 2 and 13 boosting public morale by reference to the successes, pretended or real, of the kingdom. In verse 2 examples are taken from nations around—Hamath and Calneh to the north, Gath to the south—whereby visitors might be impressed with the even greater affluence (*better*, taken in the sense of 'better off')

---

[1] Retribution is a concept almost completely rejected today, but it is central to the biblical doctrine of civic and divine justice. The Lex Talionis (*cf.* Ex. 21:23 f., Lv. 24:19, 20; Dt. 19:21; Mt. 5:38) is often denigrated as a bygone savagery, but it is nothing of the sort: it is the safeguard of equal, even-handed justice; it states that crime and punishment must balance each other exactly. It would have been a good thing for England if the Lex Talionis had been honoured in the days when people were hanged for sheep-stealing. In all its contexts in the Old Testament this principle of exact justice belongs to the law-courts; it is for the guidance of magistrates. The Lord Jesus was correcting an abuse in Mt. 5:38 whereby it had been advocated as a principle for private revenge in personal relationships. We ought also to note that the wording 'an eye for an eye', *etc.*, states a principle but does not advocate a practice. The criminal law of the Old Testament was fully aware of the possibility of commuting sentences to fines, of taking circumstances and individual cases into account, *etc.*

[2] On the verb *oppress*, *cf.* Jdg. 4:3, where a period of duress is mentioned.

and territorial extent of Israel;[3] in verse 13, it is simplest to see a reference to the Trans-Jordanian successes of Jeroboam, pointing possibly to the locations of recent victories at Lo-debar and (Ashtaroth-) Karnaim.[4] But the boast of the propagandists is hollow. Verse 3 exposes them as deliberately blinding themselves to coming calamity (*the evil day*) and as allowing the state to run into a reign of terror.[5] At the other end of the chapter, their 'boasting over nothing' (verse 13) is the third of three comparisons of absurdity: to try to drive horses up a cliff face, or plough the sea with an ox-team, and to reverse public moral values[6] (12)—all

[3] This is the simplest and most telling way of understanding verse 2. Amos mimics the government publicity hand-outs. Some commentators prefer to take the verse in a warning sense: these are examples of a by-gone, now defeated, splendour. This, however, involves dating the verse after the time of Amos, for Hamath and Calneh did not fall to the Assyrian till 738 BC and Gath even later. It also involves emending the last line of verse 2, as in NEB. If it is objected that these places were not anciently famed for their splendour and therefore not very apt proofs of the superior greatness of Israel, it may be replied that this is ever the hall-mark of specious propaganda: choose comparisons too far away for easy examination, and build them up into something impressive—hence, note that it is Hamath 'the great' and Gath 'of the Philistines'. Equally, of course, there may have been some contemporary reason for choosing these places.

[4] RSV, surely rightly, takes verse 13 to refer to places. This involves treating the consonants of the Hebrew as indicating the place referred to, *e.g.* in 2 Sa. 9:4; 17:27. The vowels which appear in the Hebrew text of Amos indicate two words capable of being translated 'not-thing'. By now we can appreciate that Amos would have been completely capable of deliberately mis-pronouncing *lō' dᵉḇar* as *lō' dābār* to make his point! 'You boast in Lo-debar—yes, you're quite right, I said "Nothing" . . .!' Hammershaimb prefers to retain Karnaim as the noun meaning 'horns', metaphorical as ever of 'strength'.

[5] In verse 3 *seat of violence* could well be 'enthronement of violence', *i.e.* 'reign of terror', as indeed the last twenty years of the northern kingdom must well have been, remembering that within ten years of the death of Jeroboam II (746 BC) there were five kings, three of them seizing power by political coups. 2 Ki. 15:16 illustrates the atrocious policies of those days.

[6] Comparison of RSV with RV indicates that there has been some emendation of the Hebrew text. In this case RSV commends itself as sensible and undoubtedly correct. Note that RV can maintain the existing Hebrew text only by inserting the keyword 'there', and in addition it involves the difficulty that the word 'oxen' appears here in the plural, a form never elsewhere found in the Old Testament, where it is always a collective, singular noun. It is obvious that the Hebrew consonants have traditionally been wrongly divided out between the words. A new division gives us two splendid examples of absurdity: to run horses up a cliff is impossible; to plough the sea, pointless.

alike have brought about the 'evil day' itself, the day when the Lord shatters the kingdom into smithereens (11).

Working into the passage from each end in this way we see how Amos is carefully balancing factor against factor: complacency against disaster; boast against exposure of its hollowness. In the same way verses 4–6 and 9, 10 balance each other. The former reveal scenes of aggravated self-indulgence: extravagant laziness (4a), improvident gluttony (4b),[7] specious frivolity (5),[8] artificial—even sacrilegious[9]—stimulation (6a) and excessive personal vanity (6b). On the other hand (9, 10) we find ten men huddled together in the terror of siege conditions, ravaged by plague, mere skeletons (*bones*) of their former well-padded selves: no deodorant society, this![1] Verse 6 pointed to the cardinal defect of the days of luxury and lolling: failure to care for the break-up of the state and the broken lives of its people; verse 10 completes the picture: they had wantonly disassociated themselves from human need (6), so they come to the point where they know that God has disassociated Himself from their need with such a deep alienation that it is no longer permissible even to use His name as a swear-word provoked by extreme disaster.[2]

We now come to the central verses (7, 8). Verse 7 sums up all that has preceded and does so with the typical pointedness of Amos. The boast of these people was their unquestioned primacy.

[7] In eating lambs and calves 'from the shepherd's point of view they were . . . manifesting a hopelessly improvident lack of concern for the future' (1B). 'It hurts the shepherd of Tekoa that good animals are used for feasts of this sort' (Hammershaimb).

[8] The gibe of Amos is that in spending idle, useless days composing songs they think they are rulers like David! *Invent* may have some such meaning as 'improvise' (in the musical sense).

[9] Hammershaimb suggests that *bowls* means 'sacrificial bowls': *i.e.* they used the sacred for the common.

[1] The whole vignette is totally lacking in the sort of detail which would enable us to be certain what situation Amos had in mind. In general the conditions of siege, with deaths from starvation and plague and inevitable resort to disposing of corpses by burning (not the customary OT procedure of burial), make sense of the verse.

[2] One has to be frankly imaginative in interpreting 'Hush! We must not mention. . . .', but it is easy to see that in a situation where the burial party find only one survivor they might be provoked to a thoughtless use of the name of God. Even this is impermissible. The sense of estrangement from God has at last bitten home to the people.

Three times the word 'first' or 'chief' comes: first of the nations (verse 1), the first (*finest*) of the unguents (6), first into captivity (7)! By all means let the proprieties be observed! This is, is it not, what they thought of themselves? It has been pride all the way, and pride will be their ruin. Thus the theme which terminates in verse 7 provides the link with verse 8: *I abhor the pride of Jacob*, and at the same time brings this whole section of the book of Amos full circle. Here again is something which antagonizes the whole divine nature (*cf.* 4:2): *The Lord* GOD *has sworn by himself (says the* LORD, *the God of hosts*) ... The two words in capitals stand for Yahweh, the divine name, the God of holiness, redemption and wrath; *Lord* means king or sovereign; *God of hosts* is God the omnipotent. When this God swears *by himself* He commits the totality of His nature (the holy One, the Redeemer and Judge), the totality of His status as the world's Sovereign Lord, and the totality of His effective power as the Omnipotent. Again, what is it that so rouses and antagonizes the Lord? Human pride. And when pride is assaulted the *strongholds* and the capital *city* (*cf.* verse 1) which are its embodiment fall as well.

Lessons of history

We have viewed this oracle as a series of concentric circles revolving round a single pivot called pride, or self-satisfaction. This disastrous quality lived first and pre-eminently in the leaders of the nation: *notable men . . . to whom the house of Israel come* (6:1). The word translated 'notable' appears as 'named' in Numbers 1:17 where, literally, we read 'marked down by name'. It refers to 'well-known' men in leadership positions. The verb 'come' appears in Exodus 18:16 in exactly the same usage, to come for the settlement of cases, the resolving of disputes or perplexities. As we try to draw out main lessons from the sections of the oracle one by one, we need to have this realization before us: it speaks first of all to leaders, and leaders never live or die to themselves, any more than anyone does, but in a particular sense they mould the destiny of those whom they lead; they involve others in the shape their leadership imposes on the organization or community or whatever it may be they lead; and just as, if their leadership comes under the blessing of God, they are never blessed alone but bring into blessing those who follow them, so also, if their leadership commands His wrath, they never go to their doom alone: when the *great house* is *smitten into fragments*, the *little house* equally is broken *into bits* (verse 11). In faithfulness, therefore, to the tone and tendency of the passage, the following four main principles are first and foremost principles for leaders, but since a leader is different only in position, responsibility and risk, and not different in kind from others, the four principles have their obvious application to all the people of God.

The first principle which emerges is that we should never be content with things as they are, for the simple reason that in every human arrangement there are seeds and forces of disaster and their most fertile breeding-ground is complacent, self-satisfied leadership. This was the situation in verses 1-3. Privilege—to live in the capital cities (1a), reputation—named and sought after (1b), comparison with others less fortunate (2a)—all these things bred complacency. Things surely could not be better; they had reached a zenith. But all the time *the evil day* was there and complacent leadership was in fact simply the incipient form of anarchy (3). Not all are called to leadership in this sense, but we are all leaders in the welfare of our own souls and the principle is of equal weight there—but how sharply and directly it speaks to those who are called to lead in the church of God! How often, in reply to a question 'How are things?', we say, 'Oh, just about the same.' But it is never true for, if nothing else, the evil day has drawn nearer!

Secondly, the welfare of the fellowship must always take primacy over the pampering of the self (verses 4-7). The word 'pampering' is vital in the last sentence. There is a godly self-care without which we shall never be equipped, physically, mentally or spiritually, to care for anyone else, but there is an ungodly self-concern which progressively blinds us to *the ruin of Joseph* (6). In these verses it is all a matter of looking after the body—bed and food in verse 4, drink and deodorants in verse 6, and, most significantly of all, in verse 5 finding non-demanding ways of filling in time with specious reasons offered for doing so. And all the while *Joseph* is going to wrack and *ruin* (6). The word literally is 'the breaking of Joseph', and its meaning is as comprehensive as that: circumstances, sorrow, finance, family, the past, the future, housing, schooling—whatever breaks the spirit and breaks the

heart! But the leadership is in bed or at a well-laden board, or
tuning up to compose a few more songs, or perhaps round at the
chemist's! It was a shrewd thrust for Amos to describe the nation
as *Joseph*—the lad who wailed his heart out in a deep pit while his
brothers sat down to eat (Gn. 37:23-25; 42:21). It is this cross-
reference which helps us to lift the words of Amos out of the
national setting in which we automatically place them and,
remembering that in his day nation and church were but two sides
of the organization of the people of God, see them as applying
directly to the church and family of God. We are all 'Josephs' to
each other, the objects of that mutual care which should mark our
fellowship; but specially to the leader: to him the crying of Joseph
must exercise the prior claim.

The third principle is that we should covet peace with God and
allow Him to dictate the terms on which peace is to be enjoyed.
The peace here referred to is the peace of daily harmonious
relationships, whereby we may be assured that God is with us and
His power operating for us. It is not, in this sense, the basic reality
of peace with God through our Lord Jesus Christ. The tragedy
of the day of reckoning for Israel (verses 7-10) was that then—and
too late—they realized what had been lost. When the crisis came
they had so long walked out of step with God that there was no
liberty to mention His name. Of all sides to the question of walking
with God Amos focuses on one alone: God opposes the proud.
What can succeed if we fall out of the power of God? What can
succeed if He, the Sovereign Yahweh, the omnipotent God (8),
turn His power against us? God opposes the proud, said James
(4:6), and even if he quoted it from Proverbs (3:34, LXX) he could
well have learnt it from this passage in Amos.

Finally (verses 11-14) Amos brings before us the necessity
to discern the things which are more excellent: the principle of
placing moral considerations above everything else. If someone
had discovered the way to enable horses to scale cliffs or to plough
and harvest the fruitless sea, what a marvel of the age this would
have been considered! When Jeroboam won his victories at
Lo-debar and Karnaim, how people marvelled and praised their
king—so it is implied! Reverse natural laws, reverse national
fortunes and the world takes note; reverse moral values and no-
one thinks anything significant has happened. Yet, purely on

the level of practical politics, once Jeroboam allowed the *justice* of his land to be turned to *poison* (12), no military prowess could henceforth save him. An enemy too strong by far held him in a pincer-grip from the far south of *the Brook of the Arabah* to the far north of *the entrance of Hamath* (14). This is the way things are in the biblical world view. Nationally, it is not the technology that makes fools of natural impossibilities (12a), nor the weaponry which extends or secures national frontiers (13), but the exactness of moral values, held in righteousness and practised with justice, that decides welfare, continuity and progress. It is equally true of a church as of a state, and we who are accustomed to say that the weapons of our warfare are not carnal should covet to live accordingly.

Why ?

When they saw Samaria in ruins in 722 BC, when mothers had been bereaved of children, husbands of wives, when there were many orphans, many pauperized, many homeless, did they ask why? The Assyrians did it, said some, and they were right (14). God did it, said some, and they were right too, both in relation to direction (8) and permission (11). Our leaders did it, was the opinion of yet more, and they too were right (1–3, 4–7). Pride did it, said Amos (8), and that was the most realistic of all appraisals of the enemy of the people.

Part Three
THE SOVEREIGN YAHWEH
Amos 7:1—9:15

General Introduction

THE sequence of teaching in the book of Amos so far would lead us to expect to find in these last chapters the vision of disaster actually falling on the people of God. This is, in fact, the case. In Part One, the roar of wrath and of coming judgment was heard; in Part Two the enemy began to encircle the land; in Part Three the predicted blow falls (*cf.* 8:1–3—what menace there is in its concluding word *silence!*—and 9:1–6).

Into this actualizing of divine judgment Amos injects two distinct features of the third part of his book. First, he repeatedly uses the title 'the Lord GOD', the Sovereign Yahweh. In the whole book of Amos this is used twenty times, of which eleven occurrences come in the last three chapters. While counting verses is a somewhat arbitrary statistic, nevertheless there are one hundred verses in the first six chapters and the title occurs nine times; there are forty-six verses in the last three chapters and the title occurs eleven times—once in every four or five verses as compared with once in every eleven or twelve verses. There is that in his message which requires him to underscore the absolute liberty of Yahweh to implement His own will, to do that which accords with His divine name. What can this be except that judgment and salvation will somehow both be secured, the overthrow of His enemies and the safety of His people? For this is what the name Yahweh means.

Secondly, in these chapters, and only here, does Amos speak of Israel as 'my people'—*i.e.* Yahweh's people: five times in the forty-six verses, once in every nine verses. Try to feel the element of surprise here! This is the Amos who laboured (the word is not too strong) to take away anything which could be abused into complacency. He never spoke of the 'God of Israel'; he dared to say that the longed-for day of Yahweh would be a day of unrelieved calamity and darkness, but now, like the striking of a clock, 'my people... my people... my people... my people... my people' rings out until, on the last occasion, it is answered by a climactic 'your God' (9:15).

Thus, as Amos ushers his hearers into the darkest valley of his prophecy and depicts all falling in ruins around and upon them, he points them upward to a God who is as sovereign to save as to judge, and he points to their own status and position as the people of that God. This is, of course, their peril as well as their privilege, for it is the ground of inevitable judgment on those who stake but cannot prove their claim (3:2) as well as the ground of eternal salvation to those whose claim is well-founded.

We can now notice that Amos once more opens and closes this part of his message on the same note. He begins with visions of total calamity which, in answer to prayer, the Lord undertakes not to implement: there will not be a total obliteration (7:1–6), *It shall not be . . . This also shall not be* (verses 3, 6). He concludes with a discriminating judgment, the destruction of all complacent sinners (9:10) and the unbroken bliss of the Messianic kingdom (9:11–15).

Amos 7:1-6
The Repentant God

SCRATCH the surface of the prophecy of Amos and out comes the doctrine of Eternal Security, which, in fully biblical terms, means that the people of God, chosen by Him of His own deliberate and free will, are also kept by Him through all the changes and chances, falls and failures of life, and are finally brought by Him into eternal and complete enjoyment of all the benefits and blessings which He, from all eternity, purposed should be theirs. Amos would not have had to make any changes in this wording were he to frame it in a credal form for his own times. He did not possess the knowledge of the full divine working in Christ Jesus, but he possessed the principle of that work in the revealed religion of the people of God. The Bible indeed speaks with one voice, not least in its insistence that God will never let His people go.

In Part One of his book, Amos wrestled to recover this great truth from current abuses, and in particular from the doctrinaire assumption that a historical fact (the Exodus, 3:2) made an eternal difference between one people and all the others on earth so that, irrespective of their manners or ways of life, they would be secure in God. He exposed to the people the hollowness of their claim to be the people of God and the inheritors of the security promised to His chosen ones.

In Part Two of his book he took his consideration of this theme further. He laid bare the sins which exposed the hollowness of current claims to belong to the elect of God, and, by contrast, those clear evidences on the basis of which a true claim could be made out.

But now, in Part Three, the matter becomes crucial. The incoming judgment, the closer it comes, is revealed as all-destructive. The question therefore is no longer who belongs to the people of God but, when all comes to all, is God prepared to stand by His promises and put a defence round the elect in the day of universal, irresistible and inescapable wrath?

The will of God

The Third Part of Amos opens with two visions of total destruction (7:1–6). In each case it is of such proportions and such timing that national survival is counted impossible: 'How can Jacob survive, being so small?' (verses 2, 5, JB). In each case also the Lord repents and promises that such a thing will not happen. The doubling makes the message emphatic. Twice over the Lord rejects the thought of a judgment of total destruction coming on His people. But the doubling also is cumulative. In verse 3 it is simply *It shall not be*, but in verse 6 there is almost a degree of warm rejoinder in *This also shall not be*. It is as if the Lord rather rounded on the praying prophet: And neither shall this be! Furthermore, in verse 3 the speaker is Yahweh, but in verse 6 'the sovereign Yahweh'; this is to say, since in Amos' theology Yahweh is in any case the sovereign God, the adjective 'sovereign' adds nothing to Him but adds the element of absolute guarantee to what He pledges to do. In this sense, then, of emphatic repetition, cumulative force and solemn divine affirmation, the idea of the total destruction of God's people is ruled out of court. It will not happen, and since it is the Lord Himself who says so, it cannot happen.[1]

[1] Mays takes a somewhat different view of these visions in context. Noting that Amos does not pray against any of the ensuing visions (7:7–9; 8:1–3; 9:1–6), he holds that it is as if Amos were saying, 'The judgment of Israel is not my will, for I have twice turned away the wrath of Yahweh by my intercession: it is Yahweh's final decree and even intercession is now forbidden me.' But Amos nowhere says that he was forbidden to pray on and it is needless to assume that any such prohibition lies behind the subsequent absence of intercession. Following through his line of argument, Mays is eventually obliged to deny the wonderful passages of hope at the end of chapter 9 to Amos, believing him to be a prophet in whose message hope, if not wholly absent, is only marginally significant. If this is the case, of course, the force of the insertion of the passages of hope is to make Amos a false prophet—though Mays, needless to say, does not hold or argue that this is the case.

Each of these visions makes its own contribution to the extent to which the Lord holds His people safe. The first (verses 1-3) is concerned with temporal calamity. There are some features of this vision which are not fully explicable in the present state of knowledge but which, fortunately, do not impair our understanding of the whole. We can only presume that *the king's mowings* was a form of Income Tax current at the time. The reference to *the latter growth* indicates that the king claimed the first grass-crop for himself. The remainder, then, would be for the farmer to use as fodder for his stock until the following year. If this grass-crop were wholly devoured by locusts, as was the case in the vision, then total ruin stared the countryside in the face. This is what the Lord forbids to happen. No earthly calamity can threaten the continuance of the people of God.

Standing as it were beside this truth, let us look forward and then back. As we look forward we see, in Amos' predictions, the destruction of the sanctuaries and the fall of the royal house (7:9), a coming 'end' in which religious ceremonies will be drowned out by cries of distress and silence will fill a city of the dead (8:3), bitter mourning (8:10), a sword pursuing every last person (9:1). Amos says all this against the same back-drop: No earthly calamity can destroy the people of God. The Lord has pledged it; it must and will be so. Such calamities may seem sweeping, destructive and indiscriminate, but they are delicate sieving operations (9:9) undertaken by a precise and almighty hand.

On this note, let us look back. Amos, in vision, saw a locust plague of deadly proportions and timing. Where did it come from? *The Lord God showed* (7:1) the answer to this question as He unveiled the springs of history: it was He who fashioned the locusts with all the delicate deliberation and artistry of a potter (for so the verb *forming* indicates). The call of Amos, therefore, to the people of God in the teaching of this vision is this: do you see troubles coming, of crisis proportions, disaster, calamity? Look through the trouble and see what hand has fashioned it and directed it, what hand now controls and limits it. The hand of the sovereign and gracious God—'the Lord Yahweh'—who has pledged beforehand that no temporal calamity can destroy His people.

The message of the second vision is significantly different. All the details here suggest the supernatural (7:4-6). The enemy is fire and the mind returns at once to chapter 1 with its repeated threat, *I will send fire* (1:4, 7, 10, *etc.*). It is, says Mays, 'the divine fire, the instrument of his wrath'. The pledge, therefore, at the heart of this vision, is that no supernatural or divine threat can imperil the people of God. Even here they are safe. Amos invites us to test the strength of this re-assurance. As he watched (7:4) *the great deep* exhausted its waters on the fire without effect. This is surely the fire of God. Just as in Exodus 3:2 it needed no fuel to feed it, so in Amos 7:4 there is no substance which can quench it.² On it swept until it concentrated its threat on *the land*. The word used here means 'the portion' or 'the allocation'. It must surely refer to that particular land which the Lord allocated to His people.³ At this point it is halted by divine decree: *This also shall not be* (7:6).

Again we may look forward through the coming prophecies of Amos. At each point the calamity is a divine act: it is He who rises *with the sword* (7:9), *will never again pass by them* (8:2), *will darken the earth* and *turn feasts into mourning* (8:9, 10), *send a famine . . . of hearing the words of the Lord* (8:11), *bring them down* (9:2), *search them out* (9:3), *command the sword, and it shall slay them* (9:4). Yet, again, it is all against the back-drop of a promise that nothing that the Lord will do can threaten the security of His people. In spite of all that seems entirely certain to overthrow it, the promise stands. The people of the Lord are as secure from supernatural threat as from natural calamity.

² There may be a quasi-supernatural dimension in Amos' reference to *the great deep*. In anqituity the 'deep' (*tᵉhōm*) was thought of in pagan culture as the home of spiritual forces opposed to the Creator God. It would be just like Amos (*cf.* 9:3) to make sport of this notion: the divine fire burning poor old Tiamat out of house and home! He had more ways than one of confessing his monotheistic faith! Some commentators (*cf.* JB with its footnote) believe the reference is to some supposed store-house or reservoir from which seas and rains alike derived their water. All this would re-inforce the notion of a completely irresistible fire: nothing known in earth or in the world of the gods can stop it.

³ Such is its meaning in Dt. 32:9; Mi. 2:4.

The mystery of prayer

This determination of God to have a people for Himself and to keep them secure is entirely mysterious to us. The only explanation offered by the Bible is that *the Lord set his love upon you and chose you . . . because the Lord loves you* (Dt. 7:7, 8). This is no explanation at all, but it is a mighty assurance. His love is an outgoing of His nature; there is some reason which makes sense to God why He should love and choose, and, since He is God, that reason can never be anything but good! Amos does not undertake to explain the inexplicable any more than the rest of the Bible, but he offers us two insights into the will of God so that we may feel the security that is ours in it and the warmth of the love it expresses.

He turns our attention to the mystery of prayer. Verses 2, 3 and 5, 6 reveal that it is by prayer that the will of God is wrought on earth. Even though (as other Scriptures tell us) God determined who should be His and that He would make and keep them as His, yet here that eternal, unchangeable, infallible decision is brought to pass only by the agency of prayer. And it is, indeed, as if the Lord wanted that prayer to be made, for otherwise why should He have allowed Amos into the secret of what He was doing (verses 1, 4)? 'Prayer,' says Pusey, 'suggested by God, moves God, the Ruler of all.' Three hundred years after Amos, Malachi (4:5) predicted the coming of the Messianic forerunner, and over seven hundred years after Amos the moment to fulfil that promise came, but the word of the Angel to the aged Zechariah was not 'Prophecy is to be fulfilled' but *Your prayer is heard* (Lk. 1:13). Prayer is a means by which the Lord of all brings His determined purposes to pass.

Before taking up the second of the two insights which Amos offers us in respect of the will of God, let us pause for a moment before this mystery of prayer. Here is a prayer which (we may say) God prompted and certainly a prayer which He heard and answered. In its way, therefore, it is a model for effective praying. There are two noteworthy things at least. First, it adopts the divine estimate of the situation: *How can Jacob stand? He is so small! . . . He is so small* (verses 2, 5). This was far from being the self-estimate of the people for whom Amos was praying! Not thus did *the notable men of the first of the nations* (6:1) understand their capacity, nor, come to that, did the prelatical Amaziah (7:10 ff.)! Prayer starts by adopting God's stance, seeing things and people as He does, focusing their needs as estimated in heaven. Secondly, prayer looks up to the divine mercy and almightiness. Amos' two intercessory words are *forgive* and *cease*. In the former case he acts from the point of view of man's sin and deserving: there is that in the nature of God to which appeal can be made, a pardoning mercy. The verb 'forgive' is used only of God in the Old Testament. It points therefore to what in its proper sense belongs exclusively to Him, the power and readiness to forgive. By the word *cease* Amos starts from man's weakness and helplessness, and he looks to that in God which is able to cope, no matter what are the dimensions of the crisis:

> Should all the hosts of death,
> And powers of hell unknown,
> Put their most dreadful forms
> Of rage and malice on,
> I shall be safe; for Christ displays
> Superior power and guardian grace.[4]

And, whatever its mystery, prayer works (verses 3, 6)!

The repentance of God

The second insight which Amos gives us into the almighty will of God comes with the words *The Lord repented* (3, 6). Under this expression (as indeed in his teaching on prayer) Amos is saying that the will of God is no harsh, unfeeling fate but is rather to be thought of as His loving concern for His frail and needy people.

The revelation of the locusts and fire is a statement of our deserving—now and always. Equally, it represents a perpetual element in the divine nature: God's ceaseless wrath against sin. We must not think that suddenly God's anger got the better of Him and flared out against His people but that, happily, Amos was on hand to pray Him into a better mind. The wrath of God is perpetual: the automatic reaction of a holy nature faced with rebellion and unholiness. But equally eternal is His determination

---

[4] Isaac Watts, 'Join all the glorious names'.

to take, save and keep a people for Himself. This is what the Scripture means when it speaks of Jesus as the Lamb slain from the foundation of the world (Rev. 13:8, RV; *cf.* 1 Pet. 1:19, 20) and of Christians as chosen in Him before the foundation of the world (Eph. 1:4). It is because we cannot unify these two revealed strands of the divine nature that the Lord graciously accommodated the truth to our powers of expression and speaks of Himself as 'repenting'. He represents Himself as hearing prayer and turning from wrath to mercy in order that we may thus understand something of what is involved in His love for us and how great is that love when He beholds us in all our need. On the one hand, there must be that in His love which satisfies and soothes His wrath: for the exercise of the one attribute cannot bludgeon the other out of existence, else there were war and not harmony in the divine nature. It has been revealed to us that it is the blood of Jesus, the great divine gift of love, which satisfies the divine wrath (Rom. 3:25). On the other hand, when the Lord looks upon His people mercy triumphs over wrath.

All this is very humanly expressed. We wrestle with the unity and unanimity of the divine nature and the subject outstrips our poor logic. Yet He who knows all allows us to see that for us, His wretched, wrath-deserving, helpless people, His love wins the day, and in that love we are safe.

Amos 7:7–9
Built to Specification

HEAVENLY realities are subject to earthly verification. This is one of the distinctives of biblical teaching. Take, for example, things which belong entirely in the divine realm. In the religion of the Ancient Near East there was a clear doctrine that the world had been created by the creator-god, but that in proposing and executing this task he did not have a clear field. There was also a god of destruction determined that something as ordered and stable as creation could not be tolerated. Before the world could be brought into being, therefore, these two gods had to fight it out, and in the event, the creator-god triumphed and was hailed as victor and king of the gods. It is most interesting to see at what point this myth peeps into the Bible: not at creation—it is one of the striking features of the Genesis story that it is free from all marks of polytheism, and especially of any suggestion of a pre-creation combat. The victory of Yahweh over all supposed gods took place at the Red Sea (*cf.* Is. 51:9–11) where Rahab, the god of chaos, was cut in pieces. Now the testimony of the Bible is that this was done on earth, before eyewitnesses (*cf.* Jos. 4:23, noting the way in which Joshua says 'us'). Consequently, while the power of Marduk, the creator-god, over Tiamat or Rahab, the chaos-god dwelling in the deep, is the subject of unproven credulity, the power of Yahweh over the forces of the waters is an observed, attested fact.

In the New Testament the same sort of importance attaches to the evidence of the empty tomb: the resurrection of Jesus from the dead is not a way of saying that 'something' happened in heaven between God and Jesus (as in Canaanite thinking 'something' happened between the creator-god and the chaos-god); the resurrection is subject to earthly verification: the testimony of people who went and saw the empty tomb and the other evidences of the reality of what had happened. Equally the miraculous stilling of the storm is the objective proof of the power of Jesus to still all storms—including the private storms of our lives—and without that objective assurance we are living in a world of make-believe.

These illustrations are capable of being extended almost endlessly, but the point is this: just as the invisible, intangible truths of God have been made certain by events and observations and have thus been brought into the realm of assured truth, so the invisible, intangible realities of our relationship with God need to be verified by observable testimony. There must be some clear evidence that we possess peace with God, forgiveness and eternal security, for in default of evidence there is only gossip and hearsay, but no assurance.

No prayer

It is into this realm that Amos brings us in the vision of the Lord standing with a plumb-line in His hand. The whole thing is earthly, full of tangibles, walls and bricks and measurements and verifiable tests. Against this, be it noted, Amos makes no prayer, for the simple reason that testing is an inseparable part of the experience of the people of God—testing designed to demonstrate the reality or the unreality of their profession. Here is the difference between this vision and the preceding two. They contained no element of test; they were efficient mechanisms of total destruction, sweeping all before them. But the plumb-line is delicate, precise, differentiating, taking note of what meets requirements and what does not. Thus the vision of the plumb-line amplifies what had hitherto been left unexplained. The Lord had turned from any thought of the total elimination of the people, but what had He turned to? The answer is now provided: a discriminating test, separating one from the other, this from that; a test not of claims as such but of evidences on which valid claims could be made. We may put it like this, within the terms of the vision itself: a person may claim to possess every building skill and qualification, but the plumb-line applied to the wall will soon reveal whether that claim is valid or bogus. It must be exactly the same with the people of God: they may well claim every heavenly and spiritual blessing and qualification, but the plumb-line of divine testing applied to certain assessable aspects of their lives and persons will soon show with what reality that claim is made. Therefore Amos does not pray, for testing such as this belongs to the very terms of reference of God's people; it is part of the constitution.

The plumb-line: what is it?

We read (7:7) that Amos saw the Lord *standing beside a wall built with a plumb-line, with a plumb-line in his hand*.[1] There are two distinct elements in this description of what Amos saw: first, the wall was 'plumb-line-built',[2] and second, the wall was subjected

---

[1] The phrase 'a wall built with a plumb-line' gives the commentators exceptional difficulty and many of them excise it from the text, *e.g.* Cripps and Hammershaimb. BHS directs (but offers no evidence) that we should read 'wall' and excise 'plumb-line'. In the Hebrew this involves the removal of only one word, but why should even this be done? The problem is one of interpretation, not one of MSS or textual study. It is assumed by the commentators mentioned (also by Mays who does not, however, discuss the phrase 'a plumb-line-wall', and by IB which advocates much more wholesale alteration of the Hebrew text) that the vision of the plumb-line is one of wholesale condemnation. The first two visions (locusts and fire) pointed to threats which the people could not survive: the plumb-line to tests which they could not pass. It is in this setting that Mays proposes that Amos' failure to pray must be construed as equivalent to being forbidden to pray: the Lord may set aside locusts and fire as the means of achieving His purpose, but He is bent on total destruction. This is a wholly unreasonable point of view. There is nothing to suggest that the plumb-line is not that mode of divine action which replaces forms of activity which the Lord has, with emphasis, ruled out of court; there is nothing to suggest that when the plumb-line is applied everyone without exception will fail the test, though, of course, if the commentators are right in identifying the plumb-line simply and exclusively with the law of God, then everyone would fail. But again it is unreasonable to explain the symbol in this restrictive way. These matters, however, must be settled by comparing one exegesis with another. That which is set out in this book is offered for examination as being the more obvious explanation in its own context, more realistic in the setting of the religion of the book of Amos, and as possessing what ought to be taken as its crowning merit, the capability of preserving the book of Amos intact up to the concluding verse of chapter 9.

[2] The Hebrew says 'a wall of plumb-line', a well-exemplified type of adjectival formula in which the second noun acts as a qualification of the first. Just as a 'man of God' is a 'godly man', so a 'wall of plumb-line' is a 'plumb-line

to a plumb-line test. In other words it possessed from the start that which was necessary if it was to pass the test to be applied to it at the end.

If we are to interpret the plumb-line correctly, then we must search for that which was initially given to the people of God and which could at the end (or at any point) be used as a yardstick to test their reality. The search is not difficult. The self-revelation of God made this one people a set-apart people: God chose them and showed Himself to them. Essentially it was the 'I am' of divine revelation which gave them being. Through all the preparatory, patriarchal years it was the re-iterated 'I am God, the God of your father' (*cf*. Gn. 46:3) which bound the family together and kept them apart from all others. This reached final and definitive proportions in the 'I am Yahweh' (*e.g.* Ex. 6:6) of the foundational Mosaic period.

The law

But a self-revelation of that nature is apt to recede into the past. How did the Lord make the revelation of Himself of contemporary relevance to His people? He did so by demanding that in the whole of daily life they should reflect His likeness: *You shall be holy; for I the Lord your God am holy* (Lv. 19:2). This passage in Leviticus is specially illuminating because, more than most, it offers an explanation of the nature and purpose of the law which the Lord gave to His people. Leviticus 19 is one of the most comprehensive statements of law for the life of the people of God. The precepts given cover virtually every department; they are intensely varied but they have one common denominator: they are given because *I am Yahweh* (19:3, 4, 10, 12, 14, 16, 18, 25, 28, 30, 31, 32, 34, 36, 37). This refrain is not primarily a statement of authority (Do this because I tell you), though it is that; it is rather a statement of the relationship between the divine Lawgiver and the law He gives: it is a reflection of His nature; the law must be what it is because He is what He is. The law is a verbal extension of the person and presence of God among His

---

wall', *i.e.* a wall built with a plumb-line, as RSV. There is no textual problem here, as to either the correctness or meaning of the words.

people; it expresses as precepts those things which exist as principles within His nature. Deuteronomy 4:7 holds these truths in perfect balance: *What great nation is there that has a god so near to it as the Lord our God is to us, whenever we call upon him? And what great nation is there, that has statutes and ordinances so righteous as all this law which I set before you this day?* The self-revelation of the Lord which made Israel what it is among all the nations was crystallized into the preceptual law and the distinctiveness of the people of God came to be shown outwardly in its life of obedience.

Redemption

But the law was neither the only nor the first element in the self-revelation of the Lord to His people. Lying even nearer to the heart of the matter was His work of redemption. The classic definition of Yahweh is not 'who gave you this law' but 'who brought you out of the land of Egypt' and it is this redeeming activity which is chosen as the proper preface to the statement of the Ten Commandments (Ex. 20:1 ff.). The two features of the movement of God in self-revelation belong together; either without the other would leave the revelation imperfect and truncated. But in chronological order it was because He was first their Redeemer, through the blood of the passover lamb, that He became their Law-giver, commanding the law as the proper pattern of life for those whom redemption had brought near to God. Again Deuteronomy gives a perfect theological expression to this: *Because the Lord loves you . . . the Lord has brought you out with a mighty hand, and redeemed you . . . Know therefore that the Lord your God is God . . . You shall therefore be careful to do the commandment, and the statutes, and the ordinances, which I command you this day* (Dt. 7:8-11). Love issues in redemption and ushers in a life of obedience to the commandments. In the life of the people of God there is a law of grace: only by the freely bestowed grace of God have they been brought to Him and only by grace can they be maintained in His presence as an accepted people. If they forsake the law of grace they lose the fellowship of their God. The law of grace was expressed in the code of sacrifices, which, we need to remember, were not given as a way by which the heathen could be reconciled to the God of Israel but as a way by which

Israel, the people redeemed by the blood of the lamb in Egypt, could be held in the fellowship of their Redeemer-God.[3]

Equally in the life of the people of God there is the grace of law. In His perfect goodness to His people, God has not left them in ignorance of the life which pleases Him. He has revealed Himself in precepts which are in themselves a way of life through which the believer can testify that *I shall walk at liberty, for I have sought thy precepts* (Ps. 119:45).

What, then, in sum, is the distinctive life of the people of God? They are brought to Him by grace, redeeming grace expressed in blood-sacrifice; they walk with Him according to the pattern of the law, the pattern of His very own life; and they are accompanied by the same redeeming grace so that they may resort to it for atonement, cleansing, forgiveness, renewal and whatever else they may need in order to remain in His holy fellowship. The grace of law and the law of grace make up the interwoven strands of the divine plumb-line.

Could Amos have believed this? Could he have believed anything else? As we saw, his rhetorical question 'Was it sacrifices . . . you brought me . . . ?' (5:25) reaffirmed the divine authorization of the cult in its proper place and use. His constant emphasis on righteousness and justice shows the strength of his grasp on the foundational importance of the law which God gave His people. When, therefore, the Lord draws near with the plumb-line, it is not to condemn all without exception through a direct application to individual life of the law, the pattern of

[3] The Old and New Testaments are here identical in principle though differing in appropriation. In the Old Testament the passover sacrifice was offered in the land of Egypt; it was the redemption-sacrifice and once that redemption was accomplished and the people left Egypt the passover sacrifice of the lamb could only be remembered, it could not be repeated. It had done its work once and for all. Because, however, the weakness of a merely animal sacrifice necessitated a repetitive system, the passover was 'remembered' by an annual sacrifice identical in kind with that offered in Egypt, and the daily efficacy of the redeeming blood was made available to the people of God through the repeated sacrifices of the Levitical code. If a stranger wished to join the people of God he did so through the appointed means of circumcision, giving access to the passover and thence to the full round of sacrifices. In the New Testament, the sacrifice of the Lamb of God, the Lord Jesus, is of eternal efficacy (Heb. 10:12, *etc.*); it is remembered in a non-sacrificial meal, indicating that what was done once and for all on the cross is constantly available for faith to appropriate simply by 'feeding' on Him.

divine life, before which each is hopelessly guilty; nor is it to isolate ceremonial sacrifice in the way in which, through Amos, He has already rejected it as a partial and unacceptable religion; it is to bind these together in biblical and due order and to declare condemned all who try to live by law and forget grace, to declare equally condemned those who have sought after the grace of the sacrifices but who have forgotten the righteousness and justice of the law, but to accept all who have constructed the fabric of their lives according to the horizontal foundation of grace and according to the vertical erectness of law. The plumb-line will try such and will pass them as approved.

The rejects

The intention of the Lord is that this discriminating plumb-line should come right into *the midst of my people Israel* (7:8). The expression 'my people' is, of course, significant. In this particular context it has the same force as we noted in 3:2. People who are brought near to God cannot avoid being tested and judged. As Mays remarks, 'the theological name "my people" makes it clear that Israel is to be judged precisely in her identity as the covenant people.' This is amplified by the following phrase: *I will never again pass by them*. The full idiom which is briefly expressed here and in 8:2 is found in Micah 7:18, *passing over transgression for the remnant*. In Amos we have the ellipsis 'pass over for them'. Comparison of the two passages shows the meaning to be 'forgive them'. No more will the Lord turn the 'blind eye' of patient forgiveness; the plumb-line is to be set up in the midst and only those who live by its standards can reckon themselves among His true and accredited people.

The first to fall before this test will be *the high places of Isaac . . . and the sanctuaries of Israel* (7:9).[4] We need not retrace in any detail the religion of the high-places and shrines. They were places

---

[4] Why 'Isaac' is specified here is not certain. Isaac is associated in Genesis only with the sanctuary of Beer-sheba (Gn. 26:33; 28:10). Calvin snorts that 'the Israelites absurdly pretended to imitate their father in their superstitions'. Maybe there was a sort of religious version of the 'Queen Elizabeth slept here' racket in Northern Israel with many shrines competing for the ancestral patronage of Isaac.

where grace was abused and law was neglected. Grace was abused first of all in its nature. The grace of God in the Mosaic tradition was God's freely given love reaching out to draw sinners to Himself. It was spiritual throughout: in its origin in God and in its benefits among men. But at the shrines the grace sought was the benefit of worldly prosperity through fertility in the land, in the stock and in the family. Grace was abused, secondly, in its appropriation, for in Scripture grace is bestowed in answer to prayer, but in the sanctuaries the blessing of God was sought by means of ritual fornication—the human fertility act being used as a visual aid to prompt the God to perform His parallel function for the world. Is it any wonder that this abuse of grace fell before the plumb-line? Furthermore, as we have seen, there was nothing more to the shrines than this, no pressure for a reformed life, no voice of the law of God calling to obedience. The shrines therefore were judged by the plumb-line and were found inadequate: they abused grace and forgot law.

The second candidate for rejection was *the house of Jeroboam* (verse 9). This politically able king—the first to be named after the founding king of the schismatic northern kingdom and the last king to achieve anything like affluence and stability for his kingdom—receives scant attention in the narrative of the book of Kings, but it is recorded that *he did what was evil in the sight of the Lord; he did not depart from all the sins of Jeroboam the son of Nebat, which he made Israel to sin* (2 Ki. 14:24). Now the sin of Jeroboam the son of Nebat—dealing with the matter broadly and not at all in detail—was basically the sin of disobedience to the law of the Lord. His kingdom was given to him upon moral conditions: *If you will hearken to all that I command you, and will walk in my ways, and do what is right in my eyes by keeping my statutes and my commandments . . . I will be with you, and will build you a sure house . . .* (1 Ki. 11:38). But Jeroboam did no such thing. Indeed his first major act was to disobey Yahweh in the matter of the shrines at Bethel and Dan and in the setting up of golden calves. Jeroboam, therefore, is the man who rejected the law of the Lord and proceeded to corrupt the grace of the Lord also.

We see in these two examples of rejection what a unity the will of God is. In the shrines, when the law of grace was abused the grace of law was forgotten; in the royal house, when the grace of law was forgotten the law of grace was abused. Both alike fall before the test of the plumb-line.

But among the people of Amos' day would there not also be those whose testimony on the one hand would be *Oh, how I love thy law . . . Through thy precepts I get understanding; therefore I hate every false way* (Ps. 119:97, 104), and on the other hand *How lovely is thy dwelling place, O Lord of hosts! . . . Even the sparrow finds a home, and the swallow a nest for herself, where she may lay her young, at thy altars, O Lord of hosts, my King and my God* (Ps. 84:1, 3)?

> Father of peace and God of love,
>   We own Thy power to save,
> That power by which our Shepherd rose
>   Victorious o'er the grave.
>
> Him from the dead Thou brought'st again,
>   When, by His sacred blood,
> Confirmed and sealed for evermore,
>   Th' eternal covenant stood.
>
> Oh, may Thy Spirit seal our souls,
>   And mould them to Thy will,
> That our weak hearts no more may stray,
>   But keep Thy precepts still.
>
> That to perfection's sacred height
>   We nearer still may rise;
> And all we think, and all we do,
>   Be pleasing in Thine eyes.[5]

[5] Philip Doddridge.

Amos 7:10–17
The Man of God

WE come now to a most interesting and vivid interlude in the
book of Amos, a personal interview between himself and an
otherwise unknown *Amaziah the priest of Bethel.* This little
piece of personal narrative about Amos reveals him at his courageous best, but, more than that, provides us with deep instruction
about the nature and function of the man of God, the experiences
he may expect to encounter, the resources on which he can draw
and the persevering fortitude which is to mark his career.[1]

The appearance of the personal narrative at this point in the
book may be accounted for along three lines. First of all, it is
chronologically in place. We may assume that it was the forth-
right prediction of 7:9 which proved to be the last straw for
Amaziah, who forthwith took the matter to court and, apparently
getting no change out of Jeroboam, decided to blunt a lance with
Amos himself. Secondly, the narrative has an authenticating
function (*cf.* 3:3–8). Amos has just given a reasoned argument for
the inevitability of the fall of the state in both its national and its
ecclesiastical establishments (7:7–9). This must have come to the
majority of his hearers as simply unbelievable. It is not a light
thing for very religious people to accept that their religion itself

---

[1] It is interesting to speculate if this narrative had a separate history before
being incorporated into the book of Amos. Mays attributes the authorship to
a disciple or group of disciples, in this way accounting for its use of the third
person singular of Amos. This may well be so. It is implied by the strictures
of Amaziah (verse 10) that Amos was a person of spreading influence. Such
people, if not Amos himself, discreetly using the third person, could well have
used this narrative as a publicity handout, or a wall-poster (*cf.* Is. 8:1; 30:8),
designed to authenticate Amos' ministry by circulating his testimony to a
divine call.

is offensive to God! For their ears also Amos recites his credentials, and the fact that he stood by the reality of his vocation to be a prophet and his commission to prophesy in the North, in the teeth of official disapproval, adds weight and gives credence to the strong possibility that he has indeed come from God to speak this unpalatable truth. Thirdly, in context, the encounter between Amos and Amaziah provides a clear example of the plumb-line in operation. It is essentially a personal test: the Lord holding His line to individual lives. So far Amos has applied it only to institutions: the church and the monarchy (7:9). As between himself and Amaziah the plumb-line will have to decide individual fates, and, as we shall see, its principles of operation remain the same. But let us allow these various strands of connection between verses 10–17 and 7–9 to take second place for a moment while we pay attention to this portrait of a man of God.

Testings are inevitable

There is no service of God without opposition, persecution and trial. This truth lies on the surface of the story before us, and it is well worth our while to face it and accept that it is so. How often servants of God are knocked off course by the onset of difficulties and oppositions! The Scripture is surely plain enough that we are not to *be surprised at the fiery ordeal which comes upon you to prove you* (1 Pet. 4:12), yet that is often exactly what we are—surprised! Amos met his tests and oppositions and so shall we. It is especially the case that encouragements seem to invite opposition. The words of Amaziah constitute 'an unintended tribute to the power and magnitude of Amos' God-given influence' (1B): *the land is not able to bear all his words.* Amos was a good strategist for the word of God. He preached where the people were, at the pilgrimage shrines, and the message and influence radiated out. Amaziah and his like began to tremble. Amos and his friends would not have been real if someone among them had not lamented that opposition should have come 'just as things were beginning to go well'. But of course! Satan also is a good strategist! He knows when and how to hit so as to give the most alarm and create the most despondency.

Amos was tested in three ways. The first test was misrepresentation (7:10, 11). Amaziah presents Amos' message in such a way that a small collection of facts, many of them true, give a wholly false impression of the man, his message and (particularly) his motives. He is charged with conspiracy (*i.e.* his loyalty is made suspect—a favourite trick with those who wish to discredit someone and who yet know that the plain facts in their plain meaning are not on their side!); his words are made to mean what in fact he never said—that Jeroboam would die in battle; and the concluding quotation of something he did say is given as though it was final proof of the original contention of treason. The uttering of *all kinds of evil* . . . *falsely* (Mt. 5:11) is a thing Jesus warned us we should have to face, so let us be warned.

The second test was temptation (12). This test was aimed mainly at Amos' motives in serving God. He is tempted, first, to act out of self-interest. The Hebrew translated *go, flee* includes the added emphasis 'for your own sake', implying that otherwise a very unpleasant fate will fall.[2] Secondly, he is tempted to seek success for its own sake: *flee* . . . *to the land of Judah,* implying that a message of condemnation against Israel will find a natural audience among the southerners, so that Amos is tempted to speak his message where it will be heard as distinct from where it needs to be heard. Thirdly, he is tempted by security: *eat bread there.* Amaziah takes it for granted, or pretends to take it for granted, that Amos is in the job for the money and that therefore he will be interested in knowing that in Judah stipends are better and are paid with a regularity which guarantees where the next meal is coming from. Whether Amaziah thought this to be true or false, this was the temptation which he thrust at Amos.

The third test came as a confrontation with authority (13). Amaziah clothes himself with all his ecclesiastical pride of position: the church will not have this sort of thing on its doorstep! Bethel is a Royal Chapel and a National Cathedral and people like Amos are decidedly out of place! But Amos was not the only

[2] There is nothing necessarily derogatory in the address *O seer* (12). The word is used as a synonym for 'prophet'. Possibly Amaziah intended a low-key and jocular approach, and took his cue from the fact that Amos' recent messages had been reports of visionary experience (7:1–9). 'Well, well, seen any good visions today? Look here, a word to the wise, I'd get out of the North if I were you. . . . ' We can hear it happening, not least the bit about it 'being in your own best interests'!

one to be tested by confrontations of authority. Was it not said to the apostles: *We strictly charged you not to teach in this name, yet here you have filled Jerusalem with your teaching* (Acts 5:28)? How splendid the reply: *We must obey God rather than men* (Acts 5:29)! Would not Amos have been proud of Peter?

A foundation that will hold

The spotlight moves from Amaziah (verses 10–13) to Amos (14–17) and remains there, providing us with two further facets of the man of God.

The man of God rests upon his divinely given authority. The essence of what Amos says to Amaziah can be summed up in the words 'Not I . . . the Lord'.[3] He rests his whole case on the single fact of obedience to the vocational word o' God. As against Amaziah's attempt to 'pull rank', Amos replies that he has, first, the authority of vocation, *the Lord said to me, Go*; secondly, the authority of revelation, the possession of a word from God to speak: *the Lord said . . . prophesy*; thirdly, the authority of commission: *Go . . . to my people Israel*. Amos underlines this authority by a denial and an affirmation. He denies that his authority is in any way whatsoever self-generated. He was neither by nature nor self-appointment *a prophet*, nor had he ambitions or plans such as would have made him enter the probationary stage by becoming *a prophet's son*, a member of a school or guild presided over by a senior prophet (*cf.* 2 Ki. 6:1). His life and attentions were directed in a humdrum, secular job, herding sheep and farming sycomore-figs. On the other hand he affirms that *the Lord took me*. The added words *from following the flock* imply the element of surprise and suddenness, that is to say,

---

[3] Tremendous controversy surrounds the translation of 7:14. The heart of the matter is that the Hebrew expresses no verb in verse 14 and in most cases where this happens the correct assumption is that the present tense of the verb 'to be' is to be understood. Hence RSV, NEB. The problem in this seems to be that it makes Amos deny in verse 14 what he most emphatically affirms (as basic to his whole case) in verse 15: 'I am no prophet . . . The Lord said to me "Go, prophesy" . . .' *i.e.* (more literally) 'Go, fulfil a prophet's role'. Faced with this contradiction it seems much more reasonable to adopt a past tense in verse 14, as RV, JB, giving a wholly intelligible and indeed forceful rendering.

while he was (contentedly) engaged in his daily concerns, he was arrested, apprehended, conscripted. An authoritative hand from outside gripped him and he became what he was not before and what he would never have made himself.

It is no wonder then that Amos was 'the prophet who feared no man'. He knew where he stood with God. When the moment of testing came and especially when a strong human authority pressed him to give up, surely we can sense the thoughts rising unbidden: But I have a vocation from God to obey, a word from God to speak, a work from God to do. This is what holds the man of God firm in the time of trial and opposition: he is where he is by appointment.

And having done all, to stand

The third aspect of the man of God which we find in this portrait of Amos is that he abides faithful to the Word of God (16, 17). It is deeply impressive to hear Amos take the initiative: *Now therefore hear the word of the Lord.* Amaziah had said *Never again prophesy at Bethel,* and Amos replied *Now therefore hear the word of the Lord.* But he makes the matter so much more emphatic by repeating the sentiments of Amaziah: *You say, Do not prophesy . . . Therefore thus says the Lord.* Truly Amos is faithful to his own earlier words: *The Lord* GOD (the sovereign Yahweh) *has spoken; who can but prophesy?* Again, please do not think of him being loud, hectoring or unfeeling in his reply to Amaziah. The product of a deep sense of authority and of a deep respect for the Word of God is at its best and purest the quiet word of reason and respect, never the word of ill-manners or abuse, never the word of vociferous controversy. The wrath of man cannot accomplish the righteous purposes of God (Jas. 1:19).

Hear then how Amos describes the word which has so gripped him that he cannot but speak it. *You say, Do not prophesy . . . do not preach . . .* (16). The first prohibition points to the divine origin of the word: it is a word of prophecy, that is to say, it is a 'Thus says Yahweh'; it is a word God has fashioned and given to man to speak. The second prohibition points to the human helpfulness and benefit of the word. *Do not preach* is, literally, 'do not drop, trickle, drip your word' (*cf.* RV). It speaks of that which is gentle, welcome, refreshing, like a waft of rain on dry ground.[4] What a beautiful and wonderful description of the Word of God and of the preacher's task! Very far, this, from the scolding which has sometimes passed for preaching; very far, this, from the ministry which leaves the people of God battered and bruised! How we need to learn today that the Word of God is this gentle dropping from God to refresh, bless and quicken souls and that those who handle it need to be equally gentle, applying the coolness and balm of divine promises!

But gentle as it is and requiring a gentle ministry, the Word of God has a steely insistence on being heard and requires an insistent ministry. No matter how much the Amaziah's of this world say *Do not prophesy*—or, to put the matter for today, Do not preach the Bible—the reply must always be the same: *Therefore thus says the Lord* (17). The man of God abides faithful to the Word of God.

The Word, the divider

The word to Amaziah, though ministered with the gentleness of lightly falling rain, was harsh and judgmental. It first touches those dearest to Amaziah, for it is true that we cannot go to doom alone and, in the plan of God, the family is bound in a unity and solidarity with great potential for good and for ill. His wife is degraded, his children killed. The land which he sought to defend from the ill-effects of Amos' ministry (10) is occupied and carved up among the enemy. He himself loses all that is dear to him in his priestly vocation: no shrine to attend, and around him all the ceremonial uncleanness which it was his life's duty to avoid. And the word which he rejected he will live to see fulfilled in the captivity of the nation.

Unpretentious causes provoked these terrible catastrophes for Amaziah. He rejected the word of the Lord and the Lord rejected

---

[4] IB seems to think the word needs to be guarded from a contemptuous meaning, but there is no case of its use in the Old Testament where any sneering note is necessarily heard. It is part of the prophet's stock-in-trade vocabulary. Pusey associates the word with the purposes of God to fructify and fertilize by His word – 'a gentle dew or soft rain, not beating down but refreshing . . . sinking in . . . softening even hard ground . . .; gentle, so as they can bear it . . .'

him (*cf.* 1 Sa. 15:23). There is no mention here of his being a leading light in a false religion. His priesthood is referred to obliquely (17) without any suggestion of opprobrium or penalty attaching to it. Such things are not brought into the case. Only one factor operates. Amos prophesied and Amaziah replied *Do not prophesy.* He heard the word of the Lord but he did not listen, accept and obey. And the Lord of the plumb-line drew near and measured these two men. One was taken and one was left, because one bowed before the word and the other did not.

Amos 8:1-10
The Autumn of Opportunity

SPRING, summer and then autumn, so runs the gradual process of maturing in the realm of nature, and here, as often in the Bible, it depicts the ripening of human conduct and character to its full development either of good or ill.

A basket of summer fruit must have been a familiar sight to Amos. In the fall of the year the Feast of Booths was kept (*cf.* Dt. 16:13 ff.) at which token offerings of all the prosperity which the Lord had given to His people were brought in thankfulness and joy to Him. Like all the feasts of Israel it was given a historical orientation so that it also recalled to the people the fact that they had been gathered in themselves from among the nations to be the people of God (*cf.* Lv. 23:39 ff.). The sense of prosperity, with its attendant buoyancy towards the future, joy and the reminder of belonging to the unique people of the Lord would have filled the minds of the worshippers as they came bearing their harvest hampers to the shrines of Israel.

Into this situation came a bitter word from the Lord: Ripe? Ripe indeed—for judgment! The vision in verses 1-3 depends for its meaning on a pun in the Hebrew. In reply to the Lord's question (2), Amos replies *qayiṣ, then the Lord said . . . qêṣ*. In sound these two words are virtually identical and the transition from one to the other would come with natural ease to the subtle and perceptive mind of Amos. They came into the presence of God not just with ripe fruit but as ripe fruit, ripened over all the months and years of moral and spiritual probation which He had afforded them (*cf.* 4:6-11) and now, sadly, ready for a particularly dreadful harvest-time.[1]

[1] NEB brings out the thought of the steadily maturing processes of divine

The end

This then is the situation. Their religion had utterly failed to alert them to a God of judgment and therefore the fact would spring upon them all unready, when their expectancies were all geared to diametrically opposite outcomes. This theme of the sudden onset of disaster appears in the illustrations which Amos uses: *songs* become *wailings* (3), the solid *land* is felt to *tremble, rise* and *be tossed* (8), *the sun* sets *at noon* and *the earth* becomes dark *in broad daylight* (9), *feasts* are turned into *mourning, songs into lamentation* of a particularly *bitter* kind (10).

Something of the structure of the passage has begun to appear as we have focused on these illustrations. Amos begins and ends the oracle by showing the divine Agent (2b, 7) and the desolation of the day (3, 8–10). In verses 2b and 7, though the Hebrew wording differs, the sentiment is identical, namely that the Lord can never forgive or forget. The exact expression in verse 2b has occurred earlier at 7:8b, where we discerned it to mean 'I will never forgive them'. This determination in the mind of God brings terror and death into the experience of people. How lightly expressions like 'God-forsaken' are used! They are part of terminology of casual blasphemy in cultures where religious formalism prevails or where the mass of the population is in a post-religious phase. Neither formal religion nor post-religious man can take seriously the possibility that such a thing could ever happen. Surely God is not like this! But He is! Let Him but just decide that probation is over, that the 'one year more' (*cf.* Lk. 13:1–8) of life's last opportunity has run to its autumnal harvest-time, then for a time the air will be filled by the wailings of lost grace (3a; *cf.* Ex. 12:30) until the death which sin brings has had its way (3b) and a silence even more terrible than the wail enfolds all (3c).

The re-affirmation of these things comes in verses 7–10. May we not imagine that, in the minds of those who heard Amos, incipient disbelief, the reaction to his first announcement in verses 2b, 3, has now become frank incredulity, incredulity that such a disproportionate result should rise from such a negligible

judgment: '. . . ripe summer fruit . . . The time is ripe . . .'; JB focuses on the moral state of the people: ' . . . ripe fruit . . . My people is ripe. . . .'

cause—why, the sins of verses 4–6 are not even real sins; they are just the way life is lived and has to be lived in this hard world: where's the sin in being a successful businessman? Surely it's a bit hard if religion is going to insist on one's losing money to one's competitors! Surely that is religious mania!

But more about that presently: for the moment let us simply notice that Amos will not leave the question of the reward of sin alone. It has to be faced. Once more the Agent is the Lord (7), and He asserts the eternal impossibility of His forgetting these sins. To make the matter more emphatic He swears *by the pride of Jacob*. The irony of it! He has sworn *by his holiness* (4:2)—His own basic and unchanging nature—and they took no notice; he has sworn *by himself* (6:8), amplifying the oath by calling their attention to His omnipotence as Redeemer-Judge, but they took no notice. Are these grounds of oath-taking perhaps too uncertain for them? Well, then, here is something that is surely imperishable: *the pride of Jacob*. Their own obduracy may succeed where the divine changelessness has failed![2]

What are the marks of a society which has reached the autumn of probation and concerning which God has drawn the line of finality? Total insecurity (8, 9), sorrow, death and eternal bitterness (10). It is entirely allowable to treat verses 8 and 9 as metaphorical of a society which has suffered the loss of stability and regularity, that is to say, where absolutes are no longer recognized and rules are there to break, where, maybe, human personality is showing more and more signs of breakdown and unreliability. This is abundantly true: the further man gets from his moorings in God the further he gets from all moorings.

[2] Mays prefers to be uncertain of the interpretation here. The 'strangeness' of such an oath formula unseats him. 13, Hammershaimb and Pusey take *the pride of Jacob* as descriptive of Yahweh, either as that on which they prided themselves or as that which was in fact true about them even though they did not recognize it. All this seems unimpressive. Cripps holds firmly to the ironical interpretation and Driver leans to it, but Gwynn dismisses it as 'artificial'. Calvin goes along a line of his own. Translating the phrase (as is allowable) 'the excellency of Jacob', the 'excellence' which the Lord sees is the special place into which He had brought this people by adoption: 'I swear by the benefits I conferred on you that I will not allow that which is justly precious in my sight to be disgracefully profaned'. Calvin's certainty is delicious: 'This', he says, 'is the meaning', but he fails to carry Harper (*International Critical Commentary*) who decides that Amos is speaking 'scornfully', *i.e.* the ironic interpretation proffered above.

But there is equally—indeed primarily—a dimension here of the biblical doctrine of world conservation. When man gets out of step with God, 'nature' gets out of step with man and is corrupted and polluted from its purity. Thus, in Genesis 3, the breach between God and man had its immediate corollary in the thorns, thistles and sweat which thenceforward marked man's relationship with his physical environment (Gn. 3:17 ff.). The Old Testament follows this teaching through consistently. The very land itself becomes polluted by the sins of its inhabitants (*cf.* Je 3:1-3), and its beauties are destroyed by human pride (Is. 2.12-17) We see this in action wherever once-beautiful valleys are disfigured by the slag-heaps and debris of industrial covetousness or wherever rivers become the running sores of careless pollution.[3] Was it God, the Creator of the atom, who released its awesome power to blind, maim and pollute? What will the end of all this be in the day when common grace is withdrawn and man is left to his sin?

That day will come and, when it does, there is nothing that man can do about it. When it comes hope dies. Amos speaks of conscious efforts being made then to show an awareness of sin (10b): the putting on of *sackcloth* (*cf.* Jon. 3:6) and the shaving of the head as a sign of mourning (*cf.* Mi. 1:16), but it will then be all to no avail: it is a grief which time will not heal. The grief will be as intense as that for a beloved. In the ordinary course even such a grief loses its intensity, but the grief of the lost sinner remains and *the end of it*, *i.e.*, literally, 'its afterwards', the outcome, the aftermath, remains exactly as in the *bitter day* when the blow first fell.

It is a terrible picture, but it is what Amos says, and the Bible nowhere says anything different.

The inner circle of sin

The people of whom this grim forecast is made are described in their characteristic attitudes in verse 5, where the introductory

[3] Passages such as Am. 9:13; *cf.* Is. 11:6 ff., *etc.* are, as we shall see, the other side of the same coin. They are not overdrawn pictures of 'pie in the sky' but the product of taking the doctrine of creation seriously. When relationships between God and man are again perfect there will be a new heaven and a new earth, and 'nature' will delight to give what it withheld from sinners.

verb *saying* has the force in context of 'being, as they are, the sort of people who say . . .'. As we examine the details of this verse we discover the sin behind all sin.

First, these people loved gain more than they loved God (5a). Typically of the times, they are described as attentive to religious forms. Their seat would never be empty at the festival of the *new moon* (*cf.* 1 Sa. 20:18) nor would they dream of profaning *the sabbath* by commerce, but at no point in the festivities did religion oust business or the church replace the office in the affections. The holy day was a duty but not a delight, a day away but not a day off: financial preoccupations won hands down.

Again (5b) they loved gain more than they loved honesty. They used a *small ephah* (*i.e.* of smaller capacity than was standard) for measuring out goods purchased and a *great shekel* (*i.e.* heavier than the Department of Weights and Measures authorized) for weighing the money taken in exchange. They sold less than they ought for more than they ought, 'giving short measure in the bushel and taking overweight in the silver' (NEB), thus dealing *deceitfully with false balances.*[4]

The sin behind all sin is covetousness, gain for self. Amos first mentioned it as the sin of self-pleasing in society and religion (4:1-5); he returned to it in the form of self-satisfaction (6:1-3) and self-indulgence (6:4-6). Now for the third time he exposes that which moves the Lord to the extreme infliction of His wrath, in the form of self-advantage. Because all had to be turned to the advantage of self, they despised the grace of God who had given them the new moon and sabbath days of feast and rest, and they disobeyed the law of God who had commanded even-handed justice in all the transactions of life (*cf.* Lv. 19:35, 36). Let us note carefully this delineation of their sin: it is an offence exposed by the plumb-line of God, for their lives neither rested on the level foundation of grace nor were constructed according to the upright of law.

In this way 8:1-10 is integrated into the foregoing teaching of 7:7 ff., and we may develop it in a way which shows this relationship. What was the characteristic manifestation of this

---

[4] Mays interestingly records the finding of shops in Tirzah with two sets of weights, one for buying and one for selling. This find is dated in the eighth century.

sin behind all sin, the sin of self-advantage? The verse in which
Amos describes their covetousness (8:5) lies bracketed between
two virtually identical statements pointing to a predatory and
insensitive attitude towards the helpless among men (4, 6). It
would seem therefore that, as the plumb-line operates separating
the true members of the people of God from those who cannot
verify their claim, there are three marks of truth which the
former possess and which the latter lack. The first is to be discerned, inwardly, in their personal attitude towards sin and
holiness (7:7–9): the plumb-line given to them to build the
fabric of life consisted of the law of God for their obedience and
the grace of God available in blood-sacrifice to cover their disobedience. Personal life constructed on this pattern hallmarks
the true people of God. Secondly, the encounter between Amos
and Amaziah stressed the upward dimension of hearing and
obeying the word of God (7:10–17), and in 8:1–10 the third
dimension of a truly godly life appears, outwardly, a concern
for the helpless and needy among men. Failure in any of the
three cases brings heavy and disastrous divine judgment (7:9,
17; 8:3, 8–10), but there is an element of divine anger reserved
for this last failure which takes it far and away beyond the threats
in the other two cases. How the Lord hates inhumanity!

Three separate sins are specified: domineering (4), treating as
means and not ends (6a) and exploitation (6c). The unrelenting
nature of their domineering of the *needy* (the uninfluential person,
easy to be pushed around, *cf.* on 4:1) and *poor*[5] is such that Amos
sees this class—the class of independent but unaffluent people—
simply disappearing from the land. They do this (6a) by using
paltry debts, such as that for a pair of shoes, as justification for
selling a person into slavery. That is to say, the poor (here the
same word as in 4:1) is every bit as much a piece of merchandise
as the nearest sack of grain, something to become the means of
the highest possible profit. He is no longer a person but only a
thing. And as a thing he can be treated with the utmost scorn.
They will even force him to buy *the refuse of the wheat,* *i.e.* that
which has 'fallen' and (presumably) has been swept up at the end
of the day and is put aside for re-sale! They looked at people

[5] A different word is used in 8:4 from that in 8:6a or 4:1; it means much
what 'underdog' signifies to us.

and saw things; they looked at others and thought about themselves, and that turned out to be the sin above all sins.

God hates inhumanity

When Jesus painted a picture of a servant who lost mercy because he failed to show mercy (Mt. 18:23–35), He informed us that He was allowing us to look into the very heart of God the Father. *So also*, He said, *my heavenly Father will do to every one of you, if you do not forgive your brother from your heart* (Mt. 18:35). He speaks of *my heavenly Father*, that is to say, He speaks from His own position of unique knowledge of who and what the Father is (Mt. 11:27), and He says that His Father, the God and Father of our Lord Jesus Christ, will not forgive the unforgiving or give mercy to the unmerciful. He put it another way around when He said: *As you did it not to one of the least of these, you did it not to me*—a sin which, in the estimate of Jesus, brought its agents *into eternal punishment* (Mt. 25:45, 46). It is as though Jesus said: 'What do you mean when you say you love Me? You are saying that you love the mercy which freely reaches out to the helpless, the needy, the thankless. But it is clear that you do not love that mercy, for you do not practise it!' But putting these sentiments on the lips of Jesus merely adds weight to what is a biblical truth. Yahweh is the God who heard the cry of the needy in their helplessness before the oppressor (Ex. 2:23), heard their groaning (2:24), saw their affliction and felt the burden of their sorrows (Ex. 3:7), with the result that He himself came down to deliver (Ex. 3:8) and in doing so made a name for Himself (2 Sa. 7:23). He is that sort of God and no-one can claim to love Him who does not love that sort of life. It is not just illogical that people should love mercy when they seek it from God for themselves and hate it when required to show it to others. The Scripture says that it is impossible. The unforgiving cannot be forgiven, the unmerciful cannot receive mercy.

The impotence of God

There is, then, one thing which the Almighty cannot do: He cannot bestow mercy on those who do not show mercy. Nothing

is left for those who turn their faces away from the needy—
or who exploit the needy for their own gain—than that God will
turn His face away from them. This is the grim but biblically
realistic truth of Amos 8:1–10. The plumb-line hangs vertical
in the unmoving hand of God, a mute summons to eternal
wrath to flash forth, terrifyingly, disastrously, unendingly against
those who are pitiless towards the poor, the central evidence of
false religion (*cf.* Jas. 1:27) and dead faith (*cf.* Jas. 2:14–17).[6]

[6] The centrality of pitilessness, or failure to pity, as the sin above all sin is
strikingly seen in the over-all pattern of Amos 7–9. We recall that the theme
of this passage is the distinction between those who can rightly claim to be
the people of God and those who, whatever they say, cannot produce evidence
to verify such a claim. The central teaching of the passage is given in 7:7—
8:10. If people are to pass the test of the plumb-line then their lives must be
personally built on its foundations of law and grace, obedience and repentance being the outstanding characteristics of such a life (7:7–9); it must show
the characteristic, Godward, of recognizing and obeying His word (7:10–17);
it must be marked outwardly by concern for the needy (8:1–10). Observe
now the pattern of the whole:

a Prologue (7:1–6): Decisive rejection of total destruction t the people ot
    God
  b The manifestation of the people ot God: personal convictions about
      holiness and sin (7:7–9)
    c The manifestation of the people of God: response to the Word of
        God (7:10–17)
      d The manifestation of the people of God: concern for the needy
          among men (8:1–10)
      *c*¹ The famine of the Word of God: a hunger that came too late (8:11–14)
    *b*¹ The Lord's war against pretence and against complacency in the matter
        of sin and holiness (9:1–10)
*a*¹ Epilogue (9:11–15): The announcement and enjoyment of the eternal
    inheritance of the people of God.

The main purpose in putting this analysis here is to show how the whole pivots
round section *d*. As God, plumb-line in hand, surveys His people, this is His
central enquiry. As in the teaching of Jesus, nothing reveals more clearly
either membership of His people or ripeness for judgment than the attitude
adopted towards the helpless and hopeless, because, of course, this reveals
whether or not we resemble Him whom we claim to worship.

It may be remarked incidentally that this sort of analytical study of the
books of the prophets is happily becoming slightly less uncommon and
suspect than heretofore. An outstanding example is to be found in the treatment of the prophecies of Zechariah in Joyce G. Baldwin, *Haggai, Zechariah,
Malachi* (Tyndale Press, 1972). See also Zephaniah in J. H. Eaton, *Obadiah,
Nahum, Habakkuk, Zephaniah* (SCM Press, 1961).

Amos 8:11-14
The Day of the Cults

GOD'S judgments work out in the ordinary and the humdrum. They are not confined to great supernatural explosions of wrath at the 'last day' as if the Lord were merely waiting in the wings of life's drama, until the curtain finally falls. He is God the Creator and therefore His judgments will be seen within the operations of human and physical nature. Thus, as we have seen, we can take 8:8, 9 both metaphorically and literally. When we see society opening at the seams, old bonds weakening, old norms relaxing, old absolutes rejected, when we see the human person not as able as hitherto to stand the strains of life and there are more breakdowns, more suicides, God is telling man, collectively and individually, that life apart from Him is not possible, that inherited spiritual capital drains away and, left to himself, man becomes progressively unable to cope. Correspondingly, the evidences of his sinful alienation from God infect the world around him, its resources are squandered, its treasures rifled, its beauties ravaged and its powers tapped for its own destruction. The judgments of God work out, as we have said, in the unrecognized humdrum of life.

The grace of forewarning

Another aspect of the almost imperceptible judgments of God is the withdrawal of blessings which have been despised. A particular example of this lies before us in these verses, but before we examine it, let us notice that judgment does not come unheralded. Through Amos, God offers not an analysis of an existing peril but a forewarning of a coming one. *The days are coming*, He says

(8:11). It is in this way that Old Testament prediction is moral and not simply a sop to carnal curiosity about the future. It tells about the future in order to prepare for the future. It says *the days are coming* in order that the interim before they come may be filled to the utmost profit and the threatened dangers may not strike home upon an unsheltered, unready people. We can even put the same truth the other way around: the very nature of morality requires some knowledge of the future. Paul is correct when he says that if there is no life to come then we would be best advised to eat and drink, for tomorrow we die (1 Cor. 15:32); Isaiah was even more sharply correct when he first used those words (Is. 22:13), namely that if there is to be no great continuance in this life, then let us give ourselves to merriment. Only the awareness of some foreseen good or evil suffices to guide man effectively in the present.

The Lord takes us at this level and proffers the grace of forewarning: particularly forewarning that the truth of God can be forfeited without remedy, but that it is never forfeited without tragic consequence.

When the fence is down

The Lord had earlier sent famine and drought upon His people to bring them to repentance (4:6–8), without result. The hardness of impenitence will now have its way with them. They will lose the truth in *a famine . . . of hearing the words of the Lord* (8:11). And when that blessing is withdrawn, there is no way to recover it (12). Amos anticipated a belated concern for the truth, just as he foresaw a belated repentance (10), but it will be all to no effect. The verb *wander* (12) is used of the rolling gait of drunkards (Is. 28:7), of the swaying of trees in the wind (Is. 7:2), of lips quivering in agitation (1 Sa. 1:13). So here, as those who hardly know what they are doing or who are 'flapping' in panic or agitation, they traverse the land to discover what once they had so lightly regarded. But the day is too far gone and the truth has gone with it.

The vacuum does not, however, remain unfilled. The cults press in eagerly to fill it (14), not one but in quantity, and the people who would not hear the Word of God taste the poor fare of man-made religion

In the parable of the vineyard, Isaiah portrays what happens when the fence comes down. It is an illustration of the judgments of God working out in the natural order of providence (Is. 5:5): when God's protection goes, the beasts are ready to maraud. And just as man is powerless to recover the truth, so he is powerless to recognize and to resist error.

These things are for our learning. Have we got a Bible still in our hands? Let us prize it, read it and commit its precious truths to heart and mind. It is not an inalienable possession; it may not be ours for ever. Is the Bible still preached in our church? Let us love to hear the Word of God; let us be urgent to bring others within earshot of it. It is not our guaranteed privilege; the voice of the preacher could be silenced. The truth of God is our only fence against error. In this as in everything else the way of strength is to keep close to God and to fear much, much more the peril of falling out of His power and truth than of falling into the power and error of Satan.

There may be a warning against the peril of pride in all this, and it is important enough to state it even if it is no more than a possibility that this is what Amos intended. He sees these poor bewildered, agitated searchers hastening this way and that. *From sea to sea* may mean from the Dead Sea in the south to the Mediterranean on the west, with the compass points being completed in the references to *north* and *east*, *i.e.* they search round the whole country. But *from sea to sea* may equally mean from the Dead Sea as the eastern boundary, to the Mediterranean on the west, thence to the *north* and back to the *east* where they started, with a deliberate omission of the south, because that would have meant Jerusalem and the truth of Yahweh enshrined there which had been schismatically rejected two hundred years earlier. It would have meant the admission of error and the humbling of pride. Without a doubt Amos' main purpose is to show the aimless helplessness of man without the revealed truth of God to hold him steady and still, but there is a typical Amos-like thrust in what is left unsaid: 'Ah yes, you will go everywhere but where you know the truth is, everywhere but where your pride would be humbled. You would rather stay in error yet have the pride of being known as a seeker of the truth than find the truth at the expense of losing your pride.'

Where the blow falls heaviest

In this famine of the truth, Amos sees the young as being specially the sufferers (13, 14). When truth goes, both hope and fulfilment go with it. The coming generation is the hope of the future but it comes as heir to the present generation and, for all its brimming energy and confidence, is not sufficient in itself for the strains of life: *fair virgins and . . . young men shall faint*; nor is youth sufficient in itself, for all its certainty, to recognize error: it is the youth of the nation who get hooked after Ashimah of Samaria, the god of Dan and the way of Beer-sheba. The very readiness for something new which is proper to their youth makes them fair game for the religious quacks and isms, fads and fancies. Yet, as Amos sees it, they are fainting with thirst, *i.e.* with an undiagnosed longing for God's truth (for this is what the metaphor of thirst means in this passage), but the earlier generation has deprived them of the possibility of finding it. The errors of one generation have become the dogmas of the next, the truth is one step further out of sight and the new generation one step further from reality.

Trusteeship

All this is surely written to give us admonitory guidance. The truth is to be held, guarded and transmitted. Amos would say it to us; Paul said it to Timothy,[1] putting it positively in terms of holding, committing, studying, abiding in and preaching. The word of Amos is more negative: there are errors against which we must guard the truth. As he sees it, this is no bare intellectualism. He speaks (14) of things which imperil worship as well as and because they imperil truth: that is to say, they make inroads into our total life with God. Jesus had the same comprehensive view when He gave His approval to Isaiah's dictum that *in vain do they worship me, teaching as doctrines the precepts of men* (Mk. 7:7). In worship neither sincerity nor antiquity will suffice. Men think, says Calvin, 'that any zeal for religion, however preposterous, is sufficient. But they do not realize that true religion ought to be

[1] *Cf.* 2 Tim. 1:13, 14; 2:1, 2, 15; 3:10-17; 4:1-5.

conformed to God's will as to a universal rule . . . that no religion is genuine unless it be joined with truth.'[2]

First, then, the truth and worship of God must be guarded against importation. This is the first element in the list of pseudo-religions in verse 14. Into the religion of Samaria had come the worship of the goddess Ashimah.[3] According to 2 Kings 17:30 Ashimah (spelt slightly differently there) was worshipped by the later foreign settlers in Samaria, the men of Hamath. But Hamath had been in contact with Israel since David's day (2 Sa. 8:9), and in the time of Amos had been captured by Jeroboam II (2 Ki. 14:28). There is nothing anachronistic about the reference here, therefore, and we may with justification understand the reference to be to the importation of a foreign cult. In Samaria, therefore, there was either syncretism or an acceptance of a multi-faith situation, and neither of these would accord with Amos' theology or with truth. Syncretism takes the characteristic features of many religions and attempts to fuse them into one 'great religion' which will presumably attract and hold the adherents of the previously separated systems. The multi-faith approach is less sophisticated, simply tolerating side by side the worship of different gods—though it may, of course, be more sophisticated in saying that these are simply different names for the same God and that Yahweh was worshipped 'incognito' in all that was true in the worship of Ashimah.

The names may sound strange in our ears, but the facts ought not to be and the warning still stands. When we studied[4] the meaning of the holiness of Yahweh we saw that it involved holding Him alone to have a proper claim to be God and also recognizing that He is a different sort of God from all other claimants. There is this exclusivism about the God of the Bible. The 'Yah-

---

[2] J. Calvin, *Institutes of the Christian Religion* (Clarke, 1959), pp. 49, 50.

[3] *Ashimah of Samaria* involves a slight but sensible emendation of the vowels of the Hebrew text which as it stands reads 'the guilt of Samaria'. Amos was quite capable of allowing the two words to fall into a deliberate confusion so as to produce a compound idea: 'your guilty worship of Ashimah'. Some prefer a rather more extensive emendation (though not excessive): 'the Asherah of Samaria'. This would refer to the general importation of Canaanite elements into Samaria's religion and theology. Asherah was a Canaanite mother-goddess, the name also being used for the image made for her. *Cf.* 1 Ki. 15:13; 18:19; 2 Ki. 23:4. See NBD, art. 'Asherah'.

[4] See pp. 89 ff., above.

weh' of the Old Testament becomes the Holy Trinity of the New and there is no other God, nor is a like nature claimed by any other supposed god. Anything which blurs these distinctions must be resisted. It is our task to transmit the biblical deposit of truth unalloyed to those who follow us and we cannot do so—any more than the people of Amos' day could—if we admit syncretism or acquiesce in multi-faith services and the like.

Secondly, we have to guard the truth and worship of God against corruption. *Dan* (14b) was one of the schismatic and corrupt sanctuaries set up by Jeroboam I (1 Ki. 12:29). It was depraved much more in its tendencies and influence than in anything Jeroboam actually did. For example, the golden calves were a pedestal for the invisible throne of Yahweh just as were the cherubim in the Jerusalem shrine. In their idea therefore they could hardly be called heretical, but inevitably, as we have seen, their visibility wrought a popular identification between the invisible God and the sort of symbol with which He was identified. In effect therefore Yahweh became a fertility deity. This sort of defect ran through the cult Jeroboam set up. His central feast was 'like' the feast in Judah (1 Ki. 12:32), but its motivation was erroneous: Jeroboam stands in the Bible as the man who sought to make religion serve the ends of politics. The cult was a technique for establishing his own monarchy (1 Ki. 12:26–30): even God became a means to an end. This has good claim to being considered as 'the sin of Jeroboam the son of Nebat, who made Israel to sin'. The truth and worship of God must be safeguarded from that (however small) which detracts from the God who is revealed in Scripture, and responsibility rests with each worshipper to purify the thoughts and motives of his own heart so that God is worshipped for what He is and not for what we want from Him.

The third matter on which Amos focuses is by no means easy or certain in interpretation. RSV expresses what the Hebrew says: *As the way of Beer-sheba lives* (14c), an odd and elsewhere unexemplified expression.[5] NEB 'By the sacred way to Beersheba' offers what can surely be the only possible interpretation: some reli-

---

[5] JB 'By your Beloved's life, Beersheba' represents a small emendation, adopted by IB and strongly suggested by Hammershaimb. Presumably 'Beloved' would be Yahweh and the charge the same as that against Dan.

gious merit or benefit was thought to accrue from the journey itself and people began to 'swear by it'.[6] Let us accept this as a good and likely understanding. It tells us that true religion must be safeguarded from superstition. It is very understandable that a thing as laborious as the journey from Israel through Judah to Beer-sheba would be looked upon as no small duty accomplished for the sake of religion and God. From this it is a small step to superstitious veneration for the doing of the thing. Superstition is a non-moral technique for securing God's blessing: walking the road to Beer-sheba brought its own, automatic rewards. And in this sense there is very little which cannot become a superstition whereby we say 'God must bless me because I have done . . . '. But slot-machine religion finds no place in the Bible.

Man lives by every word which proceeds out of the mouth of God. If this food is withdrawn or corrupted there is no other way of satisfaction or security. In this regard verse 14 must be taken as defining the people of verse 13, as indeed the Hebrew requires. Why are these folk suffering from thirst? Because they have only the cults to satisfy them and they remain unsatisfied. But more, at the end, they *fall, and never rise again*. Nothing but the Word of God can sustain and keep secure for all eternity. It is in keeping with what we have seen of the over-all pattern of these chapters that the notion of eternal security—that preoccupation of Amos —should find its way back into his teaching here. Religion as such (14) can only lead to the eternal loss of falling and never rising. But by contrast those who live by the Word live for ever.

[6] Pusey notes that according to 2 Ki. 23:8 there was a clearance of high places from Geba (N. Judah) to Beer-sheba (S. Judah) and suggests that perhaps this was along a pilgrim route with sacred 'stations' at intervals.

Amos 9:1–10
The War on Pretence

THE final vision which Amos relates is different from all the others. In those the Lord dealt with his prophet by symbols of the true, often inviting Amos to say what he saw and then going on to explain its meaning. But here it is as though a veil were drawn away from the future and the prophet saw in reality the coming destruction—in its true, inner reality, that is, with the Lord Himself as its chief Agent.

In order to bring this scene into focus let us return to how it all began. One hundred and eighty years before the time of Amos, in the year 931/930 BC, Jeroboam I led off the ten northern tribes to make them into the kingdom of Israel. Even though he had come into his kingdom on a wave of popular feeling, Jeroboam knew that his position was essentially insecure. People were disaffected by the exactions of Solomon's later years and the final blow was the refusal of Rehoboam to negotiate a more favourable constitution. But, as Jeroboam saw it, if the people continued to make annual pilgrimages to Jerusalem (1 Ki. 12:26 f.) they would remember only the golden days of David and soon the claims of the old dynasty would re-exert themselves and he would be cast off with the same alacrity as he had been accepted. To mend this situation he devised 'the sin of Jeroboam': the use of religion in the interests of politics. He contrived a feast of which we are told three main facts: first, that it took place on the fifteenth day of the eighth month (1 Ki. 12:32); secondly, that it was *like the feast that was in Judah* (1 Ki. 12:32); and thirdly, that Jeroboam himself officiated at the altar or, at the very least, stood prominently at the altar during the ceremonies. Three times the Hebrew uses the same expression which appears in RSV as *he offered sacrifices on the altar* (1 Ki. 12:32) . . . *He went up to the altar . . and went up to the altar . . .* (33). Very possibly the first of these three phrases should be harmonized with the other two: Jeroboam went up (the altar steps and stood) by the altar. This is the position in which he is at once found (1 Ki. 13:1) by the man of God out of Judah: *Jeroboam was standing by the altar to burn incense.* The whole thing was a counterfeit: a counterfeit feast on a counterfeit altar to prop up a counterfeit monarchy!

The years pass. By the grim coincidences of God another Jeroboam is on the throne of Israel and another man of God out of Judah, not an anonymous prophet but Amos, is there to see him take his stand by the altar. One vision is about to be succeeded by another, the autumnal presentation of the ripe fruits (8:1) by the great autumnal and royal festival on the fifteenth day of the eighth month. Amos watches Jeroboam but even as he watches the scene changes. 'I saw the Sovereign One who had taken His stand by the altar' (*cf.* 9:1). The counterfeit is replaced by the real, the human by the divine, the king who had come to prop up his dynasty by the King who had come to throw it down. The day of pretence was over and the war on pretence had begun. Long, long ago Samson had pulled the temple of Dagon down from below, but when the Sovereign calls up His forces the building receives great shattering blows from above, on *the capitals,* driving them down upon their own *thresholds* until the whole edifice crumbles in on its occupants' *heads.* Many rush away from the downfall, but none escape (1b).

There is no supernatural refuge (2), neither down in *Sheol,* the place of the dead, nor in *heaven,* the abode of God; there is no natural refuge (3), neither in the highest places of *Carmel* nor in *the bottom of the sea.* In the day of their affluence they wrapped the comforts of false religion and heathen gods around them, but in the day of their calamity they find that there is no God but One and that even were there a monstrous deity hidden in the deep it would turn out to be His servant! There is no political refuge (4): they may lose their sovereignty in the overthrow of the kingdom and change their place and their state, becoming slaves in a foreign land, but even so they will not escape from the pursuing vengeance. Not only the serpent in the deep but also *the*

sword on earth works to His bidding and His *eyes* are *upon them for evil and not for good.*
This disastrous and inescapable judgment is underwritten by the very nature of God Himself. He is of power to do what He has threatened. We may note the impressive link between verses 1 and 5, forgetting the verses for a moment which lie between: 'I saw the Sovereign One . . . and the Sovereign One is Yahweh the omnipotent. . . .'[1] Omnipotence is forthwith described (5, 6). God can speak with certainty that there will be no escape for these people anywhere in His universe, because He is God of the whole. He has absolute mastery over all the earth in its physical substance (5a), its human inhabitants (5b) and its condition at any time (5c); the celestial (6a) and the terrestrial (6b) are equally open to His use, and all the elements, represented here by water and earth (6c), are His to do what He wills with.

This then is what the Lord thinks of pretence; this is how He reacts to it; this is His judgment upon it. The essence of the pretence is the throwing of a cloak of religion over a life motivated towards self. This was the sin of the first Jeroboam and of the last Jeroboam (2 Ki. 14:23, 24). God and religion were tools whereby self could be secured and life made secure for self.

By understanding verses 1–6 in this way, they form the perfect background for verses 7–10. We have discerned in the opening vision and oracle the picture of a relentless war of extermination. We have imaginatively suggested that it is being pursued against spiritual pretence. When we turn in verses 7–10 to discover who it is upon whom the eyes of the Lord (note the connecting idea in verses 4b, 8a) are set with such hostility, we discover that it is precisely those who are living in a spiritual dream-world, forgetful of holiness, sin and its reward, fancying that a date in history has put God eternally in their debt and that irrespective of character they may count on His co-operation. To

---

[1] It is, perhaps, worth mentioning again how important and helpful it is to note the way in which divine names and titles are printed in English Bibles. Capital letters, LORD or GOD, always signify the divine name, Yahweh, the personal name of God, God revealed at the Exodus as Redeemer and Judge. The form Lord, on the other hand, translates a noun meaning 'king' or 'sovereign'. JB has courageously and properly broken with long tradition and uses the divine name, Yahweh.

them, as to the two Jeroboams, God is a prop of the establishment. Let us examine verses 7–10 to see if this is so.

Israel and the nations

Verses 7–10 fall into two sections. The first (7, 8a) sets Israel among the nations with a view to showing where the line of distinction is to be drawn and where it is not to be drawn.

The message of verse 7 is plain: the same divine government operates over all the earth. We must not treat verse 7a as though it stood in splendid isolation in the centre of an otherwise blank page. It must be held in close connection with 7b and in the same way, as we shall presently see, 7 must be wedded to 8a. The Lord does not say that from now on Israel has a changed status in His sight, whereby everything formerly possessed by way of privilege has been withdrawn and the adoption as sons has been annulled. It is this sort of reasoning which has led many commentators to see in Amos the prophet who proclaimed the end of the covenant relationship and some, indeed, to find in verse 7 a different author from the Amos who laid such stress on the Exodus in 3:2.

There is, and there always has been, and there always will be a sense in which there is no difference between Israel and any other nation—even enemy nations of the past and present such as the Philistines and the Syrians—and it is this, that the Lord is alike the Agent in every national history, every racial migration. In this regard it is no more a privilege to be an Israelite than to be a Hottentot. One Lord rules all, appointing the place they shall leave, the distance they shall move and the spot where they shall settle. The verse is not a statement of denial (You are no longer my people in the sense you once were) but of affirmation: You along with all other peoples are equally and in precisely the same sense subject to My sovereign decrees.

In context, this is addressed to the complacency which pretended godliness while caring only for self. We can best illustrate it this way. There used to be a song, very popular in its day, which said 'And man shall live for evermore because of Christmas day'. Now, stated like that, this is simply not true. The mere fact of a date on the calendar, a change of enumeration from BC to AD, a wondrous birth in a stable—this by itself does not guarantee eternal life to anybody, let alone, as the song said, to everybody. Clearly the people of Amos' day were treating the Exodus like that. There was a date in their calendar, a big event in their past and they were living in the bland assumption that something which God did in the ancestral past put Him eternally on their side and they on His. Not a bit of it, says the Lord, every nation has a date like that in its past. Sometime, somewhere, they have all had national migrations and the Lord is responsible for each and every one of them in precisely the same sense as He brought Israel out of Egypt.

This is not, of course, to say that history does not matter. It matters tremendously. The Exodus can confer no benefit at all on Israel if it never happened, and if they associate benefits with an unreal event, the benefits partake of exactly the same unreality. Just as for us, if benefits are associated, say, with the resurrection of Jesus and He never in fact rose, then the benefits are phoney, we are deceived and still in our sins (cf. 1 Cor. 15:17). History is vitally important as an underwriting of truth, but the historical fact, the date on the calendar, does not make spiritual alterations in individual lives whereby they can say: 'I was born on this side of the Exodus and therefore I must of necessity possess certain benefits.' They can say 'Therefore I may possess them', but that is a different story. The Exodus as a historical fact enshrines no more of God than does the coming of the Philistines from Caphtor or the Syrians from Kir and no more brings automatic benefit than do those other divinely engineered events. A historical act of God can by His will become a means of blessing but does not ever of itself convey the blessing. In this sense the Israel of the Exodus is level pegging with the Philistines who came from Caphtor or the Ethiopians who, for all Amos tells us, never went anywhere!

One divine government rules all, and (8a) one moral providence observes all, and judges all. The Lord does not look on people in the light of their historical past but in the light of their moral present. Every nation is equally under this moral scrutiny. Again there is no difference between Israel and the nations. But once more let us stress that this is not a negative, as if to say, 'You do not possess the special relationship you once enjoyed.' Amos is not talking about privileges removed. It is positive: You stand where you have always stood, alongside every other kingdom, subject to the moral enquiry of a holy and all-seeing God. Again, therefore, there is no benefit gained by appeal to the remote and historical past. The Lord says, I am not looking for a lesson in history, I am examining the facts of life and character. And at this point, as Amos has already taught (3:2), Israel is in fact worse off than any of the nations, for alone (and thanks to the Exodus, indeed) Israel had been taught how sinners might become aware of their sin, through the law of God, and be cleansed from their sin through the grace of God in the blood sacrifices.

The Israel within Israel

We can now take our study on to verses 8b–10. We observe first the pledge which God makes: *I will not utterly destroy the house of Jacob* (8b). This, of course, is what we should expect from the teaching of the total context, for this part of Amos began with the repeated assurance that the mind of God was set against any total destruction of His people (7:1–6). It is what we should expect from the immediate context, for we were not able to consider verse 8a without recalling that the Exodus set before the people the possibility of living conformably to a holy God and surely we might expect that some would do so and would pass the plumb-line test? It is what we would expect of a sovereign God whose name is Yahweh: though He must sovereignly judge, can He fail sovereignly to save? It stands to reason in every way that He will not utterly destroy the house of Jacob. There will ever be a remnant according to grace.

Secondly, there is the sifting which God makes: *I will . . . shake the house of Israel among all the nations as one shakes with a sieve, but* (and) *no pebble shall fall upon the earth* (9). The sieve, like the plumb-line in another context, is an instrument of discrimination. It gathers out impurities and leaves intact that which passes the grade. *No pebble* will remain. The *but* of RSV is interpretatively mistaken; the 'and' of NEB is correct. It is not the sieve's purpose to safeguard the pebbles but to cast them off, leaving the purged soil. So the Lord purposes to deal with His people: tossed they shall be, but it is purposeful, discriminatory and purgative.

In the third place, there is the distinction which God makes (10). If God were to say simply *All the sinners of my people shall die*, then indeed commentators would be right who see in Amos the end of the covenant relationship. For none could survive that test. But, in context, it would not be the test of a sieve! For the very use by the Lord of the metaphor of sieving implies that there are not only impurities to be purged out but good soil to be safeguarded. Thus His edict is not against sinners as such, but against one particular category of sinner: *who say, 'Evil shall not overtake or meet us'.* These look into the past and they see nothing to make them alarmed, nothing in their past to give rise to a calamitous judgment from God to overtake or catch up with them. Likewise, they look into the future and find no cause for alarm: there is no calamity rushing to meet them. They are sinners, but they are not aware that sin constitutes a threat or needs a remedy. They are sinners, but they think nothing of the law of God before which they stand condemned nor of the grace of God by which they could be redeemed. They are complacent, careless sinners living in a world of pretence and make-believe.

By contrast, what of the Israel within Israel? How would they be distinguished? The true people of God is a company of sinners bearing the mark of moral and spiritual concern. They know about the sieve and are concerned to be found making the grade; they know about the plumb-line and are concerned ever to hold their sinful selves within the compass of grace and to live lives conformably to law. They will remain sinners, but they will ever be sinners longing to war a good warfare against their sin, longing for holiness, loving the law of their God and resting on His grace. And they will be found worthy. The war which rages against pretence, fought with all the power of divine omnipotence, never hurts a hair of their heads.

Amos 9:11-15
The End of the Long Night

AMOS opened the third part of his book with the Lord saying 'no' to the thought of the total destruction of His people (7:1-6); he concludes with the divine 'never' which promises eternal inheritance of the possession He purposes to give them (9:15). The opening passage by implication commits the Lord God to discriminatory judgments—the judgment of the plumb-line (7:7-9)—but the concluding passage takes us beyond the moment of discrimination (9:9) to the glories that lie in wait for those who have lived conformably to the law and the grace of God, the people of obedience and repentance. In this oracle of surpassing beauty and attractiveness, Amos deals with five cardinal features of the coming day of the Lord: the king (11), the nations (12), the earth (13), the people (14) and the land (15).

The king: the end of the eclipse

The prophets gazed forward into the future in the light of what appeared to them the golden features of the past. Ezekiel the priest saw a perfect priestly system (Ezk. 40-48); Hosea, the man who loved hiᵉ wife, saw a perfect marriage (Ho. 2:14 ff.). But the hope which gripped more minds than any other was the ful-filment of the Davidic ideal. It was these Jerusalem traditions which excited Amos, the prophet from Tekoa in Judah.[1]

[1] The Davidic ideal in fact runs right throughout the prophetic literature, figuring even in prophets who also entertain other, dove-tailing, hopes. *E.g.* Is. 1:26; 9:1-7; 11:1 ff.; 55:3; Je. 23:5; 33:14 ff.; Ezk. 34:23 ff.; 37:24, 25; Ho. 3:5 (*cf.* 1:11); *etc.* Prophets of Judah, Israel and of the Exile all unite to foresee the coming David. The two sections of the people of God, Judah and Israel, went into captivity separately, but the prophets never

The expression Amos uses is interesting and somewhat unusual: *the booth of David* (11). In much of its usage in the Old Testament 'booth' signifies that which is flimsy or temporary, or that which offers shade but no protection. Some commentators have therefore seen in the phrase *the booth of David* a symbol of that which in itself can only collapse, but which in the hand of God will become glorious and strong. This may well be so, and it certainly fits in with the emphasis which the four verbs of verse 11 place on the activity of the Lord as the sole Agent in total restoration, lifting the fallen (11a), mending the broken (11b), replacing the destroyed (11c) and reviving the glories of the past (11d). But, while retaining all this note of divine action, and indeed without contradicting the correct notion that the monarchy of David was from the start doomed by the sinfulness of its founder and that nothing but the hand of God could raise it to glory, *booth* is mostly used in the Old Testament in connection with the Feast of Booths, and this would be an extremely significant thought in context. It was at the counterfeit of the Feast of Booths that Jeroboam I stood at the altar (1 Ki. 12:32), deliberately mimicking the feast held in Judah one month earlier (Lv. 23:33, 34). This indicates that Booths was a feast at which the king took a central place, acting out his role as middleman between the Lord and the people, possibly even fulfilling his function as the priest after the order of Melchizedek.[2] Along this line of thought, the raising up of *the booth of David* signifies the bringing in of the perfect royal Mediator, the king who will be everything that was ever wished for in a royal priest. This very much fits in with the use of *booth* (RSV *pavilion*) in Isaiah

---

envisage separate returns from captivity and in the Messianic future they see one people under one divine King.

[2] This cannot be more than a surmise, but it offers a fruitful line of thought. Jos. 10:1 names the king of Jerusalem Adoni-zedek, a name of exactly the same formation and meaning as Melchi-zedek (Gn. 14:18 ff.). It is a reasonable supposition that when David captured Jerusalem (2 Sa. 5:6 ff.) he found the royal priesthood of Melchizedek still intact and functioning there. His own traditions would tell him that this priesthood had been recognized by Abram as a valid priesthood of Yahweh, and it would have been automatic for him to accept for himself the role of the Melchizedek priest. This would explain his expectation that the Davidic Messiah would fulfil this role (Ps. 110), and is the perfect background to the Melchizedek priesthood of Jesus, born of David's line in the tribe of Judah.

4:5, 6, where, overshadowed by the cloud and fire signifying God's own presence, it will provide a place of refuge and refreshment. Isaiah 32:1, 2 links this with the reign of the Messianic king. The conjunction of these three lines of thought concerning *the booth of David* is that by the act of God a king will reign whose mediatorial work will be fully acceptable to the Lord and whose presence will bring safety and refreshment to his people.[3]

The nations: the end of the separation

Messianic hope in the Old Testament is essentially universal, as one would expect, seeing that its roots are the divine promises especially to Eve (Gn. 3:15) and Abram (Gn. 12:1 ff.).[4] Amos is no exception. He sees the nations involved in the privileges of the reign of the new David (12). Three questions will help us to appreciate what he is teaching: Why is Edom singled out?

[3] The idea of the *fallen* booth has given rise to much controversy. Those who see here the final fall of the Davidic monarchy when Jerusalem was taken by the Babylonians in 586 BC usually wish to date Amos 9:11-15 after that date, *e.g.* Mays. If this is done it becomes an exceptionally tricky problem to explain why such a passage became attached to the book of Amos. Those who hold Amos to be a prophet without a message of hope say that a later editor attached this passage to adapt Amos' message to his own day. But, in point of fact, he would not be adapting but contradicting! He would be exposing Amos as a false prophet who threatened a wholesale disaster which had not in fact happened. On the other hand, if the attachment of an oracle of hope is justified on the ground that Amos' message is not without hope, then there is no good reason for denying the passage to Amos himself. If others could see the relevance, why should he be thought so temperamentally cussed as to exclude all brightness from the future? But could Amos have spoken of a *fallen booth* prior to 586 BC? Since he has predicted the coming of fire on Jerusalem (2:5) and seen in Zion the same destructive complacency as in Samaria (6:1), is it too much to believe that he took his own prophecies seriously and then looked beyond them to a hope yet to come? Of course, the *fallen booth* may look back to the time of the great schism of the northern tribes under Jeroboam I. This lived in the memory of monarchists in Judah as a time of supreme tragedy (*cf.* Is. 7:17). If this is the meaning there is no chronological problem in attributing the oracle to Amos. Alternatively (though this is far less likely) the words may mean 'the falling booth', referring to the present, and foreseeable, decrepit and tottering condition of the Davidic dynasty.

[4] *Cf.* NBD, art. 'Messiah'.

What privilege is specified by the words *called by my name*? And what does the word *possess* mean?

Edom was used symbolically by the prophets as an embodiment of the hostility of the world to the kingdom of God. This was in keeping with its attitude from the first (*cf.* Nu. 20:14) to the last (*cf.* Am. 1:11). The overthrow of Edom therefore speaks of a real and complete end of all opposition. But it also speaks of the presence and power of the new David, for alone of the kings David had conquered and held Edom (2 Sa. 8:14). Thus when *Edom* falls, all worldly opposition is clearly and finally ended, and the second and greater David will certainly have arrived. The fall of Edom is one of the signs of the Messiah.

But the stress in this verse does not lie on overthrow but on incorporation. To be sure, in keeping with the general run of prediction, Amos speaks of *the remnant of Edom*. The great battle has taken place (*cf.* Is. 34) leaving only a remnant. But Amos does not dwell on this. Edom and *all the nations* are *called by my name*. Isaiah 4:1 shows that this is a piece of marriage terminology. It therefore speaks of intimate oneness. Genesis 48:16 uses it of the adoption of two boys from the status of grandsons to that of sons. In Deuteronomy 28:9, 10 and Jeremiah 15:16 it speaks of the special relationship—and the fruits of that relationship—as enjoyed by the people of God themselves. In 1 Kings 8:43 and elsewhere it is applied to the house built for God by Solomon and with which He was graciously pleased to identify Himself. And now all this is to apply to *the nations*. In other words, at last *the Gentiles are fellow heirs, members of the same body, and partakers of the promise in Christ Jesus through the gospel* (Eph. 3:6).

But at first sight the verb *possess* seems an odd choice if Amos has in mind to express a relationship of equality of privilege. If we trace the thought of being 'called by the name' back to its origin in Old Testament practice we find that it was the way in which credit was taken for some particular conquest. Thus Joab summoned David to the fall of Rabbah of Ammon *lest I take the city, and it be called by my name* (2 Sa. 12:28). We have thus in Amos 9:12 a complex of thoughts. The verb *possess* signifies a conquest. The people of God demonstrate a superior power. But the conquest is followed by an equality of citizenship in that it is not their name but the name of their God by which the

Gentiles are called. What the Old Testament thus saw in its own terms as military expansion, the New Testament, following the lead of Jesus who said, *If my kingship were of this world, my servants would fight* (Jn. 18:36), teaches us to see as the missionary expansion of the church. At the Council of Jerusalem James used this very passage of Amos as scriptural justification for the decision that the Gentiles were eligible for co-equal membership in the things of the Lord Jesus (Acts 15:12-19). Clearly, missionary expansion involves a submission followed by an equality. The convert must use some terminology involving recognition that truth has replaced his earlier falsehoods, forgiveness has replaced guiltiness, peace with God has replaced fear and dread of the tomb, power has replaced helplessness, and that he has come into all these benefits and blessings by submitting to the truth as declared to him by someone else.[5] In these terms, then, Amos has a world-wide vision. The particularity of the people of the covenant is preserved by the verb *possess*: the people of God are ever distinct in their privileges but are intent to make those privileges the common, equal experience of all who will obey the gospel.

The earth: the end of the curse

If the Messiah is the second David, He is also the second Adam reigning in a restored Eden. We have already noted that this is the idea behind all the passages which speak of the natural bounty of the Messianic kingdom. Amos shares in this hope also. The terms of his vision are plain: the earth will yield a lavish and spontaneous abundance. It will be so lavish that the time available will not suffice to gather in either the corn crops or the vintage. In each case the sower of seed for the next crop will find the reaper of the last crop still at work. The abundance will be so lavish that it will seem as if the very mountains and hills are themselves oozing with *sweet wine* (13).

The significance of this is very wonderful. It has sometimes been said or implied that there is a tension between the thought of Amos, with his emphasis on righteousness and on keeping up standards in conduct and character, and the thought of this

[5] *Cf.* Rom. 10:3; 15:18; 16:26, *etc.*

verse with its frank delight in the good things of the earth.[6] But
the frame of reference of this prediction is that provided by
Genesis 2 and 3, or Deuteronomy 28 and 29. The very physical
fabric and potencies of nature partake of the holy character of
the God who made them. They go into revolt and reverse when
man perverts his relationship with their Creator. When, therefore,
the adversity of nature is gone, and all the powers of nature are
operating in favour of man and for his enrichment, this is not,
and in the Bible cannot be, any sort of purely materialistic
Golden Age. It means that basic spiritual and moral realities
have been put to rights. All is well between God and man. On
man's side the rebellion is over, on God's side there has been a
great reconciliation and the whole creation is liberated and its
energies 'pent up for the centuries during which sin abounded
and death reigned, . . . explode in one triumphant burgeoning as
nature hastens to lay its tribute at the feet of Him whose right
it is to reign' (NBCR, p. 741). The curse is gone (Gn. 3:17, 18) and
Eden is restored.

The people: the end of disappointment and frustration

The theme of verse 14 is different from that of verse 13, even
though the terminology and basic thoughts are the same. Verse
13 points to abundance; 14 to the enjoyment of it by the people.
We will feel the force of this by comparing it with 5:11. There the
people *built houses . . . but shall not dwell in them . . . have planted
vineyards, but . . . shall not drink their wine*. That is to say, they set
out to achieve security (houses) and satisfaction (vineyards) but
they are disappointed in their hope and frustrated in their aims.
The reason is that their life of social carelessness is at war with

---

[6] Edghill (*Westminster Commentary*) cannot see how the prophet of righteousness could delight in this way in a merely worldly prosperity. Cripps fails
to see how Amos could have presented a picture of this glowing future without stressing the repentance on which alone in his teaching it would come
about. Of course, Cripps is the author of his own problem here in insisting
on severing these verses from the prophecy of Amos. In other words, he
first severs them from what Amos teaches and then complains that they do not
contain that teaching! IB, while holding the verses to be a later addition, sensibly recognizes that they now belong to the Amos-corpus and must not be
thought to teach the coming of a golden age except on conditions which
Amos could accept.

their personal ambitions and desires. Sin brings disappointment and frustration. But as Amos looks forward he sees the day when the power of sin will be destroyed. It will no longer blight, disappoint and frustrate the people. It is 5:11 in reverse: houses shall be built and inhabited; vineyards planted and enjoyed.

The land: the end of insecurity

Amos 9:11-15 falls into two sections. In verses 11, 12 we saw the king and the kingdom; in 13-15 the theme is life and liberty within the kingdom, the experience of its citizens. In this connection Amos has shown us two things: these are people who have been delivered from the presence of sin: the curse has been removed (13) and throughout the whole realm of God nature flaunts the fact that sin is gone; secondly, these are people who have been delivered from the power of sin, for their lives are never now blighted by the frustration of their hopes. What they plan they achieve. No alien force can rob them of their prize.

There is one final truth about the citizens of the kingdom: they are set free from the penalty of sin. They cannot ever be robbed of their inheritance (15). The land is theirs for ever. This is not typology; it is one of the facts of Old Testament history that the inheritance is lost by sin. Let the people play false with their God and they lose the land which He gave to them (*cf.* Dt. 28:58-68). But if they cannot now lose the land for ever, why, then, the penalty of sin has been lifted and they will never again feel the weight of it. How it must have rejoiced Amos, who wrestled and wrestled again with the doctrine of the security of the people of God, to write this last word in his book!

Yet it is not quite the last word. To promise eternal security is one thing, to guarantee it is another. Can he, and they, and we be absolutely certain that the time will come when the king will reign over a world-wide company, when sin's presence, power and penalty will have been removed from the scene, when abundance, satisfaction and security will be the order of the day? Is it not too idealistic to be real, too good to be true, too impossible ever to be achieved? No, because this is not a vision of what would be ideal, nor even an aspiration after it, but a pledge from God that it will happen. Amos opened his book with *the words of Amos* (1:1); he ends with *says the Lord your God.* For the second time only in his tripartite message he uses the words 'your God' (*cf.* 4:12). What do they mean? It would be true enough to say that they speak of our commitment to Him, whereby we might say that we have taken the Lord to be 'our God' (*cf.* Dt. 26:17), but that is not faithful enough to the theme of this section. It was not man who in 7:1–6 declared that the edict of total destruction had been disannulled. It was God. And at the end it is God who commits Himself to raise up the king in his kingdom (9:11), to restore the fortunes of His people (14) and plant them with eternal security in their inheritance (15). *Says your God*—the God who has committed Himself to you!

It is not out of the question. Nothing could be more certain, more realistic to hope for. The day will come when He will reign and sin will be no more, for *God is not man, that he should lie, or a son of man, that he should repent. Has he said, and will he not do it? Or has he spoken, and will he not fulfil it?* (Nu. 23:19).

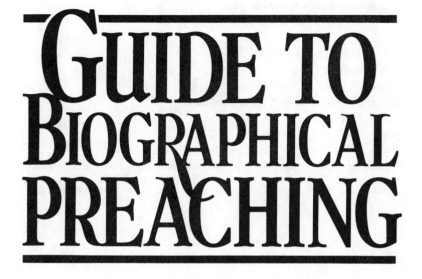

ROY E. DE BRAND

BROADMAN PRESS
Nashville, Tennessee

© Copyright 1988 • Broadman Press
All Rights Reserved
4221-19
ISBN: 0-8054-2119-X
Dewey Decimal Classification: 251
Subject Heading: PREACHING
Library of Congress Catalog Number: 87-37487
Printed in the United States of America

To my mother-in-law
Lou,
And in memory of my father-in-law
Buford,
Whose love and faithfulness rival
Many of the people of the Bible.

Contents

Contents

Preface

This book was born out of necessity. In the fall of 1984, my second year of teaching homiletics, I was scheduled to teach a course entitled "Preaching on Bible Characters." I had taken such a course from Jesse J. Northcutt at Southwestern Seminary. It was a blessing to me then and subsequently, I wanted to teach biographical preaching to my students. In preparation for teaching it, I discovered there was no textbook available. The book we used as a text with Dr. Northcutt, Faris Whitesell's *Preaching on Bible Characters,* was out of print and had been for several years. Andrew Blackwood's *Biographical Preaching for Today,* of the same vintage as Whitesell's, was also out of print. I knew Dr. Northcutt still taught biographical preaching at Southwestern, so I phoned him. "I don't use a textbook," he told me, "there's nothing in print."

"Why don't you write one?" I asked.

"No, I'm too old. Why don't you?"

So I did.

Dr. Northcutt gave me carte blanche permission to use notes I took in his class and some other good suggestions. I am deeply indebted to this man of God.

The purpose of this book is to guide preachers, whether beginners or veterans, into the rich and rewarding field of biographical preaching. I consider it in some ways an extension and update of the work of Whitesell and Blackwood, as you will see when you read. My work is not a revision of theirs but a new version of similar subjects with my own touches added. I am indebted to them likewise.

Please regard this book in its entirety as suggestive, not exhaustive. Hopefully it will either open some new ground or replow some fallow fields for all who read it. My feelings wouldn't be hurt if it became a textbook for college and/or seminary preaching courses. This, too, is a reason for writing it. But it need not be limited to beginning preachers. I would have enjoyed having a book like this at any point along my nearly seventeen years of pastoral ministry in local churches. I hope active pastors, seasoned pros of preaching, will find it helpful and encouraging.

As I write this I realize I am a debtor, not only to Northcutt, Whitesell, and Blackwood already mentioned but also to my family for their encouraging support. When I would walk into the house after a long day of writing and announce the completion of another chapter, their cheers were uplifting. I am indebted to the administration and faculty of North American Baptist Seminary in Sioux Falls, South Dakota, for time and trust to write; to Donna Fodness, secretary to the faculty at NABS, for typing all this. It's most appropriate for me to acknowledge that I write as debtor. Thank you to each person who has contributed to my work and life.

As your biography is written daily, may it be enriched by studying and preaching on the lives of Bible characters.

—*Roy E. De Brand*

1
What Is Biographical Preaching?

Preaching on Bible characters is one of the most exciting and rewarding of all the ways to preach. But before we can preach biographically, get too excited about it, or reap its rich rewards, we need a basic understanding of its nature and what there is about it that should excite and reward us. Such an understanding is gained by looking at some classical and contemporary definitions and dimensions of biographical preaching. What is it?

Classical Definition and Dimensions

The nature of biographical preaching was best described by the prolific Andrew W. Blackwood when he wrote, "The biographical sermon . . . grows out of the facts concerning a biblical character, as these facts throw light upon the problems of the man in the pew."[1] This definition deals with two important dimensions of biographical preaching.

Two Dimensions of Biographical Preaching

First, it's based on the revealed truth of God's Word about a person.—This is what Blackwood called "the facts concerning a biblical character." These are the facts given in the Bible. They're based on the historical manifestation of actual events, often with interpretive information supplied by the biblical author. These facts give insight to the person who is their subject. The people of the Bible were real. They lived in a cultural, social, political, geographical, and temporal context. Careful study and interpretation reveals the "facts concerning a biblical character," and from these facts we develop the biographical sermon. Bible-centered biography is the matrix of this sermon category.

The second dimension of Blackwood's definition deals with the contemporary significance or applicability of biographical preaching.—The meaning of the Bible isn't isolated in history. From the revealed facts about Bible people comes interpretation casting light, meeting needs, and speaking head-on to the problems of persons in the pews today. The revealed truth about Bible people reveals truth for our own lives. Relevance is the hallmark of biographical preaching.

Without both dimensions present there can be no biographical sermon. Both are essential to the nature of preaching on Bible characters. Otherwise it may be a Bible study unapplied or a contemporary problem explored and exposed, but it takes revealed truth about a Bible character addressing current needs to be a biographical sermon.

Halford Luccock, Yale's master of sermon creativity, underscored these two basic dimensions of biographical preaching when he wrote:

> The characters of the Old Testament and the New walk our streets; their temperaments and problems are ours; and the way they meet them, for good or evil, comes close to us when brought close by the preacher. . . . The people of the Bible are all about us in modern clothes; they are the most effective instruments on which the preacher can lay his hands.[2]

Our Definition and Dimensions

Our contemporary working definition is based on this classical understanding of the nature of biographical preaching and its two dimensions. Biographical preaching is the use of the Bible for sermons that interpret the life or some aspect of the life of a biblical person for contemporary significance.

Bible Based

This means the biographical sermon must be Bible based. It interprets the biblical material about the person selected to discover the unique meaning, character, personality, strengths, weaknesses, attitudes, motivations, significance, or some other aspect of his or her life. The biographical preacher should stay with the biblical material. Let the sermon develop from the text as directly and naturally as possible. Don't use the Bible as a springboard to preach your own ideas. Interpret, don't interpolate! The biblical material on the person you are dealing with should dictate the direction and development of your sermon.

Your text for the sermon, then, is composed of the biblical material about the person you're preaching on, whether it's a single passage or two or more. You obviously would not read as part of your sermon every verse in the Bible on Moses or Paul if you were preaching a whole life biographical sermon on one of them. You would summarize or narrate multipassages into a brief, easy-to-handle text. The true text, however, would indeed encompass all the biblical material on the person, even though you wouldn't actually "read the text" to your congregation. In a direct biblical sermon the substance and development of the sermon comes from and follows the order of the text regardless of its length or location(s). It uses the Scripture in the sermon with the same meaning and purpose it had in its scriptural setting.[3] The text controls the sermon. We will deal in more detail with how to do this in chapters 5 and 6.

Person Centered

Our working definition also means the biographical sermon is person centered. It primarily deals with the *person* in Scripture and only secondarily with events, ideas, or other circumstances. It may be based on the person's entire life (all that's recorded in the Bible) or only a portion of that life. It may focus on some unique aspect, contribution, or characteristic of the person. This will be discussed in a later chapter.

Obviously, there's more in the Bible about some persons than others. You wouldn't want to preach a six-week series on Tertius (Rom. 16:22) or Demas (Philem. 24, Col. 4:14, 2 Tim. 4:10), but you could easily preach that long or longer on Abraham or Simon Peter. Neither would you want to overlook the interesting possibilities of a single sermon on all the Bible has to say about a minor character. Harry Emerson Fosdick preached a wonderful New Year's sermon entitled: "The Power to See it Through," based on the three New Testament references to Demas.[4] And F. B. Meyer preached twenty-one sermons on Joseph, twenty-eight about Moses, twenty-one on Paul, to name but a few series he did on major characters.[5] So the possibilities for biographical sermons are as numerous as there are people mentioned in the Bible, major and minor, named or unnamed. The fact that there are virtually unlimited biblical resources for biographical sermons should be exciting to busy, idea-seeking preachers. This is the good news inherent in the nature of biographical preaching.

Objective of Biographical Sermons

The objective of biographical preaching is to bring life to people today in light of the lives of people in the Bible. This objective is reached by matching contemporary needs to Bible persons who shed light on our needs. Whether the major objective of a particular sermon is evangelistic, consecrative, devotional, doctrinal, ethical, or supportive, it can be reached through biographical preaching.[6] Someone in the Bible addresses or exemplifies each need we have in our lives. Once the need is seen in the lives of our people, or the preacher discovers the need is addressed in the life of the Bible character, the major and specific objective for the sermon becomes clear. This gives the sermon focus, purpose, and clarity for direction of development.

Origination from Biblical Material

Sometimes ideas for biographical sermons originate from the biblical material. Let's say you are reading devotionally from the Bible, or just reading it casually, or maybe you're doing an in-depth study of a particular passage. All of a sudden it occurs to you the passage has something to say to your congregation from the life of a character in the passage. You go from text to need. This is the best way to begin a biographical sermon.

Origination from Congregational Needs

At other times, biographical sermon ideas begin when you perceive a need in your congregation and go to the Bible to look for a character who somehow meets or addresses the contemporary need. Maybe the Bible person faced a similar situation to the one(s) occasioning the current need. Or maybe the Bible character exemplified the extreme opposite attitude to the one you need to address, and you preach a positive lesson from a negative example. With this method you go from need to text. Be very careful, though, that the text really addresses the need in some way. Never superimpose a meaning onto a text. Both text and need have to say the same thing to be valid for a biblical sermon. If they don't match, then stick with the idea and find a true text for it, or chuck the idea and preach the text. Don't strain to achieve an unnatural connection between text and idea. There are too many good combinations to have to force ideas upon the Bible.

For every contemporary need there is likely a parallel in the Bible. So, whether you begin with a text speaking to a need or go from a need to a text, you can end up with a direct biblical, biographical sermon to meet a pressing need in the lives of your hearers. The creative combinations are endless! This, too, is reason for the preacher to celebrate, as it's one of the rewards of biographical preaching.

Interesting and Rewarding

Biographical preaching can be interesting and rewarding for both preacher and listener. It can address human need on an identifiable level as few other types of sermons can. It offers a unique variety of sermonic purpose and form. Some of the greatest preachers have used it effectively as a major method. C. C. Roach summarized the nature of biographical preaching well when he wrote:

> In the Bible . . . there is this wealth of biographical material waiting to be preached. It is as we bring to life again the personalities of the Bible that we make the ideas,

for which they lived and died, live again for our congregation also. This is the opportunity and task of the preacher.[7]

The nature of biographical preaching is Bible based and person centered. By its very nature it is of great value and importance to the preacher. We turn our attention next to some specific values to excite and reward those who choose to use this homiletical variety.

Notes

1. Andrew W. Blackwood, *Preaching from the Bible* (New York: Abingdon-Cokesbury Press, 1941), p. 52. A similar definition is given in Blackwood's *Biographical Preaching for Today* (New York: Abingdon Press, 1954), p. 17.

2. Halford E. Luccock, *In the Minister's Workshop* (New York: Abingdon-Cokesbury Press, 1944), pp. 156-157.

3. H. C. Brown, *A Quest for Reformation in Preaching* (Waco: Word Books, 1968), p. 71.

4. Harry Emerson Fosdick, *Riverside Sermons* (New York: Harper & Row, 1958), pp. 28-37.

5. Meyer was a prolific preacher of biographical sermons, widely published. Fleming H. Revell published volumes by Meyer on Abraham, David, Elijah, Israel, John, Joseph, Joshua, Moses, Paul, etc. Marshall, Morgan & Scott of London published Meyer on Peter and other characters. Other publishers issued or reissued his biographical sermons. A few minutes in the author's card files of a good theological library will reveal a gold mine of Meyer materials.

6. H. C. Brown, H. Gordon Clinard, and Jesse J. Northcutt, *Steps to the Sermon* (Nashville: Broadman Press, 1963), pp. 16-18.

7. Corwin C. Roach, *Preaching Values in the Bible* (Louisville, Ky.: Cloister Press, 1946), p. 123.

2
Why Do It?

Once we understand the nature of biographical preaching perhaps our next questions are: "Why do it? What are the values of biographical preaching?" This chapter will explore why biographical preaching should be a major plank in every preacher's platform by looking at seven major values of biographical preaching. There are many reasons to preach on Bible characters.

Coincides with the Nature of the Bible

The first and foremost value of biographical preaching is the fact that it coincides with the nature of the Bible. The Bible is a book about God's dealings with people.

Person Centered

The Bible is person centered. It's aimed at the constructive meeting of human needs. Yes, there are great ideas and significant events in the Bible, but for the most part they're presented in the context of the lives of real people. The Bible is about how people dealt with their circumstances. Some overcame. Others were overcome. We can learn from them all. Therefore, the Bible has much to teach us about facing our circumstances, whatever they may be. And one great way to communicate these biblical truths to people in need is through biographical preaching.

Abundant Material

Since the Bible is primarily concerned with God's relationship with people and vice versa, it abounds with biographical materials begging to be preached. From Adam in the garden to the victorious Christ in New Jerusalem, people occupy the pages of God's Word. This fact is borne out in Faris D. Whitesell's bench-mark book of three decades ago: *Preaching on Bible Characters.*[1] In his sixth chapter, Whitesell listed "every name of any significance in the Bible."[2] There are at least 433 listed. Most are named, whether major or minor characters. Some are unnamed, such as the two blind men of Matthew 9 and the three would-be disciples in Luke 9:57-62. Whitesell identified the relative importance of these Bible people by asterisks—no asterisk indicating minor importance (Abdon, Crispus, Enos, Korah, and so forth); one asterisk indicating medium importance (Abel, Bathsheba, Laban, and so forth); two asterisks indicating major importance (Gideon, Isaac, Luke, and so forth); and three asterisks indicating maximum importance (David, Moses, Peter, and so forth).

Five asterisks are reserved for Jesus, appropriately in a class by Himself. The list and indications of relative importance are helpful. Of the 433 characters, 241 were interpreted by Whitesell as being of minor importance, 109 of medium importance, 61 of major importance, and 21 of maximum importance. Then there's Jesus. In addition to their names, Whitesell gave the reference of where they're found in the Bible, and an identification of who they were (Abel*, Genesis 4, second son of Adam;

killed by Cain).[3] This is a very helpful index for biographical preaching. Whitesell wrote:

> Some of these persons are of such minor importance that a preacher would never preach on them unless he were looking for some singular trait or statement. But most of them can be the subject of profitable sermons, and a whole series of sermons can be preached about many of them.[4]

From this and other lists, and from our general Bible reading and knowledge, we can readily see the rich resources for biographical sermons the Bible provides, a strong reason to preach biographically.

People Like People

A second major reason to preach biographical sermons is because people are interested in people. This has always been true. We're interested in why and how people act, think, behave, feel, believe, and worship as they do. Because of this universal interest biographical preaching has human appeal. Your listeners will find it interesting and informative because it's about people much like themselves, removed only by time, not traits. Biographical preaching is interesting for the same reasons airports and malls are—the people in them! And it isn't only your listeners who will find character sermons fun. They are rewarding for the preacher, too. The people of the Bible were real people, and our task is to discover their realness and relate it to the realities we face and struggle to live with day by day. That should be interesting to anybody and exciting for both preacher and listener. People like people. This basic value of biographical preaching adds appeal to this way of preaching.

Identification with Real People and Needs

A third value of biographical preaching is that we can identify with the people of the Bible.

Bible People: Human and Real

They were very human and real, just like we are. Our problems today are like theirs were. They have something to say to us out of their experiences. These experiences range the whole gamut of human vices and victories, feelings and failures, faith and frustrations. There is no experience of the twentieth century that does not have some root of relationship to Bible people and their experiences. Properly interpreted, the Bible is a book of realism based on actual occurrences in the lives of people living long ago that can speak to real needs today. This makes biographical preaching an effective way to deal with the kinds of problems our people face.

Biblical Experiences Similar to Ours

We more easily identify with those who know what we are experiencing because they have experienced it themselves. And we more readily accept our faults and failures if we realize they are not ours exclusively. Bible characters represent for us people we can identify with as they illustrate to us timeless truths that relate to contemporary circumstances. Biographical preaching is relevant to real-life situations today. The truth of God's Word can be presented more effectively in the reality of human experience than in the realm of mere theory. We identify with flesh and blood more than with ideas, abstractions, and principles. We preachers need to hear our people say, "If you want me to understand something and relate to it, let me see it in real life. How did others deal with it?" When we *show* them, by using the real people of biblical history, they readily identify and are helped. People really do identify with others of similar plight. Because of this fact, biographical sermons can be especially relevant.

Easy to Prepare and Preach

The fourth major value of biographical preaching is also good news to busy pastors and preachers. Biographical sermons are relatively easy to prepare and preach! They are based on the oldest method of conveying truth—the story. Since such narration involves movement, characterization, setting, and sequence, it's more easily remembered by both preacher and listener. The preacher can be freer from notes than with other forms of preaching. This enhances eye contact, communication, and interest. These are compelling reasons to preach on Bible characters. Biographical sermons are not easy, but they are easier than some other kinds of sermons. With the resurgence of interest in narrative and inductive preaching in contemporary homiletical writing and study, there is an abundance of material to enhance the biographical preacher's style. Maybe the time saved preparing the actual sermon can be reinvested in the study of these forms of preaching.[5]

Tremendous Teaching Value

Fifth, biographical sermons should be preached because they have tremendous teaching value. They carry the automatic bonus of example. And who will deny the awesome power of human example? We learn from others. Sometimes the lessons are positive and we emulate them. Other times we learn what not to do, think, or say from the example of others. Often both positive and negative lessons can be learned from the same Bible character.

For example, we could benefit by learning from King David's noble deeds, high aspirations, and deep worship of God. We can also learn much about what to avoid from the examples of his terrible sins against Uriah and Bathsheba. Likewise we can learn from David's deep remorse and repentance for his sin (Ps. 51). Many aspects of these biblical characters lodge in each of us. Careful interpretation can lead them out to show us the way to live, or not to live as the case may be. Hold forth the virtues to be imitated and expose the vices to be eliminated by preaching the tremendous examples found in lives of Bible characters.

Variety

The sixth major value of biographical preaching is the infinite variety it offers. Sermons on Bible characters can be as varied as contemporary needs and their historical antecedents. You find every emotion, sin, problem, joy, pain, and scheme in persons in the Bible as you find in persons today. There's no end to the variety of biographical sermons. Preaching them is limited only by the preacher's stifled creativity, lack of effort, or inability to identify needs and answers to them. A later chapter will present types of biographical sermons. Suffice it to say here there can be an infinite variety of approaches.

The needs of your people vary. Biographical sermons can address them as needed. People in your congregation and people in the Bible are unique in personality. Biographical preaching allows you the variety to address this uniqueness. Such sermons can take many creative forms —narrative, first person, monologue, dialogue, talk backs, interview, sermon interruptions. Be imaginative! Variety is one of the abiding values of biographical preaching. Be creative. Discover your own varieties of biographical sermons.

How God Deals with People

Biographical sermons are valuable because they can show us how God deals with people. This is the seventh and final major value. We can learn about God by looking at how He related to the heroes, cowards, saints, sinners, faithful, and fickle folks of the Bible. We can find ourselves among them. How did God approach people? How did He deal with people in trying circumstances? How did He bring down the haughty? Elevate the downcast? As previously mentioned, we identify with real people and real needs. But what we can learn about God from these people and their experiences is of much more value than what we can learn about them or ourselves. Learning about God and how He relates to people in various circumstances is, in fact, the major value for us from preaching on Bible characters. No matter the human values or personal lessons, it all comes down to this: what does this tell me about God and my relationship to Him?

God Worked

One need in each biographical sermon is to interpret God's role in the life or experience of the Bible person. What was this person's relationship to God? Maybe it wasn't constant. What was it in various times, places, circumstances? How did it change? Why? When? Or did it remain the same?

We must get back into the text to figure out God's role in the past. This involves the application of the historical, language, and theological hermeneutical principles. It also requires the interpreter to listen to the text to hear what is in it, to see its truths, and to move from ancient truth and experience to contemporary need in a direct and clear way. Only when we accurately and adequately exegete a text can we determine how God worked in people, with people, and for people in the past. Until we understand that, we can't understand God's dealings with people, with *us,* today.[6]

God Works

When we clearly see how God worked in His dealings with people in the past, we can cross the hermeneutical bridge to how God deals with people today. God works in people's lives. How He does so involves the theological and practical hermeneutical principles. We must interpret God's dealings with us and our congregations, based on how He dealt with others in the past. The same principles apply. It's an exciting adventure, and a basic value of biographical preaching, to determine that God still works, and how God works in our lives. Making this discovery is one of the richest rewards of biographical preaching, for both preacher and listener.

Values Suggested by Others

Obviously the seven values of biographical preaching discussed in this chapter thus far aren't the only values of this form. Helpful insights exist for us from several other sources.

Caldwell

In his book: *Preaching Angles,* Frank H. Caldwell devoted one chapter to "biographical and autobiographical angles."[7] The approaches he suggested offer further values of biographical preaching. He pointed out the benefits of sermons on Bible characters dealing with their psychological foundations, character development, virtues to be emulated, faults to be avoided, resolution of conflicts, exhibiting common relationships in an uncommon way, and diversity in unity as a series theme.[8] He also presented a brief section on the "autobiographical angle," or first-person biographical sermon.[9] He gave helpful illustrations of each of these types or approaches to biographical preaching, extolling the virtues of their value.

Whitesell

Whitesell gave fifteen "advantages of Bible character sermons" in chapter 1 of *Preaching on Bible Characters.* Each of them points to the value of biographical preaching. Summarized, these advantages are:

1. Perhaps the easiest way to preach the Bible.
2. Appeal to people.
3. Bible people illustrate truths applicable to life today.
4. Arouse interest in Bible reading.
5. Develops preacher's imagination and dramatic abilities.
6. Abstract doctrines can be taught against realistic background.
7. Search for sermon illustrations is lessened.
8. Variety.
9. Holds preacher to Bible and helps him know it better.
10. Provides material for other sermons.
11. Freshness.
12. Patterns after divine example.
13. Remembered longer.
14. Gives indirect approach to difficult subjects.
15. Fitting for special occasions and audiences.[10]

Great Preachers Were Biographical

To this extensive list and the values already indicated in this chapter, one more advantage should be added. All the great preachers have preached on Bible characters. Many voices that once rang out great biographical sermons are silent now: Clarence E. Macartney, Clovis G. Chappell, F. B. Meyer, George W. Truett, F. W. Robertson, and Alexander Whyte. But their biographical sermons live on in print, still widely read (and no doubt plagiarized) today. They are mute testimony to the value of biographical preaching.

Today's Best Are Biographical

Many of today's best known preachers preach about Bible characters frequently: Charles Swindoll, Stuart Briscoe, Billy Graham, Robert Schuller, James Cleland, and Frederick Speakman. Many people have come to know Christ through biographical preaching through the ages and today. Thousands more were enriched for living. The same results must be our goals. They can be achieved by realizing and utilizing the rich values available through biographical preaching.

Notes

1. Faris D. Whitesell, *Preaching on Bible Characters* (Grand Rapids: Baker Book House, 1955).
2. Ibid., pp. 123-136.
3. Ibid., p. 123.
4. Ibid.
5. On the current interest in narrative preaching see Alton H. McEachern, "Narrative Preaching" in James C. Barry, comp., *Preaching in Today's World* (Nashville: Broadman Press, 1984), pp. 151-164; Frederick Buechner, *Telling the Truth* (New York: Harper & Row, 1977); Richard A. Jensen, *Telling the Story* (Minneapolis: Augsburg, 1980); Eugene L. Lowry, *Doing Time in the Pulpit*

(Nashville: Abingdon, 1985); H. Stephen Shoemaker, *Retelling the Biblical Story* (Nashville: Broadman Press, 1985); and Edmund A. Steimle, Morris J. Niedenthal, and Charles L. Rice, *Preaching the Story* (Philadelphia: Fortress Press, 1980); among others. The works of Fred Craddock, *As One Without Authority* (Nashville: Abingdon, 1983), and *Overhearing the Gospel* (Nashville: Abingdon, 1978), are in the forefront of the interest on inductive preaching. See also Ralph L. Lewis and Gregg Lewis, *Inductive Preaching* (Westchester, Ill.: Crossway Books, 1983), among others. Richard Eslinger's *A New Hearing* (Nashville: Abingdon, 1987) deals with both narrative and inductive methods.

6. See Charles Rice, "Shaping Sermons by the Interplay of Text and Metaphor," in Don M. Wardlaw, ed., *Preaching Biblically* (Philadelphia: Westminster Press, 1983), pp. 103-105.

7. Frank H. Caldwell, *Preaching Angles* (Nashville: Abingdon Press, 1954), pp. 49-72.

8. Ibid., pp. 49-70.

9. Ibid., pp. 70-72.

10. Whitesell, pp. 13-22.

3
Some Dangers of Biographical Preaching

The popularity and ease of both preaching and hearing biographical sermons should raise a small red flag of concern in several vital areas. Biographical preaching has its dangers. Here are seven suggested things to beware of.

Ease

Beware of not taking preparation seriously! Since biographical sermons are relatively easy to prepare and preach, the ogre of ease lurks in the preacher's study.

Putting Off Preparation

One may be tempted to put off preparation until late in the week, in favor of more pleasurable pursuits. After all, biographical preaching is easy, isn't it? All you have to do is read up on the life of a Bible person, tell his or her story, and draw some simple applications. Why knock yourself out on Tuesday or Thursday when Saturday night or even Sunday morning will do?

Hasty Preparation

The bane of preaching is the "Saturday-night special," the sermon hastily prepared just prior to its delivery, with no real thought or serious study given to it. If church pews are filled with spiritual pygmies, it's because they're filled

with undernourished members who have been fed on a
diet of sermons without substance, messages without
meat. Let the preacher beware of not allowing adequate
time for a message to mature or of not seriously studying
God's Word for sermon preparation. Time spent in the
study will be rewarded in the pulpit. The people will
recognize when we are adequately prepared, and they
will appreciate it. They also recognize when we aren't,
and wish we were, even more than we do.

Serious Preparation Needed

Sermon preparation is as sacred a task as sermon delivery. The Holy Spirit has an affinity for the prepared mind.
Taking sermon preparation seriously removes the guilt of
not preparing. But most of all, serious study opens the
truths of God's Word to preacher and people alike. We are
to "preach the word" (2 Tim. 4:2). How can we preach it
unless we take the task seriously with our schedules and
study?

In his book: *Preaching,* Fred Craddock called for a life
of study for the preacher, not just study for specific sermons. He said:

> Time spent in study is never *getting away* from daily
> work but *getting into* daily work [italics his]. The hours of
> study bear directly and immediately on who the minister
> is and the minister's influence by word and action. It is in
> the study that so much of the minister's formation of char-
> acter and faith takes place.[1]

He goes on to point out that study is an act of obedience,
a time of worship, a broadening and protective influence,
a freeing experience, and a homiletical act.[2] Beware the
danger of ease in biographical preaching!

Eisegesis

Beware the danger of eisegesis in biographical preaching! The goal of Bible study for preaching is exegesis, literally "to lead out of" God's Word the truth revealed in it. The opposite of exegesis is eisegesis, leading or reading into the Bible rather than getting truth out of it. Eisegesis is an ever-present danger in biographical preaching for precisely the same reasons biographical preaching is of value (see chapter 2). It is person centered and relevant to people's needs. And because it is, the temptation arises to take the needs of our people and "read them into" the lives of Bible characters. Don't do that. Don't stretch the text to fit the need by speculative psychologizing or maudlin moralizing in light of what we understand today. Exegete the true characteristics, strengths, and weaknesses of the Bible person you're dealing with and apply them appropriately. Or, if you start with a need and seek a text, be sure the traits you are concerned with are truly in the Bible character, by exegesis, and not superimposed or supplanted there.

Elizabeth Achtemeier spoke to the issue of eisegesis pointedly in the midst of a discussion on the misuse of the text in experimental sermon forms. Though her particular application was to the misuse of the text in first-person biographical sermons, her words apply to all types of biographical preaching. She said:

> Unless extremely well done on the basis of sound historical and exegetical study, they inevitably psychologize the text, adding details never meant to be there, and thus introducing elements which alter and misrepresent the biblical passage . . . sermons should not ignore the fruits of that scholarly endeavor. . . . It is difficult to research the concrete details of the historical situation of Peter or Paul

or some other biblical character, and then to use those as the details of the sermon. But only if such research is done should a . . . sermon be attempted.[3]

Careful exegesis reveals truth. Careless eisegesis reaps travesty. Beware the danger of eisegesis!

Isolation

Beware of isolating the biographical sermon in the past! Since biographical preaching is set in biblical history, there's the danger of confining the sermon to its historical setting by failing to connect it to contemporary needs. Twentieth century situations may not be much like first-century AD or eighth-century BC situations, but the Bible person in his or her historical context has something to say to our day. We must be sure their message is heard, rather than just studying and talking about them, isolating them in the past. Walter C. Kaiser, Jr., said:

> Nothing can be more discouraging or disheartening for contemporary believers gathered to hear the Word of God than to listen to a simple recounting or bare description of an Old Testament Gospel narrative. This kind of preaching is nothing more than narrating a "B.C. story" or "first-century A.D. homily." It does not attempt to come to terms with the truth taught by the writer of the narrative. It is, then, a poor excuse for expository preaching.
> What is needed on such narrative portions is some method for pointing out the abiding means and continuing significance for all believers at all times.[4]

Use the Present Tense

One way to make biographical preaching contemporary and avoid the danger of isolating the Bible characters and their lessons in the past is to phrase sermon titles and major points in the present tense. This directs the truth the sermon proclaims to the contemporary audience. It speaks *to* people today, not merely *about* people in the past. Base it on the Bible person and truth, but address it to people and needs today.

How to miss the point.—Let's say you're going to preach a sermon on Jacob wrestling with the angel at Jabbok's ford (Gen. 32:22-32). You might entitle your sermon: "When Jacob Wrestled an Angel." The main points might be developed like this:

1. Jacob struggled (32:22-25)
2. Jacob was changed (32:26-28)
3. Jacob was blessed (32:29-32)

This title and points are typical of many biographical sermons. They're isolated in the past. So Jacob wrestled an angel, struggled, was changed, and blessed. So what? How does that relate to me?

How to make the point.—Now take the same character and text but entitle the sermon: "When God Confronts Us." It's already more appealing. You have the congregation's attention with an interesting title. Or call it, "What Happens When God Confronts Us?" Then phrase your main points of development from the text like this:

1. When God confronts us it sometimes causes struggle (32:22-25).
2. God's confrontation calls us to change (32:26-28).
3. We receive God's blessing when He confronts us (32:29-32).

You still develop the sermon using Jacob's experiences of struggle, change, and blessing as the basis, but you contemporize the truth by simple, yet useful, changes in style. Therefore, your speak to your people out of the experiences of the Bible people. It is a more effective way of biographical preaching. The truth is not relegated to the past. The sermon interprets the biblical record for contemporary relevance. It is not merely a history lesson, it is where we are. Don't isolate the biographical sermon in the past.

Overuse

Beware the temptation to overuse preaching biographically! It's such an enjoyable way to preach you may be tempted to neglect other types of sermons your people need to hear, and the Bible begs to be preached in a variety of ways. Don't get locked into any one mold or method. Be open. Be creative. Variety isn't only the spice of life, it's essential to interesting preaching. Preach the whole counsel of God (Acts 20:27).

How Often?

How often should we preach on a Bible character? It depends on the situation. In some places once a month would be too often while in other churches it wouldn't be. Once a quarter probably wouldn't be too frequent almost anywhere. One of the most tragic mistakes preachers make is becoming predictable. Plan biographical sermons carefully into your preaching schedule, but space them out enough so they're always fresh and appealing. Too much of anything, even good things like biographical sermons, is undesirable. You will know how often you can or can't preach on Bible characters.

Biographical Series

An exception to the previous paragraph is when you're preaching a series of biographical sermons. There are many exciting biographical series possible. Trial and error will help you determine how long a series should continue.

For example, one of the best series we can do is on the twelve apostles. But how do we structure it? You could do it on twelve consecutive Sunday mornings. The danger here is keeping it fresh and appealing. Many might think three months of apostles in a row is too much of a good thing. So you might select six consecutive Sunday mornings and evenings. The only problem with this is over half of your people will probably only hear half of the sermons because they aren't present on Sunday evenings! Maybe a better way is to plan to do three or four in a row on Sunday mornings, then change the emphasis for a Sunday or two, then get back to the series for a Sunday or two or three, and so forth. The varieties are endless. You must decide the best way for any preaching series you attempt. Series are a great way to preach.

Plan Ahead

The important thing to keep in mind in avoiding the danger of overusing biographical preaching is planning ahead. Planning is always an important part of preaching. Some preachers plan their sermons a year (or more) ahead, some by six months, some by quarters, some by the month. The trap to avoid is not planning. Plan your sermons in advance. Include biographical sermons in the plan. Avoid overuse.

Proof texting

Beware of proof texting, of using verses out of context and apart from their immediate and natural meaning! Don't make them sound like they're saying something they really aren't. Careful exegesis can help you avoid this deadly trap. Integrity demands more than a superficial use of Scripture and calls for honesty in the way we use it. The Bible is God's Word, not ours to change, abuse, or misuse.

A college student attended a revival meeting. The evangelist preached on the second coming of Christ, using numerous verses and current events to point to His soon return. He quoted Matthew 24:6*a*, as proof of the imminence of Christ's return, "You will hear of wars and rumors of wars." He then elaborated on all the skirmishes taking place at that very moment and how these were signs of the Parousia. He was very convincing. However, the college student looked up Matthew 24:6 and read the whole verse and the surrounding verses. He found out it said the exact opposite of the way the evangelist used it! "You will hear of wars and rumors of wars; see that you are not alarmed; for this must take place, but the end is not yet." After the meeting, the brash student suggested to the brash evangelist that he read the rest of the verse. We must avoid careless or dishonest proof texting at all costs!

Imagination

Beware also the danger of unidentified imagination! Imagination in preaching can be a wonderful thing. Indeed, a sermon without it can be as dry as dust. Imagination creates interest. It completes implications in Scripture and fills in details often omitted. But be sure your hearers know when you're using imagination, so they won't think something is from Scripture when it isn't. A simple statement like, "Imagine with me now Moses in the court of the great Pharaoh," or "I can see Jesus in my imagination, walking" will adequately identify when you're using imagination. It is OK to go "off the page" or "between the lines." Just be sure you and they know when you do. Again, integrity must be our guide. Work carefully on when to use imagination, how much to use, and how to differentiate it from the facts.

Plagiarism

One final danger to be avoided in all preaching in general and biographical preaching in particular is plagiarism, using unidentified sources. There are legitimate uses of what others have written or said. These require identifying the sources quoted or paraphrased. But to use someone else's words as if they were your own is downright stealing. When you find something someone has written or said that's so good you feel you must use it, then do. Just don't steal it. Give credit where credit is due.

This isn't to suggest that every line of a sermon or every idea be footnoted. There is such a thing as public-domain information. The astute preacher will know when integrity demands that a source be identified. To know it should be, but not do it, is plagiarism.[5]

The dangers of ease, eisegesis, isolation, overuse, proof texting, unidentified imagination, and plagiarism are present realities in biographical preaching. Avoid them! But the values far outweigh the dangers. Don't let the carelessness or abuses of others or the potential dangers deter you from employing this interesting and effective way to preach. To beware means to become aware of: awaken to the danger. Avoid the dangers but not the whole realm of biographical preaching. It's a God-honoring, Bible-based, person-centered, need-oriented way to preach the Word!

Notes

1. Fred B. Craddock, *Preaching* (Nashville: Abingdon Press, 1985), p. 70.
2. Ibid., pp. 70-71.
3. Elizabeth Achtemeier, *Creative Preaching* (Nashville: Abingdon Press, 1980), pp. 81-82.
4. Walter C. Kaiser, Jr., *Toward an Exegetical Theology* (Grand Rapids: Baker Book House, 1981), p. 197.
5. An excellent section on plagiarism is in George E. Sweazey's, *Preaching the Good News* (Englewood Cliffs, N.J.: Prentice-Hall, 1976), pp. 187-189. Sweazey defines plagiarism and also deals with common domain material, specific material now in public domain, and material needing acknowledgement. This whole section is insightful. See also James W. Cox, *Preaching* (New York: Harper & Row, 1985), pp. 123-124, on plagiarism, borrowing material, and originality.

4
Major Types of Biographical Sermons

The creative possibilities for types of biographical sermons are virtually limitless for both the beginning and the experienced preacher. In fact, any preacher with a lively imagination will be well served by preaching on Bible characters.[1] The various possible types of biographical sermons are so extensive it would be impossible to describe them all. This chapter will deal with a few major types for your consideration, hoping to fuel your creative fire for developing your own biographical sermons.

Whitesell's Categories

In his second chapter of *Preaching on Bible Characters*, Faris Whitesell identified two unacceptable types of biographical sermon organization, three basic types, and twenty-two particular types. It would be helpful here to review his categories briefly.

Unacceptable Types

Whitesell found running commentary and topical analysis unacceptable as types of biographical sermons. He found the running commentary type of sermonic organization deficient because, he said, it fails to draw out specific ideas from Scripture and apply them. "Perhaps this should not be called organization at all," he stated, observ-

ing a pace too fast to allow development of applicatory
ideas and organization too loose to be memorable to the
hearers.[2]

Topical analysis, when the preacher picks out and
preaches on the main ideas, was also unacceptable to
Whitesell. He commented:

> Such sermons are usually disjointed and illogical. The
> points represent breaks in thought rather than well-
> planned progressive steps stemming out from a central
> idea or proposition. . . . These points . . . do not constitute
> organization. It is doubtful they help the audience.
>
> The topical analysis takes the points in the order in
> which they occur in the Bible, regardless of their classifica-
> tion. Once in a while such an analysis may yield a good
> sermon outline, but usually not.[3]

Basic Types

Whitesell named three types of sermons that were basic
to all biographical preaching. These general categories
included the subject analysis sermon, the thematic analysis sermon, and the propositional analysis sermon.[4] Each
of his twenty-two particular types of biographical sermons, given below, would be related to one of these three
basic types.

Subject analysis.—Related to biographical sermons,
this basic type of organization simply uses the name of the
Bible character as the subject of the sermon. The subject
controls the sermon, not narrowed by a particular theme
or proposition. The sermon points are aspects of the subject, in this case the Bible person, as delineated by the
preacher.

As examples of this type of sermon construction Whitesell cited Jonah as the subject, with the sermon body organized as follows:

1. Who was Jonah?
2. What did he do?
3. What is his significance?

Or, on the same subject, as follows:

1. Jonah's career
2. Jonah's character
3. Jonah's contributions.[5]

Thematic analysis.—The thematic sermon, according to Whitesell, narrows the subject down by adding modifying terms or by limiting areas of discussion. Whereas the subject analysis sermon would treat Jonah's whole life, as illustrated above, a thematic analysis sermon would take only one aspect of his life, say the revival in Nineveh, as the theme of the sermon. His outline would look like this:

1. The call for this revival
2. The causes of this revival
3. The course of the revival
4. The consequences of the revival.[6]

By the way, consider how much more contemporary appeal this outline would have if, instead of "the call for this revival" and giving a historical explanation of Jonah's time, it were dubbed "the call for revival."

The preacher might also choose to organize a sermon around Jonah's prayer, repentance, disobedience, preaching, or bigotry. Whatever the theme, Whitesell like thematic sermons better than subject sermons, pointing out that thematic sermons are easier to prepare and preach and more interesting than subject analysis sermons.[7]

Propositional analysis.—Whitesell's third basic type of biographical sermon construction further refined the two previous types and was thus preferred by him. Using this method, the sermon is built around a proposition—a specific affirmation, question, or exhortation in the form of a complete sentence. This is the same as the classical homiletical proposition, thesis, or key sentence, as it has been called by various homileticians, containing the gist or idea of the sermon in a single sentence or statement. Whitesell saw the advantages of propositional construction as being more interesting, easier, organized tighter, stabler structurally, more logical, more symmetrical, and clean, and more easily remembered by both preacher and audience. Therefore, he advised, "most sermons should be propositional."[8] He cited an example, continuing Jonah as the subject and demonstrating how a sermon should proceed from the proposition.[9]

Based on these three types of construction, Whitesell turned his attention to particular types of biographical sermons. It would serve us well to look at them briefly.

Particular Types

Since there were twenty-two particular types of biographical sermons categorized by Whitesell, some well defined and illustrated and others merely described, let it suffice here to merely list them:

1. Character analysis
2. Career analysis
3. Activity analysis
4. Place analysis
5. Crisis analysis
6. Relationship analysis
7. Contribution analysis
8. Greatness analysis
9. Reward analysis
10. Type analysis

11. Perspective analysis
12. Group analysis
13. Lessons analysis
14. Life-principle analysis
15. Key-event analysis
16. Single-event analysis
17. Key-text analysis
18. Recurring-idea analysis
19. Unique-idea analysis
20. Comparison-and-contrast analysis
21. Psychological analysis
22. Series analysis.[10]

While this listing seems to be exhaustive and definitive for much biographical preaching, it is also repetitive and often leans toward the topical approach Whitesell earlier found unacceptable. This and the extensiveness of his types has caused me to wonder if categorizing biographical sermons could be simplified. Perhaps some of Whitesell's categories are so similar they could be combined, or maybe some need to be eliminated; others could be subcategories of broader types. With deep appreciation for the work of Whitesell, the following new categories are offered.

New Categories

While there are many basic types of sermons, we shall limit our discussion here to new categorizations of biographical sermons. It would seem that there are in reality only two major categories of biographical sermons on individuals, the whole life and the life portion. The first type deals with all the life of a Bible character as the Bible presents him or her. There are various ways of organizing a character's life, and these are subcategories of whole life biographical sermons. The second major category, a life-portion biographical sermon, doesn't deal with a Bible character's whole life, only some part of it. Again, there are subcategories or various ways to organize a life-portion biographical sermon. Let's look at each of these two major types in some detail and some of their possible subcategories. Then we will take a brief look at a third category with some dynamic potential.

Whole-Life Biographical Sermons

The whole-life biographical sermon seeks to interpret the entire life of a biblical person by organizing the sermon around dominant factors in the person's life. This type of sermon would take everything the Bible has to say about a particular person, however extensively or scantily he or she might be treated in the biblical material, as the true text for the message. The preacher might well select a few verses or a summary verse or verses for reading to the congregation as the text, but in reality one would consider all the biblical materials on this person the text.

There are a wide variety of ways to organize the life of a Bible character. Here are a few suggestions to think about.

Significant periods.—You might organize the whole life of a Bible person around time periods. Moses' life falls neatly into three periods of forty years each. Jesus' life can be organized into the periods of cradle, childhood, career, cross, resurrection, return—or something similar. Use your own categories. Be alliterative or not—as you wish. Many Bible characters can be preached on from the periods of their lives.

Key events.—Structure a whole life biographical sermon around the key events of the person's life. Daniel would be a good candidate for this type of sermon. Or

Samson. Or the apostle Paul. Simply analyze the person's life based on key events the person experienced and this gives you the basic order for the sermon. Don't make it a history lesson, however. State the points in a contemporary way, drawn from the events in the person's life.

Say you want to preach on Abraham, showing how the key events of his life led to a life of service. You could call your sermon: "Abraham—A Man Who Served God." Your sermon would be outlined:

1. Abraham was called.
2. Abraham was changed.
3. Abraham was challenged.
4. Abraham was confirmed.

This stifles the sermon by isolating it in the past. Yet this is the way much biographical preaching has been done. Is there a better way?

A better approach is contemporization. Instead of the past-tense given above, call it: "How to Serve God," or "Conditions for Serving the Lord," or some other title with contemporary appeal. Instead of a historical outline of Abraham's life, use these key events to speak to today's situation. Use the same ideas, but apply them to the present. Your outline might be:

1. Serving the Lord begins by hearing His call.
2. To serve God best we must let Him change us.
3. We must accept the challenge to serve the Lord.
4. Our service is confirmed by God at life's end.

You've preached the same sermon, used the same person, same material, but you've made it relevant, and much preferred over the old way. In each major point, you explain how Abraham's life was affected by this particular event. Talk about the same things you would under the old points above, but illustrate each point, apply each point, and contemporize each point in the new style. It makes for a much clearer, more forceful, and more appealing sermon.

Main places.—Another way to do a whole-life biographical sermon is to organize it around the major places in the chosen character's life. You see, we're using some of Whitesell's particular categories, reapplied to this new categorization.[11]

How about a sermon on Jacob organized around the main places mentioned in his life? In it you could picture him at home, at Bethel, in Haran, at Peniel, back to Bethel, and back home. You don't want a travelogue here. You use the places of Jacob's life to describe the inner and outer conflict he wrestled with all his life. He was up and down in morality, spirituality, family relationships, and faith. You could cover this wide range of experience by organizing a narrative sermon on Jacob around the places in his life.

A classical example of this type of biographical sermon is: "Moses—Man of Three Mountains" by Clarence E. Macartney. He dealt with the mountains of revelation, intercession, and disappointment in Moses' life.[12] DeWitt Talmage dealt with the life of Christ in a sermon entitled "From Cross to Crown," using this method.[13] These examples are worthy of study for examining main-places-whole-life sermons.

Crises.—Everybody has problems. One way to do a whole-life biographical sermon is to frame it around the crises in a Bible person's life.

Take Joseph, for example. There was the crisis of being sold into slavery by his brothers. This culminates the early stages of his life against the background of parental partiality, dreams of superiority, immaturity, and poor sibling relationships. Next were the crises of life in a foreign land: success, temptation, fidelity in the face of persecution, imprisonment, being forgotten, and receiving revelations. Then there's the crisis of leadership of Egypt, then reconciliation with his family in that context. There's so much in Joseph's life to contribute to a fascinating whole-life biographical sermon structured on crises he faced.

Chapters 37 through 50 in the Book of Genesis provide the major scriptural facts of Joseph's life. Carefully studied, they reveal a series of crises he experienced, which might be organized as mentioned in the paragraph above. Taking these as our guide, a whole-life sermon on Joseph organized around the crises he experienced might be entitled: "Faith Brings Victory in Crisis." In it you would show how Joseph's faith enabled him to be victorious over each personal crisis he faced. The thesis for this sermon is: "Faith in God enables us to be victorious over each crisis we face." This would be a supportive sermon with the specific objective of those who hear it finding strength to face crises through deepening faith in God.

In the introduction you could narrate Joseph's life, explaining how faith got him through the crises and what they were. You could relate this to some personal crises we commonly face, to a particular crisis you've faced, or that the church is facing. The sermon body would use Joseph's crises to help us deal with ours, as follows:

1. Faith brings victory in the crises of relationships (Gen. 37).
2. Faith brings victory by giving integrity over temptations (Gen. 39—40).
3. Faith brings victory in the crises of leadership (Gen. 41).

4. Faith brings victory in the crises of forgiveness and reconciliation (Gen. 42—45).

Another way to begin this same sermon would be to start with a life crisis situation and progress to Joseph as an answer to it. An inductive approach could work quite well with this type of biographical sermon.

Relationships.—A sixth way to organize a whole-life biographical sermon is around the relationships in the character's life. How did they relate to others? How did others relate to them? What was good in their relationships? Bad? Healthy? Unhealthy?

It would be fascinating to do a sermon of this type on David. A creative preacher could organize a sermon around the relationships in David's life—to his family, to King Saul, to Jonathan, to Uriah and Bathsheba, to Absalom, and, finally, to Solomon. You wouldn't necessarily have to do a six-point outline using these six relationships. How about a two-point outline utilizing David's healthy relational qualities on the one hand and his unhealthy relationships on the other? Again, keep the focus on the people you're speaking to by using the past to deal with the present. Don't do a history lesson. You might call this sermon: "The Path to Spiritual Victory." David's healthy relationships led him to God's favor, but unhealthy relationships led him to defeat. Your thesis might be: "Spiritual victory demands healthy relationships with others." Using David's good-and-poor relationships you would show:

1. Unhealthy relationships lead us down the path of spiritual defeat (David and Saul, Uriah, Bathsheba, Absalom).
2. Spiritual victory follows the path of healthy relationships (David and Jesse, Jonathan, Solomon).

Many Bible characters lend themselves naturally to a whole-life biographical sermon based on their relationships to others, and even to themselves. Explore the fascinating possibilities of this effective type of biographical preaching.

Principle(s).—Another way to organize a sermon on a Bible person's whole life is to discover a single principle, some unifying standard the person lived by. Often Scripture gives such a principle or guiding force about a Bible character. Some see Daniel 1:8 as the overarching principle Daniel lived by. "Daniel purposed in his heart that he would not defile himself with the portion of the king's meat, nor with the wine which he drank" (KJV). The RSV says, "Daniel resolved." From Daniel's deep resolution came all his ensuing actions and commitments. This does seem to be his life principle indeed.

Whitesell pointed out that there may be more than one principle a Bible person lived by, but a particular sermon would deal with only one.[14] I believe it could be equally effective to deal with more than one principle in a whole-life biographical sermon if more than one principle was readily evident in the text.

Could Luke 1:38 be the life principle of Mary, the mother of Jesus? In this verse we see that God used Mary because she surrendered herself totally to His will. In context, Mary's surrender related particularly to the miraculous conception of Jesus. But in truth, is this not the principle Mary always lived by? If so, we can organize a whole-life biographical sermon on Mary from Luke 1:38. It would be best to read Luke 1:26-38 to the congregation, focusing on the last verse as Mary's life principle. Our thesis would be: "God will use us if we will surrender our lives to His will." A consecrative major objective is evident for this sermon. The specific objective might be: "I want us to surrender ourselves to seek God's will in all matters." Our title: "How to Be Used By God."

An exegesis of Luke 1:38 shows us that the word translated "handmaid" in both the KJV and RSV is none other than *doulos* in the Greek, literally "slave." This certainly tells us something about Mary's total surrender. Further we learn that the verb "may it be" or "let it be" is a rare form of the common verb *ginomai.* This usage indicates openness to possibility, surrender, and trust. Here it's not so much submission to what's known as it is willingness to surrender to the unknown. Malcolm Tolbert said, "Unlike Zechariah, Mary does not seem to require any sign but humbly submits to the will of God for her life."[15] Tolbert's last three words *for her life* take on added significance when this verse is seen as not only a particular submission to the virgin birth but as her life principle. This is reinforced with the comment in the *Interpreter's Bible,* "Mary's words are those of humble acquiescence to God's will."[16] This was a lifelong commitment on her part, beginning here but not ending with Jesus' birth. This truth is evident throughout her life.

So, from Mary's life show, "How to Be Used By God."

    1. We can be used by God only if we're willing and ready to be.
       (In this you'd show how Mary was properly prepared by her purity, faith, humility, attitude, and how these affected later actions.)
    2. God can use us when we're unquestionably obedient.
       (Give examples of Mary's obedience here and in later references.)
    3. When we're devotedly faithful, God can use us.

(Show her faith in action from subsequent experiences as well as in 1:38).

You can perhaps think of other categories than life principle(s), relationships, crises, main places, key events, and significant periods around which to construct whole-life biographical sermons. Let these six serve as suggestions to fire your imagination and give you a basis to work from. Develop your own ways to preach on the whole life of a Bible person: character analysis, main lessons they teach us, their activities, their sins, and their victories. Now you're ready to think freely, creatively, and to add your own unique style and substance. Be aware that preaching on the whole life of a Bible character is one main way to approach biographical preaching, and there are numerous ways to apply this new category. Beyond this, your imagination is your only limit! God bless you in this exciting task.

Life-Portion Biographical Sermons

The second major category of biographical sermons is based on a portion—some part—of the life of the Bible character. Like the whole-life biographical sermon, the life-portion biographical sermon is Bible based and person centered. The obvious difference is it doesn't deal with all the biblical material on a particular character but only a portion of the material; thus only a portion of the character's life is used. Some of the particular types of life-portion biographical sermons are similar to the types in the previous category, except in extent. How can we do life-portion biographical sermons?

Single circumstance.—One way to preach this type of biographical sermon is to focus on a single period, event, place, crisis, relationship, principle, or some other single circumstance in the life of a Bible character. Instead of preaching a sermon on Moses' whole life organized around the three forty-year periods, you preach from the middle period: his adult career. Or instead of each of David's relationships revealing his whole biography, you zero in on his relationship with Jonathan or Absalom and focus on what this single relationship teaches us. Be sure to keep the sermon biographical, that is, mainly on the person, not on the event, idea, or other circumstance. You simply narrow the scope of the material on a Bible character and preach on a portion of his or her life rather than the whole life.

Distinguishing characteristic.—A second type of life-portion biographical sermon is based on a single characteristic that distinguishes this person in the biblical material. One thinks of Gideon's courage or Joseph's forgiveness, for example. Deal with a portion of their lives based on analysis of their character.

This may mean you must pick one characteristic among many to focus on, or a combination of characteristics. Be sure the traits are actually there by analysis and not forced on or "read into" the character. Also, beware the temptation to see the same characteristics in each person. The key here is the question: "What is (are) the *distinguishing* characteristic(s) of this person? What sets this one apart, makes him or her different, unique?" In one preaching class, the students kept coming up with faith, courage, and commitment for each person we studied. Now, obviously, many Bible personalities are characterized by these noble traits. "But what's *different* about *this* person?" was our main question. The answer will give you the sermon. Simon Peter's strange mixture of cowardice and courage, Elisha's spirituality, Deborah's patriotism, or Jezebel's scheming would each be superb subjects for life-portion biographical sermons using their distinguishing characteristics.

Single text.—Sometimes a portion of Scripture, whether a single verse or several verses, or a whole paragraph or more speaks so profoundly to some portion of the life of a Bible person it virtually begs to be preached. Abraham's call and blessing from God in Genesis 12:1-3 is such a text. So is his offering of Isaac on the altar in Genesis 22:1-19. A few minutes reflection will call to the preacher's mind dozens of vital, important texts that lend themselves to this type of biographical life-portion sermon.

Key lesson(s).—We can learn something from each person in the Bible. Many characters teach us multiple lessons. Why not preach a life-portion biographical sermon based on a key lesson learned from the life or in the life of a Bible character? Or on several lessons they teach us?

Take Judas Iscariot, for instance. Can we learn positive lessons from him? Yes, even from Judas! Consider this sermon entitled: "Lessons Learned from a Loser." Taking Judas's general background as the context, and John 6:66-71 as the text, demonstrate four "Lessons Learned from a Loser." These are powerful lessons!

1. Profession of faith doesn't always mean possession of faith (6:66-67).
2. Those who begin well don't always end well (6:68-69).
3. Carelessness in little sins can lead to carelessness in bigger sins (6:70).
4. Judas isn't too unlike us (6:71).

These are positive lessons learned from a negative character.

On a more positive note, look at Hebrews 11:24-27 on "Faith's Choices" made by Moses.

1. All of faith's choices aren't made when we're young (11:24).
2. Sometimes faith's choices call for tremendous sacrifices (11:24-26).
3. Often faith's choices aren't the popular things to do (11:27).

Careful study of Bible characters will reveal a wide range of lessons we can learn from them. Sometimes a single, monumental lesson will stand out. Other times there will be several important things to be learned. This is an excellent and exciting way to preach biographically.

So, are you catching onto the distinction between whole life and life-portion biographical sermons? Easy isn't it? Both offer rewarding sermon possibilities. The latter is undoubtedly easier to do. But don't overlook the richness of the former. Think up your own categories or combinations. Don't miss the joy of preaching on Bible characters!

Multiple-Character Biographical Sermons

So far, our new categories of biographical sermon classification have dealt solely with sermons on individuals. It is possible to do single sermons on multiple characters. Why not do a sermon on Paul and Barnabas together, as well as on each of them separately? Or on Mary, Martha, and Lazarus? Or on those three and Jesus together in Scripture? The combinations and possibilities are endless! Don't strain to find relationships between characters, and beware of shallow typology. But what about a sermon on the similarities between Isaac and Jesus, or Elijah and John the Baptist? Someone even preached once on the lasting contributions of Karl Marx and Jesus, and how different the two are! Oh yes, beware of sensationalism in the name of interest or creativity.

Multiple-character biographical sermons is a category filled with stimulating opportunities. More than one author has written an entire volume of just such sermons.[17] Don't overlook this type of preaching in favor of always choosing the less-demanding categories.

How to select apropos subjects and prepare biographical sermons on them is the topic of the next chapter. Suffice it to say there is a wide variety of possibilities for biographical sermons on individuals or on multiple characters, on their whole lives or only portions of them, structured inductively or deductively, delivered autobiographically or biographically. Let these categories suggest to all preachers, young or old, beginner or longtimer, the exciting and rewarding opportunities of biographical preaching. The exhausting work of preaching need not exhaust creativity and interest on the part of preachers or their hearers. Biographical preaching can refresh the weariness of tired pulpiteers if we let the living truths of Bible heroes and villains live again through us.

Notes

1. See Blackwood, *Biographical Preaching for Today,* pp. 131-149 for some excellent material on exercising imagination in biographical preaching.

2. Whitesell, *Preaching on Bible Characters,* pp. 26-27.

3. Ibid., p. 27.

4. Ibid.

5. Ibid., pp. 28-29.

6. Ibid., p. 29.

7. Ibid.

8. Ibid., 29-30.

9. Ibid., p. 30.

10. Ibid., pp. 31-49. Any student of biographical preaching would be well served by studying these types carefully.

11. Ibid., p. 34.

12. Clarence E. Macartney, *The Greatest Men of the Bible* (New York: Abingdon-Cokesbury Press, 1941), pp. 41-55. Cited by Whitesell, p. 34. See also Macartney's sermon, "Joseph—Dreams, Dungeons, Diadems," pp. 98-112 in the same volume for another example.

13. T. DeWitt Talmage, *Trumpet Blasts* (Chicago: North American Publishing Co., 1892), pp. 389-401.

14. Whitesell, p. 40.

15. Malcolm O. Tolbert, "Luke," in *The Broadman Bible Commentary*, vol. 9, gen. ed. Clifton J. Allen (Nashville: Broadman Press, 1970), p. 23.

16. S. MacLean Gilmour, "Luke," in *The Interpreter's Bible*, vol. 8, ed. Nolan B. Harmon (Nashville: Abingdon Press, 1952), p. 40.

17. See G. Avery Lee, *Great Men of the Bible and the Women in Their Lives* (Waco: Word Books, 1968); and Clarence E. Macartney, *Ancient Wives and Modern Husbands* (Nashville: Cokesbury Press, 1934) for examples.

5

Steps in Preparation

Preaching is hard work. It demands much prayer, thought, and study. Biographical preaching is no exception. After you understand what biographical preaching is, the exciting values of doing it, what to beware of, and the unlimited creative possibilities for types of sermons on Bible characters, the real work begins. Your next step is the actual development of a Bible character sermon. What are these steps? Here are seven to consider.

Select the Person

Step one is selecting the Bible person(s) to be preached about. This may be done several ways. You might just pick somebody at random. Maybe a name just pops into your mind, or you've thought about the persons for a long time and always wanted to preach about them. Now is your chance. Or you might discover a person while casually reading or seriously studying Scripture. Another way is to select an individual as a part of a series of sermons or as a part of a planned program of preaching. However you make the selection, this is the first step toward a biographical sermon.

There are many neat possibilities of persons to select as subjects for biographical sermons, whether by deliberate choice or as part of a plan. Consider these suggestions.

Major Characters

Whether biographical preaching is new to you or you've been preaching for a long time, some of the best subjects for biographical sermons of any category are the major figures of the Old and New Testaments. You can hardly go wrong by selecting major Bible characters. People who hear you preach will be familiar and comfortable with them and generally enjoy hearing about them. An interesting exercise is to sit down and think of whom you consider to be the ten most important people in each Testament. Write them down. Preach about them.

Major Old Testament characters.—A seminary class in biographical preaching selected ten people they considered the most important in the Old Testament. Their list included Adam, Abraham, Sarah, Isaac, Jacob, Joseph, Moses, Joshua, Elijah, and David. Other nominees were Noah, Solomon, Samuel, Jeremiah, and Isaiah. How does this compare to your list?

In Whitesell's sixth chapter of *Preaching on Bible Characters*, the Old Testament people he considered of "maximum importance" included Abraham, Adam, Amos, Daniel, David, Elijah, Ezekiel, Isaiah, Jacob, Jeremiah, Job, Joshua, Moses, Samuel, and Solomon.[1]

Suffice it to say there are many major Old Testament characters to fuel the fires for biographical preaching.

Major New Testament people.—Whitesell listed six New Testament characters in his category of maximum importance. They are Antichrist, John the Beloved, John the Baptist, Matthew, Paul, and Peter.[2] As was mentioned earlier, Jesus was categorized as in a class by Himself. Other nominees for major New Testament figures might include Luke, Mary, Mark, and some of the apostles. There certainly are not as many major New Testament people as there are Old, but this doesn't in any way diminish their importance or interest for biographical preaching.

Any of these Old or New Testament people could be the subject for a sermon and many could support a whole series of sermons. How about a series on "Leading Ladies of the Old Testament," or "Walking with the Giants" on the greatest Old Testament men? There are some exciting possibilities here.

Secondary Characters

Another great resource for biographical sermons is people of secondary importance. These persons would be those who are fairly major but not of maximum importance. Or maybe they're important because of their relationship to a major character. Some Old Testament people in this category are Aaron, Ahab, Benjamin, Caleb, Elisha, Enoch, Ephraim, Esau, Esther, Ezra, Gideon, Hezekiah, Hosea, Joel, Jonah, Josiah, Judah, Malachi, Micah, Noah, and Ruth, to name but a few.[3]

From the New Testament you might select Andrew, Bartholomew, Barnabas, Cornelius, Judas Iscariot, Mary Magdalene, Lazarus, and/or his sisters Mary and Martha, Nathanael, Philip the apostle, Philip the deacon, Pontius Pilate, or Stephen, and so forth.

Secondary characters are excellent subjects for biographical sermons because people generally recognize their names but don't usually know as much about them as they know about major characters. They are interesting to learn more about. There is usually abundant material on them. You could even do a series of sermons including secondary characters. How about a series on famous relatives of major figures? The relatives would be secondary characters who played major roles in the lives of major people. The possibilities are numerous and exciting.[4]

Minor Characters

Preaching on minor or little-known Bible characters adds interest and variety to biographical sermon repertoires. Though there are plenty of minor characters to choose from, we should probably select one only occasionally, avoiding sensationalism and eschewing the esoteric. But there are some excellent minor people who beg to be preached about. Onesimus, Phoebe, Rahab, Cain and Abel, Rizpah, Apollos, Aquila and Priscilla, Thaddaeus, Simon of Cyrene, Simon the Zealot, the centurion at the cross, and even the numerous unnamed people in the Bible are exciting prospects for sermons on minor characters. Whitesell categorized 241 people in the Bible as being of "minor importance."[5] There is a lot of homiletical gold to be mined from this shaft.

Advantages.—One positive aspect of picking a minor character to preach on is: you will undoubtedly know more about him or her than your listeners do, especially after intense study. Also, since people are interested in people, they will like hearing about unfamiliar Bible characters. How much could the average Sunday morning churchgoer tell you about Rizpah or Balak? Yet they have fascinating stories worthy of noting. The Bible is a rich source book of interesting information in its familiar and unfamiliar parts. Don't always stick to the known trails. There's much to be discovered off the beaten track.[6]

Significant Groups

Single sermon.—You might consider a significant group of people for a single biographical sermon. If you choose a group as your subject, you would preach on things people in the group had in common—characteristics, beliefs, attitudes, problems, vices, fears—whatever you find common among them. The twelve apostles, kings of Judah or Israel, prophets, priests, Pharisees, judges, and patriarchs would be some groups you might want to look at. One preacher did a sermon cleverly entitled: "Phamous Pharisees."

Series.—Another way to preach on a significant group is to do a series of sermons on individuals within an identifiable group rather than a single sermon on the whole group. Clovis Chappell did this in *Faces about the Cross.*[7] Macartney did a series on *Mountains and Mountain Men of the Bible.*[8] More recent works have used this format also.[9]

Either a single sermon on a group or a series from a group could be very effective.

Representative People

People who represent a category also provide a rich resource for sermon subjects. There are numerous representative groups in the Bible: rich people, beggars, mothers, rogues, famous friends, enemies, people who heard God speak, great women behind great men, people who turned away from Jesus, and so forth. Again, a single sermon or series could be done from this category.

People Involved in Significant Events

There are some good possibilities for single sermons or series on people who were involved in significant events in the Bible. People at Jesus' birth or at the cross or resurrection or at Pentecost or at the Exodus could be considered. You can think of others to add to this category.

People Representing Experiences

Closely akin to several of the categories above are people representative of certain types of experiences— recipients of miracles, people who were tried in courts of law, backsliders, mourners, and people who talked to Satan. This is a good category to consider because we often have similar experiences to many of theirs. Sermons on these people speak to some of the same kinds of experiences we have, need to have, or need not to have today. Preaching on these people puts you on a good feeling level with contemporary problems, issues, and experiences. It's a good way to preach.

There are so many worthy subjects for biographical sermons! Let these categories above suggest ideas to you. Add your own ideas to them. Be aware that the first step in preparing a biographical sermon is selecting the person to preach about.

What's next?

List the Passages

The second step in preparing a biographical sermon is to find and list all the passages in the Bible dealing with the person(s) selected. A good concordance is valuable at this point. Often Bible dictionaries and encyclopedias have analyses of Bible characters with lists of Scripture references. So do many good reference Bibles, the Thompson Chain Reference Bible notable among them. From these resources and your own Bible study, make a list of all the references on the person you're dealing with.

It's good to keep a file on Bible characters and include these lists of passages for future reference.

List the passages.

Study the Passages

The third step is to do a systematic study of the passages listed and located. This step involves background study, doing a general exposition of the various passages, deciding on a text, and doing a thorough exegetical study of the chosen text. Let's look at each of the stages of studying the passage to see what is involved.

Background Study

Begin this step by examining the history, culture, location, date, religion, politics, family life, geography, and so forth, of the time the selected person lived in. Learn as much as you can about their historical background. This will greatly aid your understanding of the person and will help you avoid some of the dangers mentioned in chapter 3. This will take some time and work, but you will find it well worthwhile. If you keep careful notes on your findings you can use them in the future when you're dealing with other people from the same era.

Resources for background study include commentaries, Bible atlases, general and biblical histories, reference Bibles, Bible dictionaries and encyclopedias, journals, and specialized books on subjects such as biblical archaeology, manners and customs, biblical backgrounds, and so forth.

Expositional Study

After you study the setting and background of your character, do a general exposition of each reference you've listed on him or her. To do this, first read through each passage thoroughly from your favorite version of the Bible. If there are unfamiliar or difficult words, phrases, or ideas in a passage, look at other Bible translations and compare them, or look up their definition in a dictionary,

Bible dictionary, or theological word book.[10] You don't have to be a Hebrew or Greek scholar to understand the Bible. A good English dictionary can be extremely helpful in understanding word meanings.

You're not to the exegetical stage yet. What you want to accomplish at this stage is a thorough reading of each passage and a general understanding of what each one says and means. If you skip this step, you just might miss the very passage or idea you'd need to preach this sermon. Do not underestimate the importance of reading and understanding each passage listed. A single verse could turn out to be your text, or a long section could be. You may never know unless you do this expositional study.

Decide on a Text

Your systematic study continues as you next decide if a specific passage or if multipassages will be used as your text in preference to other passages listed. On some secondary or minor characters, you could easily use everything the Bible has to say about them as the text, provided it is not too lengthy. On most characters you would not want to do this. So, decide what your text will be. This is an extremely important step toward a direct biblical sermon and away from a topical or casual treatment of the text.

Give preference to the clear, definitive passages on the person and/or area of the person's life you want to deal with. The clearer the meaning of the passage to the direction of the message, the better.

The length and location(s) of the text is important. Whether you choose a verse, a paragraph, a longer pericope, or several passages to comprise the text, prefer the biblical material that gives clearest relationship between text and sermon. If the text is to be very short, a verse or two, or part of a verse, you undoubtedly will need to supplement it with contextual material. If you choose a long section, say Genesis 37—50 on Joseph, you will want to narrate your text, or sections of it, obviously. Many preachers believe a paragraph is an ideal length of text to be read, but we need not be limited by this opinion. Text is important, so choose it carefully.

Exegete the Text

Now you have decided on the person to preach about, found and listed all the passages about him or her, done a general study of each passage, and decided on the text. Your study proceeds by doing a detailed exegesis or in-depth analysis of the passage you will use as your text.

Read and translate.—Begin your exegesis by reading the text many times from your favorite version. Twenty or twenty-five readings is not too many. You may want to read it several times daily over several days. Let it sink into your consciousness. Absorb it. Feel its meaning and movement through utter familiarity with it. Read it aloud several times. Absorb the text.

Next read it from as many other versions as possible. As you do, compare similarities and differences in word meanings, feeling levels, and ideas. We can profit by the work of others in translation.

If you are able to, translate the passage from the original language, or at least look it over in Hebrew or Greek. Sometimes interlinear translations are helpful, but don't let them become a crutch if you can work with the languages. If you can't work with the original languages, skip from reading it in English to the next step. But if you can translate, you will usually gain insights from this discipline you can't get any other way or place.

Preliminary interpretation.—Your in-depth Bible study

continues with a preliminary interpretation of the text.
State the meaning of each verse. Don't state what it *says,*
interpret what it *means.* Paraphrase it. You don't have to
write this out, though doing so might be helpful. You also
don't have to be able to work with the ancient languages
to interpret meaning. State what you understand each
verse to mean. It is often helpful to do this orally to another person, if possible. Then you can discuss the meaning
with them.

Next, interpret the meaning of the whole text. What do
the verses together mean? What is the central idea of
them? Say it out loud or write it down. Make it as clear and
concise as possible. You may have to make several attempts at this before you get it just right. When you do,
you will have the central idea of the text(CIT). Remember
at this point that your interpretation is still preliminary.
It may or may not change as your study continues.

Research thoroughly.—Now you are ready to research
your text thoroughly. Do an in-depth analysis of the specific passage. Some tools you may need to do this include
Bibles in various translations and/or paraphrases, biblical
texts, grammars, lexicons, concordances, dictionaries, encyclopedias, atlases, critical commentaries, biblical journals, devotional commentaries, and books on special
topics. Build a good theological library made up of these
tools, or frequent a library nearby if there is one. There's
no substitute for the right tools for the job.

Use these to study the background of the text until you
understand it in its setting. For such an understanding
you may need to investigate the author, date, occasion,
purpose, style, source(s), language, special features, city of
origin, type of literature it is, and other background items
related to the text.

Next, study the perspective of the passage in relationship to other texts. This is sometimes called contextual study. What immediately precedes it? Follows it? How is it related to its immediate context? Its larger context (chapter, book, section, Testament, the Bible as a whole)? An understanding of identical, parallel, or similar passages in other locations will be helpful. Compare the text to them for similarities or differences. Then determine the weight of importance of your chosen text as it relates to other Scripture. Was this an eternal principle, a local or temporary injunction, an isolated incident, a common occurrence? Knowing these things is essential for proper interpretation.

After you know the background and perspective of the passage, do an in-depth study of the passage itself. Look at the "big picture," the passage as a whole. What is its major thrust, emphasis, meaning, and story? What subthemes seem to be in it? Direct biblical preaching demands majoring on the overall truth of the text and not on some minor aspect of it. So be sure you understand its major, central meaning. Then investigate the individual sections of the text. Study each paragraph, verse, sentence, phrase, clause, and word in it as it relates to the truth of the text as a unit. Even study shades of meaning of words. Each part of the minutia contributes to the central idea of the text like each individual brush stroke contributes to a painting.

Summary interpretation.—Finally, make a summary interpretation of the passage. This must be done on the basis of all you understand about the passage in light of your research, your own interpretational beliefs, through the leadership of the Holy Spirit. Write down the central idea of the text, what it meant to the people who first heard or read it. State the thesis of the passage, what it means now. This becomes the key sentence of the sermon. State the major objective of the passage, the purpose it speaks to that you wish to develop in this sermon.

All Bible study involves work, prayer, and thought. To these ingredients God adds illumination for understanding. The result is knowledge, wisdom, and growth. And sermons! Bible-based biographical sermons that speak to today's needs become some of the most enriching and enjoyable of all ways to preach. It's a lot of work, but well worth it!

Analyze the Person

Step four in preparing your biographical sermon calls for analyzing your chosen Bible character in light of the particular text. Read out of this passage what it says is truly in the person as revealed here. If you are dealing with Simon Peter, for instance, different traits will be evident if your text is Matthew 14 (walking on the water), than if your text is Acts 2 (Pentecost). Don't overlap or borrow traits from another text. However, if you are doing a whole-life biographical sermon on Peter, a wide range of characteristics would be evident from the broader text: fear, cowardice, impetuosity, courage, faith, and so forth. So, stick with your text and glean from it the truths and traits it presents.

As you analyze the person, ask yourself, "Who was this person? What was he like? How did he behave, function, and relate? What relationship did he have with God? What character traits are revealed in this passage? What mental, emotional, physical, psychological, logical, and personality characteristics are evident?" Maybe you can think of other questions to ask. Don't be afraid to ask the tough questions about Bible characters! Only by doing so will we get the insightful answers we need for meaningful biographical sermons. Analyze the person carefully and prayerfully.

Character Traits

Character analysis tells us about the personality of the figure we are dealing with. We all have certain traits and some are more evident at various times. Look at the following lists and determine if any of the traits given are revealed in the text before you on your chosen person. This list is only meant to be suggestive, not exhaustive. It's given in no particular order of priority.

Positive traits.—Courageous, confident, realistic, disciplined, patient, well balanced, uses good judgment, openminded, fair, relaxed, spontaneous, tolerant, flexible, warm, personable, even-tempered, loving, forgiving, zealous, self-motivated, self-confident, caring, concerned, sincere, committed, feels deeply, shares openly, generous, kind, self-respect, dignity, orderly, reliable, productive, creative, resourceful, growing, encouraging, sense of humor, and faithful.

A person of good character, with good mental and emotional health, feels comfortable about himself, feels right about other people, and is able to meet the demands of life. Does this text reveal any of these positive qualities about your subject?

Negative traits.—One of the beautiful things about the way the Bible presents the people in it is that it doesn't sugar-coat them. It shows them as they really were, warts and all. They were human, and as such had negative qualities as well as positive ones. Does your text present any of the negative traits about the person you are dealing with?

Fearful, bitter, vindictive, grasping, impatient, unrealistically wishful, goes to extremes, prejudiced, closed-minded, lazy, apathetic, driven, compulsive, inflexible, intolerant, indecisive, hostile, rude, overdependent, addicted, obsessed, vacillating, self-deceiving, sneaky, cheater, inconsistent, unfeeling, exploitive, wasteful, egotistical, liar, dishonest, bland, ill-tempered, and condemnatory.

People who manifest these traits are often bowled over by their own emotions and have little emotional management. Their interpersonal relationships are shallow and short-lived. They can't seem to handle problems, responsibilities, new experiences, and ideas. Are these traits evident from your text? If so, they speak volumes about the person's character. This can be the substance of some insightful biographical preaching.

From the positive and/or negative traits revealed in your text you should be able to do a meaningful character sketch of your subject. This will be immensely helpful to you in preaching on this person.

Analyze Relationships

We need not only to look at the individual as a person, but also at this person in relationship to others. How did he/she relate to family? Superiors? Subordinates? Friends? Allies? Enemies? The present? The past? The future? What does the text tell you about how this person related? Don't presuppose that you know. Dig out the person's relationships. This will tell you a great deal that will be helpful in preaching on them.

Analyze Contributions, Lessons

Draw any conclusions you can from the text on what we can learn from this person, positively or negatively. What contributions to life, history, or faith did this person make? What lessons does she teach? How can we live more effectively today in light of what we can learn from this person? How can we avoid her mistakes, emulate her virtues? How does this apply to me, my family, my congregation, to the world-at-large? How can I use these insights in a sermon?

Many counselors try not to analyze people in counseling sessions to avoid pigeonholing them, thereby limiting their understanding of them instead of enhancing it. We must be cautious here, too. But at the same time analyzing the person's character traits, relationships, and contributions is necessary for meaningful biographical preaching. Proceed with caution in this arena, but do proceed. Avoid psychologizing and moralizing on that basis, but seriously attempt to understand the person's makeup. We can't effectively preach what we do not understand.

Write Out Your Preliminary Page

Now you're ready to formulate a plan for how you will preach from this text on this Bible character as you understand him or her. This step formalizes each of the previous steps in preparation. It needs to be written and will undoubtedly take several drafts to get it just the way you want it. We'll call this written plan the preliminary page (see Appendix 1). On it you will list your text, the central idea of the text, your sermon thesis (what Whitesell called the proposition),[11] the purpose of this sermon including major and specific objectives, the type biographical sermon it will be, the title of the sermon, and its outline. In this fifth step, let's look in detail at each of the items from text through specific objective. Then we'll deal with the type of biographical sermon it will be and the title and outline separately, as major steps 6 and 7.

Text

The first item on your preliminary page should be the text. List the reference fully, including book, chapter, verse(s), and version, in that order. If you use this method consistently then you can file sermons by text and find them easily. Since everything that follows flows from the text in a biblical sermon, it's important to list it first.

Central Idea of the Text

The second item on your preliminary page should be the written out CIT. This should be a complete sentence in past tense and as brief as possible. No more than fifteen words is ideal. It needs to be in past tense because you're interpreting what the text meant to those who first heard, read, or experienced it. Make it as directly biblical as possible. State the meaning of the text clearly and concisely. H. C. Brown, Jr., called for formulating an accurate CIT when he wrote:

> Apart from the natural, grammatical and historical meaning of the passage, the minister cannot preach authentic Biblical sermons. The historical meaning, the "then" of Scripture, serves as the only adequate basis for formulating the present tense application, the "now" of Scripture. ... The central idea of the text describes the true historical meaning of the passage.[14]

Thesis

The thesis comes next. Various homileticians have called this the proposition, theme sentence, topic statement, affirmation, main idea, main truth, or thesis. It's the sermon in a sentence, a concisely worded direct interpretation of both the text and CIT, phrased in the present tense. This is the present and eternal truth of the passage. The thesis is the truth of the text to be proclaimed.

John Henry Jowett, the great British Congregationalist preacher of the late nineteenth and early twentieth century commented about the sermon thesis in his Lyman Beecher Lecture on Preaching at Yale in 1912:

> I have a conviction that no sermon is ready for preaching, not ready for writing out, until we can express its theme in a short, pregnant sentence as clear as crystal. I find the getting of that sentence is the hardest, the most exacting, and the most fruitful labour in my study. To compel oneself to fashion that sentence, to dismiss every word that is vague, ragged, ambiguous, to think oneself through to a form of words which defines the theme with scrupulous exactness—this is surely one of the most vital and essential factors in the making of a sermon: and I do not think any sermon ought to be preached or even written, until that sentence has emerged, clear and livid as a cloudless moon.[13]

Jowett's advice gives us several factors to consider when formulating the sermon thesis. First, strive for brevity (fifteen words maximum is ideal). Next, avoid redundancy, especially with the CIT. Don't simply change the verb from past tense to present tense. Phrase the thesis in a way that is appealing, clear, and forceful, yet still captures the meaning of the text and CIT. Be accurate. It may take several attempts. Write and rewrite until you get it right. This is the truth you're going to preach, so how you say it is important.

Purpose

No sermon is worth its salt that doesn't have a clear and attainable purpose. While the thesis is the truth to be preached, the purpose is the action to be taken. Every sermon should have a major purpose dictated by and the same as the general purpose of the text to guide the development of the sermon and keep it on target. There should also be a specific purpose—what you want the people who hear the sermon to do in light of it. Let's look briefly at how to formulate the purpose of the sermon for inclusion on the preliminary page.

Major purpose.—State in one word the major purpose of this sermon. Will it be evangelistic, consecrative, supportive, doctrinal, devotional, or ethical in purpose?[14] Don't try to do too much in one sermon. Select one major objective and develop the sermon to that end. The major purpose should be true to the biblical purpose of the text, the CIT, and the thesis. The major purpose of the sermon must be found in the text. While the text may have more than one purpose in it, you should zero in on only one purpose for each sermon. This makes the sermon clearer and easier to follow. List the major purpose as the fourth item on the preliminary page.

Specific purpose.—The specific purpose states concisely and clearly what you want people to do in light of this sermon. Be as specific as possible. Use a strong verb calling for action. Follow the line of direction from the text, the CIT, the thesis, and the major purpose. What do you want this audience to do as a result of hearing this sermon in this place at this time? Write it out as your fifth item on the preliminary page.

Appendix 1 is a sample preliminary page including all the items discussed above and those in steps 6 and 7 to follow. You might find it helpful. We should discipline ourselves to writing out a preliminary page for every sermon we prepare. If it isn't a biographical sermon you simply leave that particular item off and proceed from purpose to title. You can even program computers to produce the preliminary page format. Many preachers have found doing a preliminary page to be very helpful in sermon planning and preparation. It provides an excellent tool for sermon building.

What Type Biographical Sermon?

Step 6 calls for determining the type of biographical sermon that best suits this character from this text. Look at the line of direction developed on the preliminary page. If this was done carefully from the text through the specific purpose, it should suggest a particular type of biographical sermon to you. With these written items in front of you, and all the background study, exposition, exegesis, and analysis in mind, what type of biographical sermon should you do? Pick the one most appropriate and develop it.

Select a Category

Is this going to be a whole-life or a life-portion biographical sermon? Is it going to be about an individual or about multiple characters? This is the time and place to make these choices based on your study to this point. Once you make this choice you can decide on the specific type of sermon within the category.

You have done some selection of category before you get to this point. You have decided on a particular character or characters, and you have chosen a text. But you may have had only a general idea of what to do with them as far as a sermon. Now is the time to get specific, to finalize and formalize the category this sermon will fit into.

Specify Type

Along with the general category selected, you need to specify exactly which type of sermon within the category this one will be. For the sake of review and reminder let's look at the types again.

Whole-life types.—Chapter 4 described the particular types of whole-life biographical sermons as including sermons based on significant periods, key events, main places, crises, relationships, and life principle(s). Does the preliminary page lead to one of these types? If not, create your own category or combination of categories that the biblical material leads you to do.

Life-portion types.—The particular types of life-portion biographical suggested are single circumstance (which could be based on an event, place, period, activity, crisis, relationship, principle, etc.), some distinguishing characteristic(s), a single text, or a key lesson.

Multiple-character type.—If you are going to do a multiple character-type biographical sermon, you need to make note of this fact and specify the characters involved in it on the preliminary page.

Whichever particular type you decide on within a category, you need to write them on the preliminary page as the sixth item. So you might have any one of the following on your page:

Biographical sermon: Whole life, key events.
Biographical sermon: Whole life, crises.
Biographical sermon: Life portion, key text.
Biographical sermon: Life portion, adult career.
Biographical sermon: Multiple characters, David and Jonathan.
Biographical sermon: Multiple characters, Paul and Silas.

Whenever you look at this preliminary page subsequently, you will know exactly what you did in this particular sermon. It's an excellent record.

Formulate the Sermon Structure

The (sixth) and final step in preparation is to formulate the sermon structure. This includes entitling the sermon and outlining it. These are items 7 and 8 on your preliminary page.

Title

Call the sermon something interesting. A good title is more than an eye-catcher. It's an important key to the unity and cohesiveness of the sermon structure.

Make the title contemporary, not historical. Phrase it in the present tense. Instead of calling a sermon, "Job—the Man Who Made Satan Quit,"[15] you might call it, "How to Make Satan Leave You Alone." Or let your title ask a contemporary question like: "Can I Be an Encourager?" instead of, "Barnabas: Mr. Encourager."[16]

Carry the title into each of the sermon points by using the key word(s) of the title in each point, using synonyms, or by carrying the idea into each point. Use key words from the CIT, thesis, and purpose to keep the title in the line of direction from the text. Then use the key words from the title in the outline to keep the line of direction going.

The title is the seventh item on your preliminary page. Write it down.

Outline

The final item of preparation is your sermon outline, the eighth item on the preliminary page. Your outline should include an introduction, body, and conclusion. Even narrative and inductive sermons, relatively unstructured, need some plan to move them along. This plan is your outline, regardless of how simple or formal it may be.

Introduction.—As far as what you need to put on the preliminary page for your introduction goes, be sketchy. Put just enough to remind you of what will be included by way of opening sentence, illustrations, homiletical items from the preliminary page, where the text will go, and so forth. Use phrases or sentences, whatever suits your needs. A couple or three lines should be enough. Put enough to remind you of what you want to do, but briefly enough to be preliminary.

Sermon body.—Write down your sermon points as you will use them in the sermon. The number of points doesn't matter. Some sermons will have only one. Many may have three. Don't contort a text to try always to get three points out of it. Two points, four points—let the text dictate the sermon body; don't impose a structure onto it. Your sermon will have some kind of order and organization. Put it down on your preliminary page at this time.

Conclusion.—You will need to conclude your sermon. This is the place to drive home your specific purpose and thesis. As you did with the introduction, put down enough on the preliminary page to remind you of what you want to do in this conclusion. Be brief and concise. Never underestimate the importance or impact of a carefully conceived and constructed sermon conclusion.

Now you have a plan for preaching a biographical sermon. You've put a lot of time and effort into it. You selected the person, listed all the passages about this person, studied the passages, analyzed the person in light of them, wrote out a preliminary page, determined the type of biographical sermon to be preached on this person from this passage, and formulated a sermon structure. Whew! That's a lot of work. But it will be well worth it. God can use it to communicate His holy truth to people. God will honor your time spent in study as much as the time spent in delivering the sermon. God bless you for it. Maybe the Boy Scout motto, "Be Prepared," isn't a bad one for preachers either!

Notes

1. Whitesell, *Preaching on Bible Characters,* pp. 123-136.
2. Ibid.
3. See Whitesell's list on pp. 123-136 for characters with two asterisks by their name for further help in this category.
4. Characters with one asterisk by them in Whitesell's list fit this category. He listed 109 of them in the pages noted above.
5. Whitesell, pp. 123-136.
6. See Huber L. Drumwright, *Saints Alive! The Humble Heroes of the New Testament* (Nashville: Broadman Press, 1972); Basil Miller, *Meet the Little Known People of the Bible* (Dallas: Chandler Publications, 1955); A. T. Robertson, *Some Minor Characters of the New Testament* (Nashville: Southern Baptist Sunday School Board, 1928), and others.
7. Clovis G. Chappell, *Faces about the Cross* (New York: Abingdon-Cokesbury Press, 1941).
8. Clarence E. Macartney, *Mountains and Mountain Men of the Bible* (New York: Abingdon-Cokesbury Press, 1940).
9. R. Earl Allen, *Persons of the Passion* (Nashville: Broadman Press, 1972); William Barclay, *The Master's Men* (New York: Abingdon Press, 1959); Charles R. Brown, *These Twelve* (New York: Harper & Bros., 1926); H. H. Hargrove, *Personalities Around the Cross* (Grand Rapids: Baker Book House, 1963); Basil Miller, *Meet the Marred Men of the Bible* (Dallas: Chandler Pub., 1955) and *Meet the Voices of the Bible* (Dallas: Chandler Pub., 1955); Edwin McNeil Poteet, *These Shared His Passion, Cross and Power* (New York: Harper & Bros., 1948); et al.
10. Works like *Baker's Dictionary of Theology, Baker's Dictionary of Practical Theology,* Alan Richardson's *A Theological Word Book of the Bible,* or Colin Brown's three-volume *Dictionary of New Testament Theology* can be very helpful in this latter category.
11. Whitesell, p. 29.
12. Brown, *Quest,* p. 51
13. John Henry Jowett, *The Preacher: His Life and Work* (New York: George H. Doran Co., 1912; reprint ed., Grand Rapids: Baker Book House, 1968), p. 133.
14. See Brown, Clinard, and Northcutt, *Steps to the Sermon,* pp. 16-18, for definitions and elaboration on these six major objectives of preaching.

15. Macartney, *Greatest Men*, pp. 208-222.
16. Drumwright, pp. 13-18.

6
How to Do It

Even after all the time and work spent studying the text and analyzing the chosen character, even if you laboriously followed every step suggested in the previous chapter, you still don't have a sermon! You have an excellent plan for a sermon, but you can't live in a blueprint, only in a finished house. You have an excellent understanding of a Bible person, but no finished sermon to present to your people. The steps in preparation give you a framework, the basic elements and information needed for a sermon. Now you need to build a superstructure onto this framework. How do you get from plan to product, study to sermon, preliminary page to pulpit? Read on.

First you need a shape for your sermon, then some substance for it, then a way to say it. This chapter will look at how to give a biographical sermon shape using familiar forms particularly fitted to this genre. Then we will consider how to fill out the form functionally. Since the scope of this book is focused on biographical preaching and is neither a general homiletics text nor about a particular form of sermon construction, we will confine our interest to the relationship of these forms to our subject. This will not be an exhaustive study of each form per se. Anyone interested in more specific scholarship on narrative, inductive, or deductive preaching can find ample materials.

Here we assume a working knowledge of these forms and limit our presentation to a brief description of each, relating each to biographical preaching in particular.

Give It Form

Let's begin by considering biographical preaching in the forms of narrative, inductive, and deductive sermons. These three forms either naturally fit or are easily applied to sermons on Bible characters. There are other forms that could be used for biographical preaching, but we will limit our discussion here to these three. One reason for choosing these three is the current revival of interest in narrative and inductive preaching, and the ongoing interest in the most common form of sermon construction through the ages, the deductive.[1]

Narrative Biographical Preaching

Narrative biographical preaching is telling the story about or of the Bible character you have chosen. This form obviously is not limited to preaching on Bible characters, but it is naturally suited to it. And when something fits naturally and comfortably, we had better get into it.

The narrative form of the biographical sermon presents the life or a portion of the life of the Bible character you are dealing with in the form of action, characterization, setting, and sequence. It is especially appealing to people's imaginations and emotions. It draws them into the character, thus into the sermon. Truth in story form is the oldest way of communication. It is one of the best ways for communicating God's truth from the lives of Bible characters.

What is the difference between the traditional deductive method of sermon construction and narrative method? Several contemporary writers deal with this subject. Eugene Lowry is one of the most helpful. In his first chapter of *Doing Time in the Pulpit,* Lowry differentiates between these two forms as follows.[2]

Deductive Method	*Narrative Method*
Orders ideas	Orders experiences
Task-organizing	Task-shaping
Form-structure	Form-process
Focus-theme	Focus-events
Principle-substance	Principle-resolution
Product-outline	Product-plot
Means-logic, clarity	Means-ambiguity, suspense
Goal-understanding	Goal-happening

Understand that Lowry is arguing for narrative method and against deductive method, so he overstates the case. For example the goal of all deductively organized sermons isn't merely understanding. The goal of "happening" and numerous other objectives in deductive sermons can be achieved, as they can be in narrative sermons. Lowry has done some important work on narrative style, however, and the biographical preacher will find him helpful.

Narrative is an especially good way to handle large volumes of textual material. You would not want to read to a congregation all the Bible has to say about Joseph (OT), but you could narrate his story in a relatively short time. Even a portion of Moses' life, say his first forty years, would be too lengthy to read in a sermon, but what a beautiful and meaningful story to tell! Whether you are doing a whole-life, life-portion, or multiple-characters biographical sermon, the narrative method is a dynamic, useful form to do it by.

Biographical narration.—Telling the story *about* a Bible character is biographical narration. It fits any of the major categories and particular types of biographical sermons already discussed.

For example, let's look at a whole-life biographical sermon based on key events. It can be on any character. For now let's not pick one, but simply look at the category. This person obviously was born, lived, and died. In between birth and death he did something. Something happened to him. What did he do? In what sequence? With what meaning? Your answers to these questions give you the form for your sermon.

Change the analogy from events to places. Where was she born? Where did she die? Where did she go in between? What significance did these places have? What happened there? What do we learn? What meaning do these places have? Here's your form for a narrative whole-life sermon based on key places.

Apply the method to a life-portion sermon based on a crisis. Who was involved in it? What was the crisis? How did the person handle it? Learn from it? What can we learn from what the person did or didn't do, or learn or didn't learn? Tell the story of the crisis the person experienced as the basis for your narrative biographical sermon. Illustrate it. Apply it. You have your sermon in a simple, communicable form.

Narrative biography, telling the story about a person, is a useful form for any of the categories and particular types of biographical sermons. It has the automatic advantage of being fairly easy. It takes its form from the person's story and moves along with it. Not only is it easy to prepare, it's easy to listen to and follow. If it's on a more familiar character, much of the story might already be well known. If it's on a lesser-known character, people might find it interesting because they're hearing something new. The story form itself has great appeal. Most people love to hear a good story. The Bible is filled with fascinating stories, especially about people. Tell them. It's a major method for shaping biographical sermons.

Autobiographical narration.—Telling the story *of* a Bible character in first person is autobiographical narration or dramatic monologue preaching. Be aware that even this form of narrative preaching has to focus on the person to be considered biographical. One can get into character and talk about an event, place, or idea instead of being biographical. What we're interested in is the story of a person told by the preacher assuming the role of this person.

Some helpful insights on this form of preaching can be gained from Alton H. McEachern in his book: *Dramatic Monologue Preaching.*[3] He pointed out that this form makes the Word come alive, thus heightening interest and communication. He warned about unchecked imagination and the danger of anachronism, calling for careful research and preparation. "Always be faithful to the biblical material," McEachern advised, giving helpful hints on how to do this effectively.[4] His introductory "how-to" chapter is followed by fourteen autobiographical sermons worthy of examination.

To do a first-person biographical sermon, the preacher "becomes" the Bible character and tells his or her story. Using narrative style you simply relate "your" life or the portion of it you're dealing with to the congregation. The biography is itself the illustration, but you can draw in other illustrations if you so desire. Apply the truths you're telling as is appropriate. Again, the simplicity of this form belies its effectiveness and dynamism. It can be a very moving way to preach a biographical sermon.

Autobiographical narrative fits any of the categories and types of biographical sermons discussed above. Use this as the form to express the truths you have discovered about the person in the text you're dealing with. You must get a feel, a true understanding, for who this person was. How did he think, act, express himself? What did he sound like? Look like? Was he warm and personable or cold and calculating? Did he laugh or cry easily? Was he haughty or humble? These and other questions must be answered before you can adequately portray this person in an autobiographical sermon. But if you can get a feel for a character and feel comfortable using this format, it can be dynamite for you and your listeners. Why not give it a try? You just might discover some gifts you never knew you had!

The best biographical and autobiographical narrative preaching is directly related to a text. You can and should use your imagination to create context, fill in details not given in Scripture, and interpret moods, but you must always be aware of where your imagination begins and Scripture ends. On this point Jensen commented:

> Always begin with a text. Story preaching must be anchored to a given text(s) of Scripture. Our interest is not in the creative potential of our own storytelling ability. We are concerned with recasting a biblical text so that it might come alive for our hearers in new ways. . . . Your story is told in the service of the text; the text is not the excuse/springboard for your story.[5]

Biographical and autobiographical narration are two of the most effective ways to structure biographical sermons. Carefully done, they can be an expressive, even artful way to preach.[6] We got our Bible character stories from the great storytellers of old. Why not adopt this method they used so effectively to preach the same truths they proclaimed? Narrative is an excellent form for shaping biographical sermons.

Inductive Biographical Preaching

Inductive preaching organizes the sermon from a specific experience (or several experiences) to a general truth.[7] This is the exact opposite of deductive preaching, which moves from general to specific. Inductive form moves from an incident, question, or issue to the sermons' truth (thesis). The thesis refers to material previously presented. Deductive form begins with the truth and explains, illustrates, and applies it in specific areas. Inductive method has many strong advocates and much to commend it. It can be an especially effective form for preaching on Bible characters.

Centered in need.—Inductive biographical sermons would begin with some experience, question, problem, issue, or insight of living and move toward a Bible character who had a similar situation. In the first chapter we saw how a sermon idea can originate with a text that addresses a need, or with a need that seeks an answer from a text. Inductive biographical would principally be of the latter type. It would be distinctively biographical in that the preacher would address the need, answer the question, and solve the puzzle specifically through the life of a Bible person, in whole or in part.

Focused on Scripture.—Every conceivable contemporary human need is addressed in some way by someone in the Bible. For every experience we have there is a biblical parallel. God's source Book is sufficient for our living. We can preach inductively by focusing on Bible characters who give us insight. We arrive at the inductive biographical sermon by assessing the need, then asking, "Who in God's Word experienced a similar thing? What did he do about it? How did he handle it? Face it? Solve it?" These questions and many others may lead you to an inductive form. You answer the questions from the life of a Bible person.

It could be that the Bible character you are drawn to exemplifies the opposite experience or attitude you're seeking to address. You could use this inductively in a biographical sermon as well. The message is what is important. The method only takes you to the message.

One particular instance comes to mind. A pastor needed to speak on how to recover from grief. A child in his congregation had died. It was a terrible, tragic incident. Not only the child's family but the whole congregation was grieving, and couldn't seem to work through their grief. They were stuck in the depths of despair. The pastor's question, both in the study and in the sermon before his people, was: "Is there any model, any aid to help us get up from grief?" And the answer was a resounding yes, in the form of an inductive biographical sermon based on 2 Samuel 12:16-24. This was David's experience of rising from the grief of the loss of his son. David's experience wasn't typical, but, then, whose encounter with grief is? So the pastor began with the specific instance of this child's loss and the lingering grief it brought onto the whole congregation. Then he asked the key question, mentioned already. Next he related David's experience and read the text. From these verse he drew four general principles.

1. Rising up from grief demands a proper understanding of death.
2. Recovering from the depths of grief involves time and process.
3. Faith in God is essential for getting up from grief.

4. Rising from grief means remembering life goes on.

In each principle the experience of David was related, then applied to the present situation. The people felt tremendous love and support through this sermon. The response was positive and immediately evident. People were helped and ministered to. This is good preaching!

Ralph and Gregg Lewis give additional examples of inductive biographical sermons in their book *Inductive Preaching.* Here you will find an example of this method applied to a whole-life combination (key places, events, crises) biographical sermon on Moses, and to a multiple characters sermon on Abraham, Isaac, and Jacob, along with some helpful insights on this genre of preaching.[8]

The inductive method can be an extremely effective form for processing biographical sermons.

Deductive Biographical Preaching

The traditional deductive form of sermon construction can be nicely suited to biographical preaching. Deductive preaching develops the sermon by using the thesis as the controlling idea. The remainder of the sermon, whether stated before or after the thesis, supports and elaborates it. The structure of a deductive sermon generally includes an introduction, body, and conclusion. The number of "points" in the body, whether major or subpoints, varies. It is possible to have as few as one point or to have several, depending on the particular text and sermon. The important thing to remember is to let the text dictate the structure of the sermon body.

Deductive preaching has frequently gotten a bad reputation due to overuse, overorganization, and abuse. One commonly hears it derogatorily referred to as the three-points-and-a-poem method.[9] But it doesn't have to be that way. In fact it will only be that way when we get into a homiletical rut and don't deal with texts honestly or deeply enough. Deductive form can be quite effective and shouldn't be discarded. Craddock observed, "Forms of preaching should be as varied as the forms of rhetoric in the New Testament, or as the purposes of preaching, or as the situations of those who listen."[10] We must always consider any particular form of sermon construction only *a* method, never *the* method.

The preliminary-page method of preparation presented in the previous chapter leads primarily but not exclusively to the deductive form of biographical preaching. Consider all forms as you study and prepare. Follow whichever one the text most clearly supports. Often that will be the deductive form. This form has the advantages of being logical, cohesive, organized, substantive, and purposeful. It's easy to listen to and follow. Clearly presented, a deductive sermon can communicate God's truth effectively.

Deductive biographical preaching is using this method to communicate truth in sermons based on Bible characters. A past master at using this form was Frederick W. Robertson (1816-1853), the British Anglican known for his two-point sermons. Robertson never published a sermon during his brief lifetime (thirty-seven years). His entire ministry lasted only six years. He died thinking he was a failure. But after his death his sermons were gathered by his parishioners at Brighton and published. They have been widely read and influential since. Many of Robertson's sermons were biographical. One of them, entitled "Triumph Over Hindrances," was based on Zacchaeus from Luke 19:1-10. From Zacchaeus's experience with Jesus, Robertson showed, first, "The hindrances to a religious life," and, second, "The Christian triumph over difficulties." This was a rhetorically structured deductive biographical sermon with a supportive major purpose.

In part 1, Robertson dealt with Zacchaeus's circumstantial hindrances and his personal hindrances of coming to Christ. He skillfully used the text to speak to greed and guilt. In part 2, Robertson spoke of God's part and humanity's part in triumphing over difficulties, showing these from the experience of Zacchaeus with Jesus. All parts of this sermon were well organized and easily discernible: introduction, body, and conclusion. Each developed the main theme: "The successful pursuit of religion under difficulties." It is a masterpiece of deductive biographical preaching.[11]

Fosdick's frequent methodology was to begin with his thesis as his opening sentence and proceed from there. This was true even in many of his sermons on Bible characters. When his thesis wasn't his first sentence, it was still usually given early, and clearly, in the introduction.[12]

Narrative? Inductive? Deductive? Which sermon form should you use? Let the text tell you, don't take a prescribed form to a text. Careful study and thoughtful prayer will direct your sermon method on any particular text. Don't be bound to any one form. As you seek to give your biographical sermon shape, or rather let it suggest a shape to you, be awake to the variety of creative possibilities open to you. Any method that fits is viable. Apply the form as the text reveals itself. Good preaching calls for variety and creativity. Surprise your congregation with something different the next time you preach. You and they will be glad you did.

Now let's turn our attention to how to give substance to the shape of your sermon.

Fill Out the Form Functionally

No matter the method of sermon construction, when you stand to preach you don't give people divisions, you give them development. The final product of a sermon isn't its shape but its substance. Whether your style is narrative, inductive, deductive, or something else, you need meat on the sermon's skeleton. Functional development is this meat.

When you narrate a story, what are you doing? When you state a principle, what are you doing? When you illustrate, what are you doing? You are using language in a certain way. You are doing something with what you are saying. You are either explaining, illustrating, or applying. These are the functional elements of preaching.

In 1870 when John A. Broadus wrote what is now the prototype textbook of homiletics, *On the Preparation and Delivery of Sermons,* he identified four functional elements of preaching.[13] These have been revised, combined, reviled, and renewed through the decades, but the point remains that when you use language in a sermon, you're doing something with it—whatever the form of the sermon. The language of preaching has some function in the sermon. Functional analysis tells you what you are doing with the language you're using. It's the way to fill out the sermon.

Broadus identified explanation, argument (logical persuasion, not bickering), illustration, and application as the four functional elements of the sermon.[14] Here we will regard argument as a subcategory of explanation rather than dealing with it separately. Again, this not being a general homiletics text, we will confine our interest to the functional elements of explanation, illustration, and application as they relate to biographical preaching.

How do we develop biographical sermons?

Explanation

Whenever you make something plain, clear, interpret, reveal, give cause or reason for, or make something known in a sermon, you are explaining. Explanation is the functional element that develops the meaning of the text or context, in whole or any part of it. When you give exposition to a text, narrate a story, or describe a person, place, or thing, you're explaining. Explanation is the foundational functional element in any sermon. Whether you're explaining something about a text (a word meaning, situation, place, and so forth) or dealing with nontextual facts, you're using this functional element. In biographical preaching various types or subcategories of explanation are especially useful for developing the content of the sermon.

Explanation by exposition.—Exposition simply means to expose or uncover. In preaching it refers to uncovering the truth of the text. The opposite of exposition is imposition, and we never want to impose onto a text what isn't there.[15]

In biographical sermons we want to reveal truth, facts, and details about Bible characters. We can give analysis of them, explain their character traits, their backgrounds, history, setting, and culture, and so forth. We can summarize facts about them or interpret them. Exposition appeals to the intellect by presenting information about a Bible character in an objective manner.

Explanation by narration.—It's also possible to use explanation in biographical sermons by narration. Narration explains people, facts, events, places, background, relationships, and so forth, in the form of action, characterization, setting, and sequence. It is telling the story about or of the Bible person rather than an objective exposition of facts. Narration adds movement and feeling to the data. It appeals more to the imagination and emotions than does exposition.

An excellent example of explanation by narration is found in these paragraphs from C. Roy Angell's biographical sermon entitled "Rizpah":

> They took the seven sons of Saul up to the hill of Gibeah, and runners went out to summon all the Gibeonites. That was a gala day for this little remnant of Amorites. Drawn on your imagination a moment and you can see what happened. All day long they paraded back and forth in front of the seven suffering sons of Saul, snapped their fingers, hissed and ridiculed, jeered and sneered. Then the day ended, and the boys were dead.
>
> As twilight descended, a little old woman, mother of two of the sons, a concubine of Saul named Rizpah, climbed the hill of Gibeah. Sobs shook her frail frame and tears ran down her face and dropped into the hearth. When she found the two that belonged to her, I imagine she did what any American mother would have done, she kissed their bloody feet and wept her heart out. It was the law that anyone put to death could not be buried, so they had to hang there until, as Tennyson said, "the wind rattled their bones," and the vultures picked them clean, or until the beasts of the forest tore them down. That was their fate or what it was supposed to be.
>
> Night came and Rizpah spread her sackcloth on a rock to rest. But there was no rest for her, for the wild beasts of the forest smelled the blood and, snarling, they had come for their feast. What did she do? Scream in terror and run away? No, she took the sackcloth and flashed it over her head, screaming in defiance, and drove them back into the forest. Day came. Exhausted, she again spread the sackcloth to rest. A shadow, and another, and

then another careened before her. Wearily she lifted her face to see the vultures of the air that had come for their feast. Once more the sackcloth flashed her defiance. . . .

June, July, August, September, she stayed among the decaying bodies of the seven sons and drove the beasts off by night and the birds of the air by day.

Then into the silken seclusion of David's palace seeped the rumor, "Poor Rizpah. She is going mad."

David asked, "What's the matter with Rizpah?"

They answered, "Hadn't you heard? They fixed a little tent for her up there where the seven sons of Saul are and she's kept the beasts off at night and the birds of the air by day. She hasn't left her post, they've carried her things to eat."

David, remorseful, his whole heart bursting, ordered: "Take that law off the statute books now. Go get those seven sons of Saul, bring them down here and bury them in the king's burying ground. That's where they belong, all of them." That's the story.[16]

Explanation by description.—When you paint vivid word pictures of the taste, smell, feel, or sound of something or someone, you're using explanation by description. In the biographical sermon you can also describe how someone acts, their motives, emotions, and so forth. Description appeals to the senses. It draws the hearers into the picture until they feel like participants. They see this person, the subject of the biographical sermon; they seemingly hear her speak, or they see his misery or hope.

Peter Marshall drew us into a scene in Pharaoh's court where Moses pleaded God's people's cause before the King in the sermon: "Compromise in Egypt," using vivid description in the midst of narration.

For sheer drama it is difficult to find anything in history

or fiction to surpass the tug-of-war, the clash of wills, between Pharaoh and Moses. It was a struggle long drawn out. It began when God selected Moses to lead the children of Israel out of bondage in Egypt into nationhood in a homeland of their own and instructed him to go to Pharaoh and demand that he liberate the Hebrew people.

Moses made excuses to God, even as we all do. He protested that he was not the man for such a task. But God met all of his excuses, and Moses finally accepted his commission and accompanied by Aaron sought an interview with Pharaoh. He walked forward over the tiled floor to where Pharaoh sat on his stone throne with its huge carved figures for arms. Giant Nubian slaves stood behind him working the screens of palms that moved the humid air, heavy with exotic fragrance. He blinked his eyes in the bright sunshine, so bright that the shadows seemed to be etched in purple on the floor. He advanced slowly, aware of the inscriptions, the frescoes, the tiles, and the very stones eloquent with boastings and stories of conquest. In the sharp shadows sat Pharaoh, a thinly veiled sneer on his lips, his smooth chin cupped in his one hand, watching through half-shut eyes. Moses felt the threat of the hanging draperies. They were dark red—as dark as blood drying on the sand, and Moses remembered the color of it for he had seen Egyptian blood on the sand.

He was impressed with the magnificence of the palace court and the sense of Pharaoh's power. But he remembered that he had just come from an audience with Jehovah—a power greater than Pharaoh's—and he grew bold again. His courage returned and he thought of his commission. He straightened up until he looked Pharaoh right in the eye without the slightest fear and he said simply, just as it is written: "Thus saith the Lord God of Israel, Let my people go."[17]

Other types of explanation are also applicable to biographical preaching—explanation by argument, division, and transition—but exposition, narration, and description are the major subcategories of this functional element we should utilize. Use them generously and creatively to develop your biographical sermons. They will serve you well.

Illustration

Illustrations open a window of light onto the truth you are proclaiming. Basically the format for developing a sermon functionally is to make a point, explain it in relationship to the text, illustrate it, apply it, then move on to the next point. This applies to any of the sermon forms previously discussed or to any other form. It certainly applies to biographical sermons, whatever shape they take.

It is possible to use illustrations in all types of biographical sermons, even in first-person sermons. This doesn't mean it will always be easy, or even advisable, but it is possible. For example, a seminary student was preaching a first-person sermon in a delivery practicum as Judah, brother of Joseph. He was in costume. He did the sermon in narrative style. "How can I illustrate in it?" was his question to the professor. "Biblically," was the answer. So the student drew illustrations from Abraham, Adam, and "his" own family to cast light on what he was preaching about Joseph. This is a legitimate use of illustration in an autobiographical sermon.

Select fresh, creative, appealing illustrations that truly explain or apply what you're preaching about. They must be relevant to the point. The Bible is a rich source book for such illustrations. However, don't rely solely on the Bible. Use history, arts, literature, science, television, books, sports, personal experiences, and so forth, as well. Or make up illustrations. Use your imagination. Be creative. The best preachers are the best illustrators. Draw illustrations from fact, fiction, opinion, poetry, prose, quotations. Illustrate each part of the sermon. It will add interest, clarity, and appeal.

Application

The Bible characters who are the subjects of our sermons have a message for us. We must discern it carefully and pass it on faithfully. That is, we must apply the truths we discover as we prepare biographical sermons to the people or institutions they apply to. Some truths will apply to individuals, some to families, some to pastors, or deacons, or Sunday School teachers. Others will apply to the universal church, or to a specific situation within a local church. Still other applications might be made to the world-at-large. However and wherever biblical truth applies, we must directly give it voice. This is the purpose of preaching in general and biographical preaching in particular—to help people, challenge people, inform people, bless people, save people, and call people to action.

Don't assume truth is implicit in your biographical sermon. Make it explicit. Even in autobiographical preaching we can use application directly and effectively. One doesn't have to step out of character to use application in the course of a first-person sermon.[18] The preacher portraying Job can say,

> I learned to be faithful to God no matter what. Even when my family died or forsook me, I remained faithful. When my friends analyzed me, accused me, abandoned me, I was still faithful. Faithfulness is rewarded. This is a lesson I learned. And some of you need to learn the same lesson. Be faithful. Faithfulness is rewarded. When you're tempted to commit adultery, be faithful.

When you're faced with the opportunity to steal from your business, don't do it! Stay true to God. Faithfulness pays, even when it costs. Learn from me. Be faithful.

However you can use application, in whatever type of sermon, don't fail to apply the great truths of God, gleaned from the lives of Bible characters, in your biographical sermons.

The way to add substance to the shape of your biographical sermons is by functional development. Explain, illustrate, apply. This frees you for creative delivery. It puts meat on the bones of the sermon. Use the functional elements to fill out the form.

Use Your Imagination

Whatever shape your biographical sermon takes, and however you fill out this form functionally, be imaginative.

Imagination Defined

Imagination is "the mental process by which we bring together facts of experience, set them in their true or actual relationships to one another, and rearrange them in new combinations and relationships."[19] In other words, imagination is the picture-making facility of the mind. It's based on reality and deals with reality, adding creativity to reorder it into something new. Blackwood defined imagination as the "God-given ability to see and to show."[20]

Uses in Biographical Preaching

Our interest here is not in imagination in general but in its creative uses in biographical preaching. Let's look at six such uses.[21]

Fills in the blanks.—Imagination can be used in the biographical sermon to fill in details of what might have actually happened in the historical and narrative material of the Bible. Details must sometimes be constructed or reconstructed in the light of the time and place our chosen character lived. Imagination based on scholarship is the method for doing this.

Gives background.—Imagination can be used to set the context or background for a particular Bible character. Some data will be discovered in the background study. Others will have to be assumed from the general history, location, culture, and so forth, of the times. How did these factors influence this person? Help shape him or her?

Creates dialogue.—When conversation or dialogue between biblical characters isn't explicit, imagination can supply it.

Analyzes.—Imagination can be used to analyze the psychological makeup of a biblical character. Sometimes when we aren't told much about a Bible person we can still imagine what they must be like. What was his personality like? What motivated him? How can I understand him? Imagination can help supply some answers.

Contemporizes.—How do we draw twentieth-century people into the lives of first-century people or people who lived eight-hundred years before Christ? Imagination! It enables moderns to enter the experiences of ancients by drawing parallels, making contemporary application of ancient truths, and using imaginative narration and description. By using imagination we can put Saul in a business suit or an astronaut in the ark. Imagination brings a biblical character into touch with contemporary life. It creates the mood for the sermon.

Creates illustrations.—Imagination can be used to create illustrations for biographical sermons. When we can't *find* an illustration, we can always *think up* one.

Use imagination in every part of the sermon. Use it to complement each functional element. Use it to add spice and variety to your biographical sermons. Use it to expand your own consciousness and creative ability. Our goal is to communicate the gospel. If we let it grip our minds, we can't help but be imaginative in its proclamation. Pass that imagination on to others so their imaginations can get fired up on gospel truth. When we've done that, we've done a pretty good day's work!

Now your biographical sermon is created. It has preparation, form, function, and fire. It's ready to be delivered. How about some creative delivery suggestions?

Notes

1. In fact the intensity of interest in narrative and inductive is so strong on the part of some of their advocates that they would discount deductive methods entirely. To do so would be tragic in my opinion. Any way we can get God's Word across is legitimate, and many forms are needed and expedient. Let's not throw out the baby with the bath water.

2. Pages 11-28. The organization of this chart is mine.

3. Alton H. McEachern, *Dramatic Monologue Preaching* (Nashville: Broadman Press, 1984). See also Harold Freeman, *Variety in Biblical Preaching* (Waco: Word Books, 1987), pp. 47-84. Freeman also has an excellent section on narrative preaching in general on pp. 115-160.

4. McEachern, pp. 12-18.

5. Jensen, p. 151.

6. See Eugene L. Lowry, *The Homiletical Plot: The Sermon as Narrative Art Form* (Atlanta: John Knox Press, 1980), for additional information on the sermon as narrative art form.

7. Craddock, *As One Without Authority*, pp. 54, 57.

8. Lewis and Lewis, pp. 87-89.

9. The author recently heard a wag refer to a sermon as having "three poems and a point" by someone who didn't particularly care for it. Oh well, at least it had *a* point.

10. Craddock, *As One Without Authority*, p. 53.

11. Frederick W. Robertson, *Sermons Preached at Brighton,* reprint edition (New York: Harper & Brothers, n.d.), pp. 68-78.

12. Edmund H. Linn, *Preaching as Counseling: The Unique Method of Harry Emerson Fosdick* (Valley Forge: Judson Press, 1966), p. 79. See also Clyde E. Fant and William M. Pinson, *Twenty Centuries of Great Preaching,* vol. 9: *Fosdick to E. Stanley Jones* (Waco: Word Books, 1971), p. 20.

13. John A. Broadus, *On the Preparation and Delivery of Sermons,* new and revised edition edited by J. B. Weatherspoon (New York: Harper and Row, 1944), pp. 156-221.

14. Ibid.

15. John R. W. Scott, *Between Two Worlds* (Grand Rapids: Eerdmans, 1982), p. 126.

16. C. Roy Angell, *Iron Shoes* (Nashville: Broadman Press, 1953), pp. 65-67.

17. From the sermon "Compromise in Egypt," side two of the record by Peter Marshall, *Were You There?* (Waco: Word Records, 1944).

18. For the opposite view see McEachern, pp. 17-18.

19. Broadus, p. 287. See his whole chapter on imagination for some helpful insights, pp. 279-292.

20. Blackwood, *Biographical Preaching for Today,* p. 132.

21. Much of this material comes from class notes taken by the author in the course Preaching 437, fall semester 1967, Southwestern Baptist Theological Seminary, Dr. Jesse J. Northcutt, professor. Used with Dr. Northcutt's oral permission.

7
Creative Delivery Suggestions

In its final form a sermon is not an exercise in writing but an event in communication.[1] Preaching is more than a Bible study, more than merely talking about God and the things of God. Preaching is the living word of God.[2] It involves spirituality, intellect, will, emotions, cognition, words, movement, and more. Because preaching is a communicational event involving virtually every dimension of human and divine interaction, we must prepare for the delivery of a sermon every bit as carefully and thoroughly as we prepare for its structure and contents.

Our focus in this chapter is on sermon delivery suggestions specifically related to biographical preaching. This is not a textbook on general sermon delivery. Many excellent ones are available.[3] Neither is it a manual on oral preparation.[4] Our interest here is on appropriate ways to deliver biographical sermons, with an accent on creativity. Perhaps there are some ways to preach on Bible characters you haven't thought of, or need to be reminded of. Let's look at six suggestions for delivering biographical sermons creatively, then look briefly at drama in biographical preaching, and at the use of contemporary and historical biography in sermons.

Tell Their Story

We have already looked at the preparation of narrative biographical preaching in the preceding chapter. If this is the shape you choose for your sermon, how do you present it creatively?

Simple Storytelling

The most obvious way to deliver a narrative biographical sermon is simply yourself, dressed as you would regularly be dressed, all other parts of the worship service being normal, and telling the story of a Bible character. Tell it as you would tell any story ("The Three Little Pigs," and so forth), only focus the content on the chosen Bible character. There's nothing especially creative about this method of delivery, unless it's so different from the way you usually preach that your hearers will be surprised. Come to think of it, a little surprise might not hurt the average Sunday-morning congregation, would it? Why not try delivering a biographical by simply telling the story of the person you've selected?

Second-Person Narrative

A bit more creative way to tell the story of a Bible character is as a character, but not the one whose story you're telling. This method of delivery narrates the story of a Bible person as a second character. It isn't autobiographical. It is dramatic monologue. Only instead of your own story you tell someone else's. Maybe it's "deuterobiographical," to coin a term.

Do you remember Isaiah's enacted prophecy intended to discourage Judah from aligning with Egypt against Assyria in chapter 20? Do you remember what he did? He walked around Jerusalem naked for three years! Doesn't this act speak volumes about Isaiah as a person? It shows us his total obedience to God, even in the face of humiliation, and his commitment to get God's message across, no matter what. Why not preach a life-portion key event deuterobiographical sermon on Isaiah as one of his next-door neighbors, or as a person on the streets of Jerusalem, observing this disturbing act? You could begin by narrating the historical situation that occasioned Isaiah's startling deed, then move to what you observed as an eyewitness to it, then to what you learned from it about Isaiah as a person. As always, keep the focus biographical.

You can think of many other Bible characters ripe for this method of delivery: Aaron commenting on Moses, Moses speaking about Miriam, a lion talking about Daniel, Judas Iscariot discussing Jesus—on and on the list could go. This can be a fascinating way to preach biographical narratives, fitting nearly any of the categories or types of sermons previously presented.

Become the Person

Autobiographical or dramatic monologue preaching in which you personally portray the character presents many creative possibilities for delivery. You can do it in costume or not, with special lighting or not, with or without special effects such as background sounds, scenery, or music. Commenting on the creative advantages of this method Francis C. Rossow of Concordia Seminary wrote:

> Role playing, unlike so many other familiar things, has never lost its capacity for creativity. To this day I am tricked into listening whenever a pastor assumes the role of a Judas or a Peter or a Caiaphas and preaches a sermon from that perspective. There seems to be something inherently creative about first person preaching.[5]

We might use this inherent creativity in one of the two following ways.

Bible-Period Autobiography

Try preaching in costume appropriate to the period your character came from. There are ample pictures available in Bible encyclopedias, dictionaries, and so forth, and even in Sunday School classrooms, (We've all seen those children's picture sets of Bible scenes.) and quarterlies. Someone handy with a sewing machine can be a big help. Or try borrowing a costume from a local school, college, or large church. Or a costume rental place might prove helpful.

Variety needed.—Vary the way you deliver your autobiographical sermons. One pastor used this method about once a month but did it the same way each time. He put a dish towel over his head to imitate a ghutra, but wore his Sunday suit. It got old rather quickly. Variety is the spice of preaching.

You can go to elaborate lengths with costuming or keep it fairly simple. You can use beards, powdered hair, make-up, and wigs in addition to biblical-period clothes. You will surely want to remove your watch, eyeglasses, and possibly rings and other jewelry, although some jewelry may be appropriate. Don't be anachronistic. Beware of wearing contemporary clothing that might show from under your costume. This detracts from the effect.

Resources.—You undoubtedly will have persons in your church who can help you with costuming, scenery, backdrops, recorded sounds of music, or whatever you wish to utilize to create variety for this method of delivery. They can be a great resource for autobiographical preaching, and they are usually most happy to be asked. Use them as opportunity arises.

Contemporize

Another way to "become" the person is to avoid the Bible period altogether and deliver the sermon in a highly stylized contemporary fashion.

Picture this. It's time for the sermon in a Sunday evening service. The pastor isn't up front; the service is being led by someone else. The house lights go out for a moment. Then a single light comes on, and the pastor is sitting on a stool beside the pulpit. He's wearing a turtleneck sweater. He has a look of anguish on his face. He begins to speak:

> Hello. My name is Joe. Well, Joseph actually, but my friends call me Joe. I'm engaged to the sweetest, purest, most beautiful girl in the world. At least, I thought she was the purest. Mary is her name. Well, last night I went to pick Mary up for our date, and she tells me she's pregnant. Pregnant! I *know* I'm not the father. I've never touched her. Not like that, I mean. But she's pregnant.
>
> I was sick. I didn't know what to do or say. I wanted to run, cry, scream, get sick. Instead we just talked about it. We talked far into the night.
>
> Mary told me she hadn't been with a man. Any man. She said an angel of the Lord came to her and told her she, a virgin, would conceive by the Holy Spirit and bear a son, God's Son. Can you believe it?

The sermon proceeds, in first person, as "Joe" tells his story of the birth of Jesus and his feelings, reactions, and experiences. "Joe" tells us how he, too, was visited by an angel, how he came to believe, and how he learned to trust God in very unusual circumstances.

This is only one example of a way to contemporize an

autobiographical narrative sermon. Let your imagination lead you to other sermons that could be delivered this way. There are many. Why not try one?

Interview the Character

Another good way to preach on Bible characters is to use the interview method of delivery.

Do It Alone

You can do this by being both interviewer and interviewee. You might begin such a sermon by expressing a wish to talk to some Bible character personally, to ask them some questions you'd like answered from their perspective. Then you invite the audience to imagine with you that this person is present right then. Call him forward. Welcome him to the pulpit (imaginary at this point, of course). Then ask him a question.

At this point, step to the position the Bible character would be standing in if actually present, and become that person. You might want to change your voice pitch, tone, or accent when in this other role. Or not. Answer the question to the audience. Then, step back over to your first position as yourself and ask another question. Then, back to the Bible character for the answer, and so forth. This method is communicational dynamite! It can captivate an audience and communicate truth effectively.

Use Another Person

Another way to interview a Bible character is to get someone else to help you. You can be the interviewer and get someone else to play the role of the interviewee, or vice versa. Either way, this method of delivery takes more time in preparation than some others because you have to coordinate everything, and inevitably practice with your partner in the venture. But it's well worth the effort when it's done well. It's a powerful way to communicate Bible truths biographically.

One example of this method was an interview with the woman at the well of Samaria done by a pastor in a Sunday evening service. The part of the woman at the well was played by a young member especially gifted in drama. She got up an elaborate costume of the period, laden with jewelry, and a veil. The pastor began by reading John 4:1-30 to the congregation. Then he introduced the special guest and called her forward. They had rehearsed, of course.

On the platform were two chairs, a small table, and microphones. They sat down. He asked her name, then set the background of why she was at the well at noon, the relationships between Jews and Samaritans and between men and women in Jesus' day by asking questions. The main thrust of the interview concerned her own response to Jesus during their encounter and what she learned about evangelism because of it. The questions and dialogue were arranged in these two areas as follows:

Responses to Jesus	*Lessons about evangelism*
Surprise	Social contact important
Puzzlement	Establish common interest
Sarcasm	Arouse interest
Receptive	Don't go too far
Change began	Don't condemn
Conviction	Stick with main issue
Bewilderment	Confront directly
Reverence	Show love
Stunned	
Religious knowledge	
Faith	

Conversion
Barriers broken down
Told others

This interview sermon went over well with all but one staid deacon. On his way out he told the pastor he wished "we'd get back to preaching and quit this play acting!" Oh well, we can't please everyone all the time.

Voice Offstage

A creative alternative for delivering a biographical sermon is to enlist the help of another person or a recorder to be an unseen partner, a voice offstage.

Two Voices

One such sermon was done with the preacher in the role of Jonah and the voice offstage being God's. God called (in the form of a person sitting out of view in the rear vestibule with a microphone). Jonah responded. God asked Jonah to go to Nineveh and preach repentance. Jonah refused and gave his reasons. The sermon continued along the lines of the four chapters in the Book of Jonah, each time with God speaking to Jonah as He did in the Bible. It was a very effective, creative sermon.

Several Voices

How about a pulpit version of the old TV staple, "This Is Your Life"? The preacher would enact the Bible character on the platform, and others from this person's life would be the voices offstage. You could involve several people from the congregation in this sermon as voices.

Tape-recorded Voice

Another way to deliver this type of sermon is to have the voice offstage taped. It can even be your own voice. How about Job, talking to himself about what's happening? This method might require some coordination with whomever operates your sound equipment at church. Or you can buy an inexpensive foot switch for a recorder that starts the recorder playing when depressed and stops it when released. Better yet, borrow one. Use media to preach the unseen voice type of sermon.

Interrupted Sermon

You could also creatively deliver a biographical sermon by having someone interrupt it at some point during its delivery. The preacher could be the one interrupted or the interrupter. This is an especially fine method to use if you are in a church with other staff members, but it isn't limited to that. You could use anyone from the congregation if you so chose.

Here's how it works. Have a staff member, deacon, yourself, or some other person begin telling the story of a Bible character. They might be giving background, introducing the character, or reading Scripture about him or her. All of a sudden, from the back of the sanctuary or out of the middle of the congregation someone interrupts. "That's not the way it was. You weren't there. I know how it really happened." The speaker then invites the interrupter up to the front, or goes out to where he is. From this point the sermon can become a dialogue between the speaker and interrupter, or the platform can be given over entirely to the character to tell his story. Do you see the creative possibilities here?

One word of caution: clue the ushers into what's going

to happen in advance. These days, some strange things happen in church and ushers are usually trained to be watchful and protective. You don't want them to be over-protective in this instance. Let them know what's going on.

Media-enhanced Sermon

Biographical sermon delivery can be enhanced with the use of audiovisuals. There are pictures you could put into the hands of your congregation as you preach or before you preach which could augment your message. Or you could use slides of people, places, and things, great works of art, or recorded background sounds and music. Special lighting can add to your preaching technique. Films and/or videos might be used. Don't forget you want to keep your focus biographical and not on events, places, ideas, or even on the media themselves. But there are a plethora of ways to enhance biographical sermons using graphic and electronic arts. Our only limitations might be our own imaginations.

I hope these six suggestions will open the floodgates of your own creativity for ways to get the word out about Bible characters. Be creative without being sensational. Be open to new ideas, methods, forms of sermon delivery. Try new things. Don't substitute the innovative for the traditional entirely or your congregation may feel very insecure, like they never know what's coming up next. Proven methods are still needed. But don't stifle creativity either. Don't become so secure you get stale. Take these suggestions and launch out from them to new heights of creativity. You and your congregation will be glad you did.

Drama in Biographical Preaching

Creative sermon delivery calls for a certain amount of the dramatic element in many of its forms. This is evident in most of the styles of delivery suggested in this chapter. Let's look at some of the values of the dramatic elements of creative sermon delivery, especially as they relate to biographical preaching, then specifically at biographical preaching as drama.

Values of Dramatic Elements

There are some natural values inherent in the dramatic elements of various types of delivery of biographical sermons.[6]

Drama portrays character.—Drama is basically the portrayal of character. Because this is true it lends itself comfortably to biographical preaching. The best drama, whether on stage, movies, or television, is constituted by strong, identifiable characterizations. Even situation comedies like "All in the Family" and "M*A*S*H" were so popular because of their unique characters: Archie and Edith Bunker, Meathead, Hawkeye, Frank Burns, Hot Lips, Radar, and so forth. Far superseding elements like setting, costuming, and even plot, is the importance of character portrayal. This carries over into biographical preaching as well. The portrayal of character is of paramount importance in any biographical sermon. For this reason drama is of value to biographical preaching.

Person centered.—Drama is helpful to biographical preaching because it enables the preacher to think in terms of persons rather than events, places, and ideas. Since this is the goal of biographical preaching, drama is of value in this regard.

Portrayal of emotions.—Since drama particularly expresses emotions, it is valuable to biographical preaching. When we preach on Bible characters, we want to present their feelings and depth in all dimensions. It's impossible to do this without portraying their emotions. Drama is the element that enables this to happen.

One of the first things aspiring actors are told is, "Emote!" They must feel the emotions called for, then show the audience how they feel. Method acting teaches:

> The great actor should be full of feeling, and especially he should feel the thing he is portraying. He must feel an emotion not only once or twice while he is studying his part, but to a greater or lesser degree every time he plays it. . . . In the soul of a human being there are certain elements which are subject to consciousness and will. These accessible parts are capable in turn of acting on psychic processes that are involuntary.
>
> To be sure, this calls for extremely complicated creative work.[7]

When the preacher can tap into this creative art, the biographical sermon will be greatly enhanced.

Dramatic order.—Drama is helpful to biographical preaching because drama unfolds in an orderly fashion similar to the presentation of a sermon. Basically, drama is made up of three things: (1) portrayal of character, personality, (2) dialogue to portray character and/or conflict, and (3) action. The action also portrays character and/or conflict and moves toward climax. This dramatic order can enhance biographical preaching, lending to it form, movement, and climax.

Biographical Preaching as Drama

It is possible to do biographical preaching in the form of drama. A drama sermon could take the shape of a one, two, or three-act play, or a dramatic monologue. You could do a whole-life or life-portion sermon on the character chosen. You might even combine some drama with narration or have some drama going on during the course of the sermon, depicting what the preacher is saying. There are many creative ways to present a dramatic biographical sermon.[8]

One-act play.—A Bible person is presented in one act, one scene, with a minimum of characters, movement, and action. Basically, you present the character in a way that will arouse empathy in the audience. The movement is threefold: (1) set the situation and relationship of the character to it (Usually, the situation is conflict.); (2) present the involvement or complication of the situation (Usually, the situation develops to the point where it looks impossible.); (3) present the solution (Problem is resolved).

If you have any interest or ability in drama, this is a memorable way to present a Bible character.

Dramatic monologue.—The biographical sermon presented as a dramatic monologue has three characteristics: (1) it presents a dramatic moment in the life of the Bible character, or it can present the whole life; (2) it reveals the character (personality) of the Bible person; (3) it is faux dialogical in that the listeners hear what the speaker says, yet they never speak, but the speaker reacts to the listeners as if they were speaking.

Multi-act play.—It is possible to present Bible characters in two, three, or more acts. This obviously requires a great deal more time and effort. Usually more people are required, also. But if this is your desire and you have the capability, go for it. Just remember this genre requires keeping the focus on the person, not on other emphases. Don't lose the message in the method.

Drama can be a dynamic way to communicate God's

Word. It is especially suited to biographical preaching. As you plan your preaching, consider utilizing the suggestions given here. It will add a creative element to your preaching.

Using Contemporary and Historical Biography

In chapter 1, biographical preaching was defined as the use of the Bible for sermons that interpret the life or some aspect of the life of a biblical person for contemporary significance. The words *the use of the Bible* and *a biblical person* are intentional and unretractable. These elements are indispensable to the nature and content of biographical sermons. It isn't considered a sermon if it doesn't fit within the parameters of this definition. To use an extrabiblical person from history or from today as the subject of a message without any biblical relatedness would not fit the definition and, therefore, wouldn't be considered a sermon per se. Does this mean then that there is no use for contemporary and historical people in biographical preaching? Heaven forbid! There are valuable and important uses for nonbiblical biography in biographical preaching as defined, and we shall examine some of them.

In *Biographical Preaching for Today*, Andrew Blackwood acknowledged the then-current resurgence of interest in biography.[9] Although Blackwood advocated Bible-based biographical sermons, he commented, "As for examples outside the Bible, they have their place. The best of them, not many in one sermon, come from life today, or from biography, which means life interpreted in books."[10] We need to look at the place for nonbiblical biography in biographical preaching so we may keep it in proper perspective. What are some of these uses?

Illustrations

The most obvious use for contemporary and historical biography in biographical sermons is as illustrations.

Historical biography.—History is full of great people doing noble deeds and teaching lessons of enduring value we need to emulate. It is also full of dastardly people doing ignoble deeds teaching alarming lessons we need to warn against. Any preacher would be remiss in responsibility not to draw sermon illustrations from the lives of Polycarp, Luther, Calvin, Knox, Alexander the Great, Napoleon, Washington, Jefferson, Lincoln, Disraeli, Churchill, and other stellar human beings. The whole gamut of human history is a treasure trove of illustrative biography. There's nothing we can't learn from the lives of people in the past about how to live or how not to live today.

Contemporary biography.—Likewise there are living examples who should be looked to as illustrations. National and international leaders, scientists and scholars, actors and actresses, poets, philosophers, and preachers— there's no end to the possibilities. People don't have to be famous to serve in this capacity. Look about your own home. Family members can be a great source of illustration (even pets). You want to use them wisely and sparingly, but don't overlook them. How about friends, neighbors, fellow church members, civic leaders, sales people, people you meet casually like on an airplane, in a grocery store, and so forth? You don't have to look far or high to find people you can use as sermon illustrations. But you do have to look. Be open and sensitive to how you can use people in sermons. The alert preacher is always on the lookout for sermon illustrations from people's lives.

Analogy

Another way to use contemporary and historical biography in biographical sermons is analogy, showing correspondence between the Bible person and the contemporary or historical person. How do their lives compare? Overlap? What points of similarity exist between them? What differences are there? How do they agree? Disagree?

You always want to be careful comparing anybody to anybody else, for each person is unique. But there are legitimate and helpful analogies that could be drawn between certain persons past or present and Bible persons that would make splendid sermons.

One might compare someone regarded as a contemporary prophet to a biblical prophet. Or how about a great evangelist from the Bible being analogous to an evangelist from recent or distant history? Is there an analogy to be drawn between some great biblical reformer and some leader of the Protestant Reformation?

We could easily preach a biblically sound biographical sermon using some contemporary or historical person as the parallel.

Supportively

You might use people from the past or present to support some truth or point you're making. To do this you would state the truth drawn from the Bible person you're dealing with. Then you would support this truth by showing how it manifests itself in someone else's life, past or present. You could use several people's experiences to support the truth, possibly even your own. This lends credence to the truth you're proclaiming and is a legitimate use of extrabiblical people in biographical preaching.

Conclusion

This book was written to serve as a guide to biographical preaching. This is a fascinating and dynamic way to preach for all the reasons stated. Maybe the suggestions in this book will encourage you to try something new or revive something old in preaching on Bible characters. This is my fervent hope.

Use the ideas here as a springboard to new levels of creative communication. Add your own unique touches. Create your own categories, combinations, forms, and style. This isn't the final word on biographical preaching, only a hopeful encouragement to preach the old truths in some new way. The basics never change. Keep your focus on the Word of God. But we must be open to change the forms as they need changing. Become a creative change agent. Be open to the leadership of God's Holy Spirit to new avenues of communication. If you aren't preaching on Bible characters, add this genre to your repertoire. If you already are, consider the suggestions here as encouragement to keep on.

From the foundation of God's Word we can build sermons in any shape, any direction. There is no limit to where we can go and what we can do by God's Spirit.

Notes

1. John R. Claypool, *The Preaching Event* (Waco: Word Books, 1980), p. 28.
2. James Daane, *Preaching with Confidence* (Grand Rapids: Eerdmans, 1980), pp. 8-16.
3. See Charles L. Bartow, *The Preaching Moment* (Nashville: Abingdon Press, 1980); Al Fasol, *A Guide to Self-Improvement in Sermon Delivery* (Grand

Rapids: Baker Book House, 1983); Dwight E. Stevenson and Charles F. Diehl, *Reaching People from the Pulpit* (New York: Harper & Row, 1958); et al.

4. See Clyde E. Fant, *Preaching Today* (New York: Harper & Row, 1975), pp. 118-122. Here Fant advocates what he calls an "oral manuscript." This is an excellent supplement to written preparation but not a total substitute for it. Fant's ideas on the sermon brief (pp. 122-126) coupled with his oral manuscript idea make an excellent way to prepare to preach.

5. Francis C. Rossow, *Preaching the Creative Gospel Creatively* (St. Louis: Concordia Publishing House, 1983), pp. 126-127. Rossow also points to the advantage of being able to say, in character, things the preacher might not want to say as himself.

6. Based on class notes, Preaching 437, Southwestern Baptist Theological Seminary.

7. Constantin Stanislavski, *An Actor Prepares* (New York: Theatre Arts Books, 1936; Seventeenth printing, 1959), p. 13.

8. Based on class notes, Preaching 437, SWBTS.

9. Ibid., pp. 21-25.

10. Ibid., p. 21.

Appendix 1:
Sample Preliminary Page

Text: Joshua 24:14-24 (RSV)

Cit: Joshua exhorted his people to follow him in choosing undivided commitment to God's service.

Thesis: Service to God calls for the deliberate choice of total commitment.

Purpose: Major—Consecreative
Specific—I call you to commit yourselves to serve God throughout the new year.

Type of Biographical Sermon: Life portion, key event.

Title: "Choosing Our Commitment"

Outline: *Introduction*
Choices we make, large and small. Background of text. Text. Homiletical items. Look what's involved.

Sermon Body
1. Commitment is a matter of deliberate choice (24:14-15).
2. The quality of our service is determined

123

by the commitment we choose (24:16-21).

3. Our choices involve and influence the commitment of others (24:22-24).

Conclusion

Life confronts us with choices. We must choose to serve or not. Spell out specific choices. Up to you!

Appendix 2:
Whitesell's Suggestions for Biographical Series

In *Preaching on Bible Characters*, pp. 115-120, Faris Whitesell presented fifty-three suggestions for series on Bible characters. Each category had from three to sixteen names under it. While there is no need here to reprint all the names, a listing of the categories would be helpful.

Abandoned by God
Accepted by God
Apostates
Atonement, Men who made
Backsliders
Baptized Persons
Benefactors
Bold in Prayer
Boys, Famous
Compromisers
Commended by Jesus
Confessors of Christ
Confessors of Sin
Conscience, A Bad
Converts, OT
Converts, NT
Death seekers
Death, Men ready for

Fools
Forgivers of Enemies
Friendships, Notable
God, Men Who Saw
Greatest Men of OT
Greatest Men of NT
Guided, Divinely
Holders on for Blessing
Intercessors, Great
Joy of Salvation, Lost
Justified Men
Letting Go, Letting God
Lovers
Mystery Men
Pastors, Greatest Bible
Preachers, Greatest Bible
Perfect Men
Personality-Plus People

Death, Men unprepared for
Decisions, Great
Decision, Wrong
Dreamers, Great
Election—God's Chosen Men
Evangelists, NT
Excuse Makers
Faith, Saving, Examples of
Faith Tried, Examples of

Procrastinators
Rejectors of Christ
Religious Persons Needing
 Salvation
Seekers after Salvation
Tears, People of
Visions, Men of
Vow Keepers
Women, Godly

Selected Bibliography

Achtemeier, Elizabeth. *Creative Preaching.* Nashville: Abingdon Press, 1980.

Allen, R. Earl. *Persons of the Passion.* Nashville: Broadman Press, 1972.

Angell, C. Roy. *Iron Shoes.* Nashville: Broadman Press, 1953.

Barclay, William. *The Master's Men.* New York: Abingdon Press, 1959.

Barry, James C., comp. *Preaching in Today's World.* Nashville: Broadman Press, 1984.

Bartow, Charles L. *The Preaching Moment.* Nashville: Abingdon Press, 1980.

Blackwood, Andrew W. *Biographical Preaching for Today.* New York: Abingdon Press, 1954.

_____. *Preaching from the Bible.* New York: Abingdon-Cokesbury Press, 1941.ᐧ

Broadus, John A. *On the Preparation and Delivery of Sermons.* New and revised edition edited by J. B. Weatherspoon. New York: Harper and Row, 1944.

Brown, Charles R. *These Twelve.* New York: Harper & Brothers, 1926.

Brown, Colin, ed. *The New International Dictionary of New Testament Theology.* 3 vols. Grand Rapids: Zondervan, 1975.

Brown, H. C. *A Quest for Reformation in Preaching.* Waco: Word Books, 1968.

Brown, H. C.; Clinard, H. Gordon; and Northcutt, Jesse J. *Steps to the Sermon.* Nashville: Broadman Press, 1963.

Buechner, Frederick. *Telling the Truth.* New York: Harper & Row, 1977.

Caldwell, Frank H. *Preaching Angles.* Nashville: Abingdon Press, 1954.

Chappell, Clovis G. *Faces About the Cross.* New York: Abingdon-Cokesbury Press, 1941.

_____. *Sermons on Biblical Characters.* New York: Harper & Brothers, 1922._____. *Sermons on New Testament Characters.* New York: Harper & Brothers, 1924.

_____. *Sermons on Old Testament Characters.* New York: Harper & Brothers, 1925.

Claypool, John R. *The Preaching Event.* Waco: Word Books, 1980.

Cox, James W. *Preaching.* New York: Harper & Row, 1985.

Craddock, Fred B. *As One Without Authority.* Nashville: Abingdon Press, 1983.

_____. *Overhearing the Gospel.* Nashville: Abingdon Press, 1978.

_____. *Preaching.* Nashville: Abingdon Press, 1985.

Daane, James. *Preaching with Confidence.* Grand Rapids: Eerdmans, 1980.

Drumwright, Huber L. *Saints Alive! The Humble Heroes of the New Testament.* Nashville: Broadman Press, 1972.

Eslinger, Richard. *A New Hearing.* Nashville: Abingdon Press, 1987.

Fant, Clyde E. *Preaching Today.* New York: Harper & Row, 1975.

Fant, Clyde E., and Pinson, William M. *Twenty Centuries of Great Preaching.* Waco: Word Books, 1971.

Fasol, Al. *A Guide to Self-Improvement in Sermon Delivery.* Grand Rapids: Baker Book House, 1983.

Fosdick, Harry Emerson. *Riverside Sermons.* New York: Harper & Row, 1968.

Freeman, Harold. *Variety in Biblical Preaching.* Waco: Word Books, 1987.

Gilmour, S. MacLean. "Luke." In *The Interpreter's Bible,* vol. 8, pp. 3-434. Edited by Nolan B. Harmon. Nashville: Abingdon Press, 1952.

Hargrove, H. H. *Personalities around the Cross.* Grand Rapids: Baker Book House, 1963.

Harrison, Everett F., ed. *Baker's Dictionary of Theology.* Grand Rapids: Baker Book House, 1960.

Jensen, Richard A. *Telling the Story.* Minneapolis: Augsburg Press, 1980.

Jowett, John Henry. *The Preacher: His Life and Work.* New York: George H. Doran Co., 1912; reprint ed., Grand Rapids: Baker Book House, 1968.

Kaiser, Walter C., Jr. *Toward an Exegetical Theology.* Grand Rapids: Baker Book House, 1981.

Lee, G. Avery. *Great Men of the Bible and the Women in Their Lives.* Waco: Word Books, 1968.

Lewis, Ralph L., and Gregg. *Inductive Preaching.* Westchester, IL: Crossway Books, 1983.

Linn, Edmund H. *Preaching as Counseling: The Unique Method of Harry Emerson Fosdick.* Valley Forge: Judson Press, 1966.

Lowry, Eugene L. *Doing Time in the Pulpit.* Nashville: Abingdon Press, 1985.

_____. *The Homiletical Plot.* Atlanta: John Knox Press, 1980.

Luccock, Halford E. *In the Minister's Workshop.* New York: Abingdon-Cokesbury Press, 1944.

Macartney, Clarence E. *Ancient Wives and Modern Husbands.* Nashville: Cokesbury Press, 1934.

_____. *The Greatest Men of the Bible.* New York: Abingdon-Cokesbury Press, 1941.

_____. *Mountains and Mountain Men of the Bible.* New York: Abingdon-Cokesbury Press, 1940.

_____. *Trials of Great Men of the Bible.* New York: Abingdon-Cokesbury Press, 1946.

Marshall, Peter. "Compromise in Egypt." Side two of the record *Were You There?* Waco: Word Records, 1944.

McEachern, Alton H. *Dramatic Monologue Preaching.* Nashville: Broadman Press, 1984.

_____. "Narrative Preaching." In *Preaching in Today's World,* pp. 151-164. Compiled by James C. Barry. Nashville: Broadman Press, 1984.

Meyer, F. B. *Abraham; Or, the Obedience of Faith.* New York: Fleming H. Revell Co., 1950.

_____. *David: Shepherd, Psalmist, King.* New York: Fleming H. Revell Co., 1895.

_____. *Elijah, and the Secret of His Power.* Fleming H. Revell Co., n.d.

_____. *Israel: A Prince with God.* New York: Fleming H. Revell, n.d.

_____. *John the Baptist.* New York: Fleming H. Revell, 1900.

_____. *Joseph: Beloved—Hated—Exalted.* New York: Fleming H. Revell, Co., n.d.

_____. *Joshua and the Land of Promise.* New York: Fleming H. Revell Co., 1893.

_____. *Moses, the Servant of God.* New York: Fleming H. Revell Co., 1950.

_____. *Paul.* New York: Fleming H. Revell Co., 1897.

_____. *Peter: Fisherman, Disciple, Apostle*. 6th ed. London: Marshall, Morgan & Scott, 1939.

Miller, Basil. *Meet the Marred Men of the Bible*. Dallas: Chandler Publications, 1955.

_____. *Meet the Little Known People of the Bible*. Dallas: Chandler Publications, 1955.

_____. *Meet the Voices of the Bible*. Dallas: Chandler Publications, 1955.

Northcutt, Jesse J. Unpublished class notes from the course Preaching 437. Southwestern Baptist Theological Seminary. Fall, 1967.

Poteet, Edwin McNeill. *These Shared His Passion, Cross and Power*. New York: Harper & Brothers, 1948.

Rice, Charles L. "Shaping Sermons by the Interplay of Text and Metaphor." In *Preaching Biblically*, pp. 101-120. Edited by Don M. Wardlaw. Philadelphia: Westminster Press, 1983.

Richardson, Alan, ed. *A Theological Word Book of the Bible*. New York: Macmillan Co., 1950.

Roach, Corwin C. *Preaching Values in the Bible*. Louisville, KY: Cloister Press, 1946.

Robertson, A. T. *Some Minor Characters of the New Testament*. Nashville: Southern Baptist Sunday School Board, 1928.

Robertson, Frederick W. *Sermons Preached at Brighton*. Reprint edition. New York: Harper & Brothers, n.d.

Rossow, Francis C. *Preaching the Creative Gospel Creatively*. St. Louis: Concordia Publishing House, 1983.

Shoemaker, H. Stephen. *Retelling the Biblical Story*. Nashville; Broadman Press, 1985.

Stanislavski, Constantin. *An Actor Prepares*. New York: Theatre Arts Books, 1936. 17th printing, 1959.

Steimle, Edmund A.; Niedenthal, Morris J.; and Rice,

Charles L. *Preaching the Story.* Philadelphia: Fortress Press, 1980.

Stevenson, Dwight E. and Diehl, Charles F. *Reaching People from the Pulpit.* New York: Harper & Row, 1958.

Stott, John R. W. *Between Two Worlds.* Grand Rapids: Eerdmans, 1982.

Sweazey, George E. *Preaching the Good News.* Englewood Cliffs, NJ: Prentice-Hall, 1976.

Talmage, T. DeWitt. *Trumpet Blasts.* Chicago: North American Publishing Co., 1892.

Tolbert, Malcolm O. "Luke." In *The Broadman Bible Commentary,* vol. 9, pp. 1-187. General editor Clifton J. Allen. Nashville: Broadman Press, 1970.

Turnbull, Ralph G., ed. *Baker's Dictionary of Practical Theology.* Grand Rapids: Baker Book House, 1967.

Wardlaw, Don M., ed. *Preaching Biblically.* Philadelphia: Westminster Press, 1983.

Whitesell, Faris D. *Preaching on Bible Characters.* Grand Rapids: Baker Book House, 1955.

Whyte, Alexander. *Bible Characters from the Old and New Testament.* One volume edition. Grand Rapids: Zondervan, 1967.

Scripture Index

Subject Index